G000280407

XTC: SONG STORIES

The Exclusive Authorized Story Behind the Music

London

XTC: SONG STORIES

XTC and Neville Farmer

This edition published in 1998 by Helter Skelter Publishing.
Helter Skelter Limited, 4 Denmark Street, London.

First UK edition

Published by arrangement with Hyperion

First published in the USA in 1998 by Hyperion, 114 Fifth Avenue, New York, New York 10011

Printed in the United States of America

Cover design by David Zachary Cohen
Cover photograph by Kevin Westenberg

A CIP record for this book is available from the British Library

ISBN 1–900924–03–X

CONTENTS

Prologue · vii

Introduction · 1

1 · Black Music 1977/8 · 13

2 · Strong and Silent 1978 · 37

3 · Boom Dada Boom! 1979 · 59

4 · Terry and the Love Men 1980 · 87

5 · Rogue Soup 1982 · 109

6 · Off the Rails 1982 · 132

7 · Fruits Fallen from God's Garden 1983 · 141

8 · Coal Face 1984 · 159

9 · Day Passes 1986 · 177

10 · Colonels, Kings, Dukes, and Jesticles · 205

11 · Songs of Sixpence 1988 · 228

12 · The Last Balloon 1991 · 253

13 · The History of the Middle Ages 1998 · 278

Epilogue · 303

Postscript · 311

Song and Album Index · 313

PROLOGUE

It is a sad fact that most of XTC's fans have never seen them play live. I was lucky. I saw them, both with Barry Andrews and Dave Gregory, playing in Barbarella's club in Birmingham, England, in the late seventies. XTC had the most electrifying presence live, despite the hail of spit from idiot punks who thought they were paying homage and the deafening noise and suffocating heat. On both occasions I left soaked in sweat, hoarse from singing, and six inches off the ground with elation. It was an exciting time for live music and I saw some amazing bands in very small venues, but XTC were as good as any band I have seen or will ever see. When they retired from live performance, I mourned along with many other fans. But I was hooked on what they did and followed their music through its many twists and turns, having to be satisfied with the more detached medium of record or CD.

Early in 1986, Virgin's publicist, John Best, sent a white label cassette of three XTC songs to me with the words *Comments, please* scribbled on the compliment slip. It was unusual for the opinion of a hi-fi magazine editor to be requested by a record company. So I felt quite flattered, especially as I was a fan. The songs were

"Grass," "Extrovert," and "Dear God." I listened to them and called John Best immediately. "They're brilliant but they're in the wrong order," I said. " 'Dear God' is the hit." John agreed but said that they wanted to break America with the new album and were worried about offending people. "That's exactly the reason you should make it the single. The publicity will be worth it." He informed me that it wasn't even going on the album. It was to be a B side and Andy Partridge, XTC's leading man, didn't like it. "He's mad!" I said. "D'you want to tell him that to his face?" asked John. "Does Dolly Parton sleep on her back?" I answered.

"You're mad!" I told Andy when we met. "I knowwww!" he moaned, tired of being told the same thing again. But he was stubborn and didn't want to change his mind—a trait that affected much of XTC's career. We became friends, as a small number of fans had been allowed to become in the past. And I came to know about the openness, the ordinariness, the laughter, and the frustration that is XTC. Dave Gregory and Colin Moulding turned out to have the same down-to-earth manner, all of that rare breed of recording artist that does not consider itself above mere mortals. Dave and Andy even wrote record reviews for my magazine, though Andy's were florid gibberish and almost unprintable and Dave hadn't the killer instinct of a music critic.

Over the years of knowing XTC, I became party to privileged information of the type you wouldn't normally share with your best friend, a difficult position for a journalist. But Andy, Dave, and Colin seemed unconcerned and that trust ensured my loyalty to them in return. It wasn't until Andy asked me to write this book that I felt I had license to talk. Andy said, "Be open, don't hold back," and I was astonished at the frankness of the discussions we held in the book's preparation. There are still things that I have missed out. Some of them would have caused rifts in the band and other things left no mystery for the fans to savor. There are still plenty of treasures hidden in the songs to tease and tempt. That said, I tried to write the book I, as an XTC fan, would want to own; to refer to while listening to records; to study to outsmart fellow fans; to dig that bit further into a band with a very limited public image but a great deal of public affection.

My gray hairs, nervous twitch, full-time therapist, and wardrobe of designer incontinence pants are evidence of the stress caused in writing this book. But it was a labor of love. And it was only possible thanks to a gang of friends and contacts whom I feel I should thank before I progress. So, my gratitude to: Andy Partridge, Colin Moulding, and Dave Gregory for all the obvious reasons and several less obvious ones. Erica Wexler, Holly and Harry Partridge, the long-suffering Kitt Sands, Paul Bailey, and Jennifer Lang and Bob Miller at Hyperion. John Best for the personal introduction, and Malcolm Green, Jon and Chas Bridger, and Liquid Lil for making me an XTC fan in the first place. Gill Paul, Jenny Todd, Sarah Miller, and Marion Kaempfert for advice and support. Christina, Roger, and Ruby Randall-Cutler, Steve Cope, Fiona Davies, Kathy Varley, Dave Beevers, Debbie Bonham and Peter Bullick of Sound Discs, Kate Berridge, and K Newman for being stars in times of stress. Peter Gabriel for giving me the freedom to write my way instead of the way Jim Charlton taught me. John and Christina Leckie, Paul Fox, and Franne Golde, Haydn Bendall, Prairie Prince, Allan Botchinsky, Deni Bonet, and Richard Coward for illumination, illustration, and accommodation. Kelly and Imogen at Virgin. Simon Sleightholm and Becky di Gregorio for their enthusiastic and unrewarded help. Anthony MacKenzie-Farmer, Beth and Gordon Roberts, Sian, John, Amy, Ellie, Megan, and Blake O'Neill for being my family. Pam Robbins for Red Cross Parcels. And Jane Robbins—heavens above! I love you for putting up with all this! I know most of you will have skipped this bit, but if you are reading this, and you enjoy the rest of the book, offer a little prayer of thanks to them, as well. They deserve it.

Neville Farmer
John Leckie's cottage
West Wycombe
Buckinghamshire
England
January 1998

XTC: SONG STORIES

INTRODUCTION

High on Uffington Down is the image of a galloping horse, scraped through the green, English turf into the white, chalk hillside. It's an odd-looking thing, elongated, almost abstract. It was carved during the Iron Age by some ancient Picasso, a piece of naive art that wouldn't look out of place on the door of a giant refrigerator, signed *Merlin, aged 8*.

The Uffington Horse was already 1,000 years old when the Roman construction teams built the paved highway of Ermin Street to the west. It watched the pigs being herded along it from the market on Swine Dun (Pig Hill). The horse was ancient when the Celts were driven into Wales by the colonizing Saxons. It galloped as the Vikings rampaged, raped, and pillaged and as King Alfred fought back. It stood proud as the Normans invaded and laid out the property boundaries that still stand today. It stood sentinel over medieval Britain as it struggled to civilize itself. It watched the never never navvies pounding spikes into the rails of the Great Western Railway. It ran wild-eyed from the development of the M4 motorway. It is one of the great historic symbols of England. "It looks like a duck!" said the Epic Records executive, and dismissed the great monument at a stroke. "If you want a horse, we'll get our artists to draw one!"

Once again, XTC was being misunderstood. The record company sent pictures of a wild mustang and a bucking bronco and of someone trotting through a cartoon caricature "English" village. The company totally missed the point. *English Settlement* was the name of the album and the Uffington Horse was a 3,000-year-old signpost to an ancient English settlement. It was a strong visual image. XTC won the argument but didn't understand why they had to argue in the first place.

XTC is probably the most misunderstood band in an industry riddled with misunderstanding. Andy Partridge, Colin Moulding, and Dave Gregory are extremely unlikely rock stars. They talk with an English West Country drawl, unsuited to songs of '58 Chevys or surfing or hard-drinking. Dave Gregory collects guitars and carefully archives his video library. Colin Moulding is fascinated with astronomy and has two adult children. Andy Partridge collects and designs toy soldiers and invents board games and won't learn to drive.

Bands this far from the rock 'n' roll norm are not totally uncommon in Britain, but perhaps only the Kinks could claim to be more influential misfits than XTC. Even they couldn't claim to have been so consistently influential throughout their careers. Twenty years since its first record, XTC remains a productive cottage industry of musical R&D, a standard by which others gauge themselves. While they practice their hobby of creating better and better songs, shut in their back rooms and garden shed studios, the music of Partridge, Moulding, and Gregory continues to inspire musicians around the world.

Of course, even among their fans, XTC inspires misunderstanding. The national sense of irony has always got the Brits into trouble. John Lennon's infamous "more popular than Jesus" comment was a perfect example of off-the-cuff British irony, but he was taken at his word and thousands of Beatles records burned for it. XTC's frankness, coupled with smatterings of ironic comment, would always get them into trouble, too. Colin Moulding probably was being ironic when he said, "We're only making plans for Nigel. He has his future in British Steel." But did British Steel really have to wheel out a group of employees named Nigel to testify to the security of their futures? (The real irony was that they laid off most of their workforce over the following decade.)

XTC would also be misunderstood when they were speaking in earnest. Andy Partridge was questioning the existence or the motives of a deity in "Dear God," but does that mean radio stations broadcasting the song should receive bomb threats? (Again, the real irony was that Christians were making death threats because of his supposed un-Christian behavior.) Perhaps it is naive of XTC to expect the world to understand. The British always seem to think that foreigners will understand them better if they speak slowly and loudly, and they are always wrong. XTC fans worldwide consistently misread the words and the music. Probably the thing they understand least is the humor of the band. They write about bombs, poverty, dysfunctional families, war, religion. But they write about the human condition and they laugh about it. Anyone who comes from Swindon has to laugh about it. None of them comes from a wealthy background. None of them has found fortune in his career. They still live in one of England's least desirable towns, the butt of jokes. They cause trouble quietly and then chuckle about it in the pub. If ever there is anarchy in the U.K., it will probably manifest itself like this—men with country accents and middle-age spread, singing provocative songs from their hideout in Swindon.

As one sits on the 125 Express heading west, about fifty minutes out of London, the Uffington Horse can be seen atop its hill two or three miles to the left. It symbolizes the borderline between the Home Counties and the mystical West Country. It is also a warning that you are about to arrive in Swindon.

Swindon today is the fault of one of the great heroes of the

Industrial Revolution, Isambard Kingdom Brunel, a sensible man with a silly name. He was a great engineer, when the title engineer could sit proudly with general or judge or professor or pioneer. He built the world's first iron ship, the first steamliner, great bridges and tunnels, and the Great Western Railway, which linked Wales and the West Country of England to the capital. Of course, in the mid-nineteenth century you couldn't just pick a locomotive and wagons off the shelf. So Izzie had to design and build the rail industry from scratch.

To do this, he chose a flat, 350-acre area of land, halfway down the line, supplied with plenty of water, stone, clay, and land for building factories, loco sheds, furnaces, stockyards, and housing. The land he chose lay beneath a zit of a hill, crowned with the small, peaceful, no-need-to-change, leave-us-alone-we're-happy-as-we-are-thank-you, 2,000-inhabitant market town called Swindon. Izzie squeezed that zit and Swindon burst all over the upper Thames Valley.

New Swindon thrived and boomed. You could tell it was thriving because of the filth. In industrial Britain, if you couldn't breathe you were in a rich town. As the northern English phrase says, "Where there's muck, there's brass," and Swindon was neck-deep in muck. In half a century, the little town became a small city, lacking only the ecclesiastical trappings that would endow it with city status. By the end of the nineteenth century, it employed 100,000 people and was given a royal charter by Queen Vic to recognize its importance. Her boys would come to Swindon to sample the delights offered by a local pimp called Partridge and they gave him a row of cottages in thanks. Swindon built railways for the world. Swindon was a northern English industrial town displaced to the prissy countryside of the south. It was, and is, out of place.

Although Britain still reaps the benefits of being first in line for the Industrial Revolution, being wealthier than a small wet rock in the Atlantic deserves to be, the Victorian rush for industrialization left an ugly legacy. Swindon is a mess of a town. Brunel had a clear vision which had become irrelevant by the mid-twentieth century. The closure of the railway works left a large, dirty scar on the landscape and successive council planning committees made it worse, like tag teams of ham-fisted student plastic surgeons "correcting" different parts of the same face. As with most of the British population, the people of Swindon suffered this upheaval quietly. The unity they gained from the railway works was gone. Civic pride was gone. They made do. If they did protest, it was about the wrong things, striking over pay, instead of their lousy working environment or unemployment. By the late seventies, the British people were listless, bored, apathetic, stupid. They deserved Margaret Thatcher.

From this cultural void of cheap council housing estates, Victorian slums, and grimy factories came punk rock. It had an American origin, like most British pop, but it became totally British, an expression of youth frustration that horrified the press, the adult population, the authorities, and the record industry. Of course, punk was more real in some minds than others. It was as exploited as any musical form but it was a religion to many young people, suckers for any sort of cult. It filled a gaping niche. But many of the bands who turned up on "Top of the Pops" as "punks" had only cut their long hair and customized their flared trousers to fit in. They had just stopped playing glam pop covers and pretended to be angry young punks, spitting, changing their lyrical content from girls and cars to abortion and the dole.

The Helium Kidz. (CREDIT: STUDIO 70)

Punk rock could never become the revolution it promised to be. As its chief exponents earned money, they became the same as any other young rock star with more cash than sense. Most of them used the punk ideal as leverage to get a record deal. The few who survived became comfortable, fat, clever, and embarrassed by the whole thing.

If punk did anything good, though, it was to kick the British record industry squarely in the nuts. The musicians took the music back from the A&R men and made it theirs. That was exciting. It became acceptable to make records with more passion than pizazz. If Beefheart had been born ten years later and British, he'd have been a chart act.

Swindon was certainly not at the heart of the punk revolution. Its only previous link to stardom was Diana Fluck, who became British Monroe clone Diana Dors. Swindon's musical history consisted of the Garrard record deck factory and dance bands cobbled together with local musicians like drummer Johnny Partridge and singer Charlie Moulding. The few gigs in town failed to nurture a quality musical culture as in Liverpool, Birmingham, Manchester, Glasgow, or London. Swindon had no more than rather ragtag bands of kids playing to themselves in local church halls. One of these bands was the Helium Kidz, who recognized the possibilities offered by punk and headed sufficiently in that direction to attract management and regular work. By the time they became XTC, their principal writer, Andy Partridge, had penned a catalogue of punkish pop songs of variable quality and they had become Swindon's star turn. When Richard Branson signed them to his newish Virgin Records, their lineup had become Andy Partridge (guitar and vocals), Colin Moulding (bass and vocals), Barry Andrews (keyboards and backing vocals), and Terry Chambers (drums).

The original Red Hot XTC promotional leaflet.

(CREDIT: ANDY PARTRIDGE)

They were utterly naive, coming from poorish families on town's council estates. When they were offered wine at their first recording sessions in Virgin's baronial Manor Studios, Andy turned it down because he didn't know if he'd like it. Terry Chambers's idea of a good evening out was to get legless with his mates, break into a fish and chip shop to steal the cash and, finding none, to piss in the tub of precut chips in the back room. Barry Andrews was a punk monk, devoted to the cause of punkdom. Andy Partridge had been supported through his childhood by Valium and lived in a vermin-infested storeroom behind an empty shop. Colin Moulding worked as an assistant groundsman and procreated very young.

Cool Colin, assistant groundsman and father.

(CREDIT: STUDIO 70)

What they did have was curiosity, and the wicked sense of humor essential for anyone of intellect who grows up in a rundown community. What they also shared was a passionate and catholic taste for music. They quietly harbored a liking for disco, dub reggae, circus tunes, music hall, the Beatles, Free, the Kinks, Captain Beefheart, the Stooges, the Velvet Underground, the New York Dolls, Cockney Rebel, Motown, Can, David Bowie, the Groundhogs, Black Sabbath, and much, much more. These were difficult times. Punks weren't allowed to admit to any influences. So XTC kept mum when Be-Bop Deluxe or Andy Williams or Leonard Bernstein flavored their songs. But it was these influences, and their fascination with the structure of music, that raised them out of the crudity of punk to become as important as they have.

XTC soon let slip their tenuous ties to punk, along with the mad monk Andrews and, eventually, Terror Chambers. In came their local childhood guitar hero, Dave Gregory, the diabetic demon of the six-string plank, a man who could play every lick by every band they loved and could write out the dots, as well. They learned rapidly about songwriting and recording. They developed the power of lyrical expression, though not without confusing some of the more intellectually challenged of their listeners—the natural outcome of entrapping simple folks with simple pop hooklines and then telling them something that questioned their very existence.

Tasteful sophisticates, XTC in 1977. (CREDIT: STUDIO 70)

They evolved all the faster after Andy's body and mind surrendered to the pressures of touring. Retirement from live performance did not mean retirement from music. The realization that they actually liked living in Swindon, were proud to sound like a gang of English turnipbashers, is what finally established XTC as the musical institution it is. Their seclusion on Pig Hill has made them all the more mysterious. Artists will almost genuflect before asking Gregsy, as friends know Dave, to play on their records. Stars make pilgrimages to Andy's door. The producers who line up to work with XTC do so with trepidation, afeared of the difficult reputation of the band. The music industry remains in hushed awe of XTC, which is remarkable because anybody in Swindon still sees them as the stupid hayseeds from Penhill, who love a curry and a pint as much as any Brit.

There are few other bands who have managed to maintain their careers through breakups, breakdowns, early retirement, lost court cases, near bankruptcy, divorce, death threats, and living in Swindon. But XTC inspires tribute bands, tribute albums, fan conventions, Websites, fan mail, hate mail, and the admiration of almost any musician. The band that drew on more influences than a Tarantino movie has become influential itself. Even the name inspired U2, INXS, R.E.M. Just as trainspotters gather at the ends of the platforms of Swindon Station, cramming rolling stock numbers into notebooks for future processing, so have the members of XTC crammed musical knowledge into their heads. They have processed the data, chewed on it, and belched it out in a stream of diverse, extraordinary, and unique songs, seasoned but not smothered by the influence of thousands of other records.

It was only during the discussions for this book that XTC recognized some of these influences. Neither Colin nor Andy had openly admitted many of their influences to each other. Andy only now recognizes the influence of *The Rocky Horror Show* sound track on their debut, *White Music*. Writing this book was as much a revelation for them as it should be for the reader. It exposed more about their lives, their attitudes, their family problems, their songwriting, their recording methods, their bad habits, and recurring nightmares than they had dared consider. Sitting in Andy Partridge's shed studio, pausing only for bowls of chicken korma soup and Colin's sporadic bouts of flatulence, the analysis of XTC's music became a voyage of discovery. Andy asked me to write the book with them because he wanted to clear up the misunderstandings people have about XTC's music, but it actually cleared up more of their own misapprehensions about the songs and themselves. It even altered the choice of drummer for their new album.

Although this is not a biography, it exposes more through the songs than any of the band might have readily admitted. It is a chronicle of personal, political, and philosophical thoughts, anecdotes, myths, and legends. As XTC progressed from song to song, the band shed a few drops of its essence and these were captured and distilled through the pages of the book, album by album from 1977 to 1998. The discussions that led to the book were whimsical, unscientific, and scattered, and to some extent that is reflected in its pages. The spirit was more important than the structure of each song. There were few discussions of keys and chords because, most of the time, nobody had a clue what chords or keys were used. There were no grand discourses on the benefits of differing recording techniques, because this was to be more a book about music than mechanics. If a particular musical instrument warranted mention, so be it. But this was not to be an equipment list or a lyric book. It was just a long discussion about songs—about what happens when three or four mad bastards from Pig Hill get to do what they love most.

There is a risk in writing a book of this type, that the past tense might take a psychological hold. XTC's last three albums have been spread over twelve years, more than half a decade of which was spent trying to find an amicable way of leaving Virgin Records. Almost all the XTC activity of the mid-nineties was instigated by outsiders—retrospectives, biographies, conventions, Websites, tribute albums. The implication is that XTC is an historical monument, like the Uffington Horse, relying on enthusiasts to stop the grass growing over their work. But this simply isn't true. They have been busy writing, recording, and performing, often in disguise. They even gatecrashed their own tribute album, under an assumed name.

This book heralds a new era for XTC. They have a new record deal that seems to satisfy Andy. As I write, they are recording the first new album in years. There is even talk of live performance, though perhaps one shouldn't tempt fate. Meanwhile, the book serves to explode a few myths about what has gone before, to wipe clean the slate, and to give an insight to the real XTC, clever and crude, funny and fatuous, serious and silly, deep and daft.

When XTC signed the new record deal in 1997, they took the Japanese label executives who visited them to the top of the Uffington Horse. Standing in their suits on the top of the bleak hill, they probably didn't really understand its significance either. But they didn't say it looked like a duck. They just accepted that the members of XTC deserve respect for being what they are: brilliant, unpredictable, self-willed, utterly English, and barking mad.

1

BLACK MUSIC
1977/8

The race to sign XTC was hard fought. At least, by two A&R men it was. Having been turned down by Columbia, Decca, and Pye, the likely contenders were Harvest, Virgin, and Island. Island was convinced they had a deal in the bag and when one of their managers spotted a Virgin man sniffing around XTC at a London gig, fists flew. The Virgin man won. Virgin was a hip young label, the one with the guts to release the Sex Pistols albums after EMI and A&M had dropped them. There was definitely cache in being part of Richard Branson's dream.

It was barely a week after signing to Virgin that XTC found themselves in Abbey Road Studios recording their first EP with producer John Leckie. They were utterly innocent of the ways of the recording world. To be in a building full of rock memorabilia, with a producer who had engineered on Pink Floyd sessions, was too good to believe.

EMI's studios had been regarded as the Beatles' studio since they named their last recording after the street outside. It was an unlikely place, an early Victorian villa in the salubrious suburb of St. Johns Wood, built by a wealthy member of Parliament for his mistress, whom he subsequently murdered. To this day, people see her ghost walking the upstairs offices and, according to all sightings, she's still pissed off.

Studio Three was the smallest one there in those days and was situated on the ground floor to the left of the famous entrance. It was the room where "Eleanor Rigby" and "Paperback Writer" had been recorded. Appropriately, for the cheapest studio in the place, it was also where "Money" and "Taxman" had been mixed. It was hallowed ground.

Nineteen seventy-seven was not a good time for money or taxmen in Britain. Jim Callaghan's Labour government was crippled with striking unions, runaway inflation, and massive national debt. The Tories were straining at the leash to take over, with the snarling figurehead of Margaret Thatcher barking for the government to fall—this was, of course, prior to the professionally tutored softening of her vocal tones, so at that stage she still barked like Johnny Rotten with a plum in his mouth.

The biggest issue was racial tension. The British National Front was rioting against immigrants in South London, inspiring U.S.

Ambassador to the UN Andrew Young to call the Brits "little chickens" over racial matters.

Swindon was untouched by such things, so the band didn't see the problem when they called the album *Black Music*, in reference to black humor, rather than race. Virgin and their manager insisted they change it. So they called it *White Music* as in white noise. This was worse. In their naive insensitivity, they were unaware that this might be taken as a sign of white supremacist leanings. They couldn't even spell *supremacist*! Their songs were simple, discordant, power pop songs about boredom, drinking, sex, and space. They had never been heard by more than a couple of hundred drunks at one time. They had no idea of the damage that could be wrought with a few ill-chosen words. They just wanted to be pop stars.

If Andy Partridge was the front man, Barry Andrews was the band gimmick. Andy's onstage energy was highly infectious, but Barry was weird. Barry had a sound that lifted them out of the ordinary. Of all the bands to come out of so-called punk to date, only the Stranglers had relied on keyboards to shape their sound. This gave XTC an edge over all the other guitar-only wannabes.

ANDY ON BARRY'S ARRIVAL

Johnny Perkins, the previous keyboard player, just dumped us. He got his own band who were going to do what he said as opposed to him doing what I said. We tried to threaten him into staying; I shaved my head and put on a leather jacket and Colin and I went 'round to force him to stay, but he wouldn't.

We went around the music shops in Swindon and saw a card on the wall which said something like "Key-

board player. Own equipment." We dashed 'round to see him and basically had him in the band after two auditions. I say auditions, but the fact that he had his own equipment and all his own limbs meant he was in.

Barry played very differently when he came for the audition. He played more like John Lord of Deep Purple. I felt that he wasn't being right to himself and I said, "You can play how the hell you want to." The next time we got together to play, his style had completely changed. It was like he'd had a nervous breakdown. I thought, Wow, this is so good. Why didn't he play like that the other time? Why did he play like "Smoke on the Water"? And here he is playing like the young boy out of the Jetsons on amphetamines. He had his wah-wah pedal and his fuzzbox and he always played his crappy little electric organ with the lid off, not for any kind of scientific "Hey, look at my mass of guts/metropolis space age/space station keyboard innards, folks." He played it with the lid off because it kept breaking, things kept busting, and wires kept coming off. And he would immediately reach in amongst all these live wires and just do running repairs.

When he joined, we did go out and get phenomenally drunk and I remember getting back to my two room bedsit near the shunting yard and vomiting in the kitchen sink. My girlfriend was poking the lumps down the plughole with me in between mouthsful, saying, "He's in, we've found one. He's in, he's in the group, we've got one, brilliant . . . bluuuurghhh!"

The first XTC EP session, from August 28–30, 1977, featured "Science Friction." The *3D EP*'s critical acclaim convinced Virgin to take a further step and record an album. Six weeks later they were in Virgin's Manor Studios. The ancient pile was Richard Branson's productivity bonus for "Tubular Bells" success. It was a huge, 400-year-old country house set in acres of grounds outside Oxford. It was luxuriously furnished with ancient tapestries and solid oak furniture and a pair of matching Irish wolfhounds. XTC was in and out again within a fortnight, though John had to remix

Alka-Seltzers all 'round at The Manor. (CREDIT: RICHARD COWARD)

most of the tracks in Advision Studios while the band toured. He swears he made identical mixes the second time, but Virgin seemed happier.

White Music was released in February 1978. The front displayed the band dressed in black and white. Andy, in specially made white pants with black arrows, pointed his backside at the camera. Colin tried to look innocent, unaware that his fly was undone and Barry insisted on holding a can of Heineken beer, which was air-brushed out later.

Five videos were made for the album, most of them in one day. The band had one spare day to shoot the videos before rushing to the Amsterdam Hilton to join the Talking Heads' tour. They spent the previous night in the Talgarth Hotel, trying to find spiritual awareness through the bottle. On the way to the ITN

TV Studios the next morning, Colin went a curious shade of green and asked to be let out of the cab. They dropped him off on Park Lane and watched as he wandered through the six lanes of traffic to the entrance of the Dorchester Hotel, where he threw up. He caught up with them an hour later.

"Statue of Liberty" wasn't a big hit for the second single. This lack of success set Virgin on edge. It brought about the decision to slight the novice Leckie and rerecord "This Is Pop" and "Heatwave" with Robert John "Mutt" Lange for single purposes, the following February.

Despite the extra recording, the picture sleeve singles, and the low-budget videos, *White Music* only scraped into the Top 40 of the British pop chart for about a month. But it established XTC as a recording act, and that gave them better billing on the gig circuit. With a fixed wage of £25 per week apiece, their management set them on a grueling tour schedule that would have severe repercussions in future years.

WHITE MUSIC

TALKING BETWEEN THE LINES

ON XTC MUSIC

ANDY PARTRIDGE: *I've had to go back and think, What the hell was that about?*

COLIN MOULDING: *They're desperately seeking attention, these songs. I'd just look for what onomatopoeic words would go with that rhythmic explosion.*

ANDY: *It's like naive space art. Colin and I didn't know what we were singing about—genuinely! We thought we were the best thing since sliced nuclear energy. I was that nerdy, that gauche, that cack-handed. We were desperate to be futuristic and modern, but the end result is like someone had sat down in 1956 and designed a future pop group. Imagine the film* Forbidden Planet *when the monster from Id had finished tearing people up and they all go back and relax in their spaceship. They'd put on their headphones and* White Music *would come out. We were obvious and poppy and bizarre. It was all dead straight and dead unusual, stirred into some sort of nouvelle cuisine sauce. You couldn't separate those stripey swirls. We were Captain Beefheart meets the Archies.*

ON JOHN LECKIE

ANDY: *Somebody said, "John Leckie. You should work with him."*
COLIN: *He'd worked with Be-Bop Deluxe, which was one of the things we liked about him.*
ANDY: *And he mixed a few Pink Floyd things. I think he mixed "Vegetable Man" single-handed. He was tape op at the time. They'd smoked too much pot and they left him to it. He was used to winding tapes and getting cups of tea and suddenly he was all alone in a dark and spooky studio mixing "Vegetable Man." John Lennon also used to call him Lickie, and for some reason he was very proud of this. Good credentials.*
COLIN: *He was very laid back.*
ANDY: *He got very drunk one evening and confessed to us that it was the first album he'd ever produced. I think we'd got most of it recorded by then so him pulling the confidence carpet from under our feet in a drunken confessional didn't matter. We'd managed to get through doing the whole album without too much mishap and very quickly it was done, too.*

ON RECORDING PRACTICES

ANDY: *We were nervous as hell and ludicrously keen to get it right, but I didn't have much concept of what a professional recording was. I thought that when you made an album you played all the songs in that order and then you made yourself go quiet between the tracks. I thought you just played it all and there it was, straight to shellac, straight to the nation. I wrote all these charts so that I wouldn't get any lyrics wrong and so I'd know where I was. I taped them to my amp and would be glued to them, petrified that we were going to go wrong.*

COLIN: *We signed the contract and the following week we were in Abbey Road, then we finished a month of gigs and then we were in The Manor. The recording took about ten days and then there was all this mixing nonsense which we knew nothing about.*

ON PRIME MINISTERS

ANDY: *Edward Heath, the ex-prime minister, was conducting a recording of Christmas carols in the next room and we were making a racket so he came in to see what was going on. He wanted to know what this punk thing was about and so he came in with his cronies. Our publicity man, Dennis Detheridge, brought him in. We weren't allowed to take pictures, so we wired up a plant pot with a microphone. The security guys checked the place out but they didn't spot the mic. John Leckie's still got a copy of the tape somewhere.*

ON MUTT LANGE

ANDY: *I'm sure he wasn't called Mutt because of his dog but his dog was ever present. One of the things I remember from the Utopia sessions was his dog, a bassett, a converted bloodhound, something very low slung, and his balls dragged around on the brown, fluffy carpet.*

COLIN: *They were like bits of chicken skin.*

ANDY: *Mutt really cooked the groove out of us. We lost pounds of sweat during the recording. His arranging skills impressed us. He was some sort of George Martin figure who really made a musical contribution.*

ON THE MANOR

ANDY: *We couldn't believe it. There were four-poster beds and tapestries for Christ's sake. "Bloody 'ell, they've got carpet on the walls in 'ere."*

COLIN: *It was autumn and there was log smoke in the air and these huge Irish wolfhounds that my kids would jump on. I loved all the murals. I was living in a terraced house in Ferndale Road and Andy was in a flat, so this was quite an experience.*

ANDY: *This big Tudorbethan mansion and all this professional equipment to play with. They would say things like, "Do you want wine with your dinner?" I'd never had wine and I was too scared to say "Yes."*

ON SINGING

ANDY: *My style of singing then was so bloody mad. It was so contorted because I had a fear that we weren't going to make another record—I couldn't see beyond the first album—and people weren't going to be left with any impression of the singer. So I adopted a vocal style that I thought I could handle, that I thought was me. I can see, years later, that it's just an amalgam of a lot of things I thought were classic rock 'n' roll. There's the Buddy Holly hiccup, the Elvis vibrato, and the howled mannerisms of Steve Harley. Also, when you play live and you're singing through crappy PAs, you had to sound like a walrus with prostate problems to be heard.*

A FAN SPEAKS

DAVE GREGORY: White Music *was a great way to start a career. It just kicked down the door and said, "Listen to me!" It's like a Marvel comic, full of bright colors. It's very entertaining and you have to keep turning the page. When they signed, I was thrilled for them. The punk thing should really have happened a couple of years earlier because they'd been kicking around for two years. Ian Reid got them out of Swindon and presented them on the punk circuit, and after a year they got their deal. I bought* 3D EP *the day it came out. I guess I was just pleased that I could buy something by my friends at the record shop.*

WHITE MUSIC

ON THE TRACKS

3D EP

"SCIENCE FRICTION"

(Andy Partridge) (Single and EP track)

Virgin spotted "Science Friction" as a single from day one. It was a rapid, catchy, humorous piece of pop gibberish, apparently about pacifying invading aliens, a side effect of Andy's passion for comic books. But it had a deeper meaning that even Andy didn't realize. "I always thought this was a nonsense of a song. Just a play on the words *fiction* and *friction*. Years afterward it suddenly clicked what the hell it was about. As a child I had astrophobia, a fear of stars. I'd run home from Cub Scouts at the Penhill Junior School hall on a frosty night staring at the ground. I could not look up because I'd be petrified of the stars staring at me."

Like much of XTC's early music, the arrangement followed Andy's love for Johnny and the Hurricanes' "Rockin' Goose" and "Red River Rock," the type of music that would play on the rides at Edwards's traveling fair on holiday weekends. The staccato piano intro and mental guitar noise made it an attention-grabbing set opener. It was equally effective on record. Barry's fairground organ and busking alien solo decorated the song, while Andy skanked his guitar so he could be heard between drumbeats. In Abbey Road, Andy wandered the building hitting things to add to the sound, settling on a metal microphone cabinet, which it was Terry's job to hit toward the end of the song.

"She's So Square"

(Andy Partridge) (Single B side only)

Antifashion was the order of the day in the punk era. XTC had "gone up to London to get punked up" and thought themselves Swindon's icons of antifashion. Andy wrote "She's So Square" as an attack on his unhip, hippie forebears. But he was a total hypocrite. As a teenager, he had tried to be one himself. "The nearest I got was a fake buckskin jacket which I begged from my mother for my fifteenth birthday. Totally appalling! It looked like Crosby, Stills & Nash if they'd come from Russia."

"It's the New York Dolls meets Be-Bop Deluxe," admits Andy of the record. Featuring Barry on the Abbey Road Fender Rhodes and some slick Bill Nelson-ish guitar before breaking into a Dolls-style rhythm, it is, as Andy says, "A snotty little song. Just a knock at the previous generation and its icons—the Cathy McGowans."

"Dance Band"

(Colin Moulding) (Single B side only)

The workingmen's club was the focus of every industrial town in Britain—noisy, smoky, with an unspoken heirarchy and a sense of permanence. Charlie and Vera Moulding would drag their sons, Colin and Graham, down to the local club on dance nights. Everyone would dance to the Gay Gordons's "Heel to Heel and Toe to Toe" while the kids sat quietly and the adults would get steadily drunk. "And then me and me brother used to get up at the end of the night and do the 'March of the Mods,' once the band had had a few drinks," says Colin.

This vaguely inspired "Dance Band," though this was only his second-ever song and he hadn't developed the Lowryesque descriptive quality that characterizes his later lyrics. These were just words to tag onto a bass riff.

"Dance Band" attracted a lot of attention, including an early session for the BBC Radio One John Peel show in June 1977. Most importantly, it was the first XTC track to appear on television. The opening few bars of bass riff sound uncannily like Steve Harley's "Mr Soft." Colin admits the link. "There are Harleyisms in there. It was bound to come out, really. At this time I had about six personalities and none of them were my own."

"Goodnight Sucker"

(Barry Andrews and Terry Chambers) (Secret extra EP, B side only)

Uncredited on the *3D EP* but there nonetheless, "Goodnight Sucker" was a whimsy of Messrs. Andrews and Chambers with Andrews on the Abbey Road celeste and Chambers on lager. It was Andrews's idea to insult the fans for buying the record but it was Chambers's voice that said it. "Chambers does this thing like Donald Pleasance saying 'Goodnight, Suckers,' in a sticky, molester sort of voice," says Colin. "We were thinking about this production line thing which was to come out in the *Go 2* concept later and I think they were thinking along those lines when they did it."

WHITE MUSIC

"Radios In Motion"

(Andy Partridge)

Based on an earlier song, this became a set opener to vie with "Science Friction." "I'd made a tape of radio interference, radio gibber, just tuning noises, and this would play while we got ourselves plugged in, strapped on, oiled up, and rubbed down. Sandblasted!" says Andy. Radio One's John Peel session included the interference tape but John Leckie chose not to. "It's a real little thunderstorm of a song, this," says Andy. "Originally, this was a song called 'Volcano' and it was just meant to be a noisy kind of blast. The music stayed the same but it was changed to 'Radios In Motion' because we thought there was something happening in music, but we couldn't quite put our fingers on it. Lyrically it's just a long stream of buzz words—'Make 'em, shake 'em in Siam.' It doesn't mean anything, just sounds exciting. 'Bouncing off an ocean liner.' What is? That's how a lot of our songs were written. You'd load up the shotgun with a lot of good, exciting words and go *blam!* It was not structured, but the overall effect was this modern twentieth-century buckshot."

"Cross Wires"

(Colin Moulding)

"So tell me, Colin—'Everything's buzz buzz, Everything's beep beep.' Spokesman for a generation? No, spokesman for Philco," says Andy in his best BBC accent.

If the lyrics of "Cross Wires" were rubbish, nobody could have told—they were more mucus than music. Anyway, Colin was only emulating Andy. "It's sort of surrogate Partridge, really. I don't know what it was about. It's probably a bit of nonsense. The word *buzz* was the word of the moment. On my bass guitar I had painted the word *buzz* in very fast lettering. We were very into electric sounds and crackles. It comes from DC comics, I suppose." The music, on the other hand, was from the dark side of Colin's musical taste. "This is probably more related to Black Sabbath than anything else. The G to C# chord change with Terry's twin-faceted rhythm pattern, evoke the 'devil's harmony,' as it's known, the sort of wicked intervals you'd find on the first Sabbath album. That's probably why I did it, though I can only suspect. There's a bit of Arthur Brown in here and a bit of Sabbath. I was struggling for a style." He was struggling to sing it, as well. No wonder John Leckie switched off the tape machine to end it.

"This Is Pop"

(Andy Partridge) (Single and album track)

Andy's first of many attacks on the music industry was set in a milk bar similar to that in *A Clockwork Orange*. He depicted a lost soul being pummeled about his choice of music on the jukebox and faced with the problem of describing it. The term "pop music" was still considered unhip in the U.K. but as far as Andy was concerned it didn't matter whether it was Iggy Pop or the Bee Gees, it was all pop. "There was so much questioning in papers, magazines, and TV. 'What was this new phenomenon? What was this punk rock? Is it punk or new wave? What do we call this stuff?' I thought this was daft, because to me it was just ice cream. Different flavors of ice cream."

People were shocked by Andy's guitar discords, unaware that they were based on one of the most famous chords in pop. "The whole thing is based on the 'Hard Day's Night' opening chord—a bastardized version with one note difference in the opening and at the end of every chorus. Then the verses are built on that chord shape." The track was probably the quintessential Andy Partridge composition, making something catchy without following the rules. "When a song was in a certain key, we played all around that key because of the great rubs it made. Why should the ball always fit in the hole? It's great fun when it goes all around the rim sometimes, when it bangs against the edge. So people would say, 'He's playing out of tune' and I wasn't. I was just causing a bit of rub there, a bit of grind."

Virgin saw it as the big single and invested in a promo video of the band slicing records like bacon in the Booker Cash and Carry superstore in Swindon. Acknowledging that John Leckie's production had been rushed, they shelled out for a rerecording with Mutt Lange at Utopia Studios in London. "The single version we did with Mutt Lange pretty much blew the album version out of the water," says Colin. "I think it's the best recording we made until *Black Sea*. But it was about twenty or thirty times that we played it through and it was getting to the point of tears. When we got it, we could see where he was coming from, but at the time it was, 'You bastard, this is Nazism.' "

"Do What You Do"
(Colin Moulding)

One minute and fourteen seconds worth of comic jam sums up this song. It's the sort of thing that would be played behind a "Benny Hill" sketch. "I was laughing my socks off while that was playing," says Andy. "It's like someone getting a sugar high through eating too many Tutti-Fruities. Like shoving a John McLaughlin record into the blender. The sort of music that makes your insulin go haywire. It's complete and utter bollocks!"

"I had this melody as a continuous thing and I didn't really know what to do with it," says Colin. "It should really have been about ten seconds long but it sounded good live so it got in the set. It was like a clown emptying a blancmange over somebody and getting a reaction from the audience and then trying to put it over on radio."

"Statue of Liberty"
(Andy Partridge) (Single and album track)

"Statue of Liberty" was the most obvious single on *White Music* and was written with that in mind, by a cocky Partridge, two years before they signed a deal. The music, which "probably came about through hearing one of those big crunchy, three-chord guitar Lou Reed tracks like 'Sweet Jane,' " had been sitting around looking for a lyric. "It was inspired by the girlfriend ironing. She was holding up her iron, trying to get her lead untangled. Stood there at the board holding her arm straight up, waggling this lead. And I said, 'You look like the Statue of Liberty,' and I thought, Oh yeah, that's the lyric I need for this bit of music."

"It's a bit more cartoony than 'Sweet Jane' with the organ and the Wurlitzer piano," argues Colin. "This tune was the real football crowd, scarf-waving number at gigs. We had people climbing on stage putting their arms 'round Andy and singing into the microphone with him."

When Andy, an impressive illustrator, saw the uninspired single sleeve, with its poorly cropped photo of the statue and the XTC logo in red, he almost came to blows with the Virgin in-house artist and swore he would be involved in all future sleeve design. It was his idea that spawned the award-winning *Fossil Fuel* cover. But he rarely got what he wanted from videos. To this day, he doesn't believe XTC has made a good video.

"All Along the Watchtower"
(Bob Dylan)

The only cover version on *White Music* was an odd but effective choice. For a band that was hanging onto the bandwagon of punk, covering a Bob Dylan song was perverse. But Andy wanted to sing a song that had a sense of scale in its lyrics and, as yet, he was unable to write that way himself. His choice came down to this or "Citadel" by the Rolling Stones, but Barry didn't know "Citadel."

This was also an opportunity for Andy to put down the guitar and play rock star. "Andy liked occasionally to do a bit of an Iggy Pop and not be fettered by a guitar 'round his neck," says Colin. With Andy on his harmonica and the mic, space was left in the arrangement to experiment. Dub reggae impacted on a lot of post-punk U.K. bands and XTC had honed "Watchtower" during live shows into a sort of cod "self-dubbery." Andy recalls Rupie Edwards's "Irie Feelin' " as an influence and, at the time, John Peel's influential late-night radio show would always include a sprinkling of genuine dub tracks. But the track which really opened them up to the possibilities of dub was a lot less cool. "Laugh as you may, but David Essex came out with 'Rock On,' which was played in a dub style. It was just very empty and everything had these little echoes that were making part of the rhythm. I thought that was fantastic and I became interested in the whole idea of leaving holes in music after that," admits Andy. " 'Life Is Good In the Greenhouse' is also influenced by David Essex," says Colin.

John Leckie had seen them play this live and preferred to record it that way. So they stood around the drums and played and sang it live. It wasn't a true dub, it was just a matter of different musicians leaving holes in their playing, while Andy self-edited Bob's words, sounding more as though he was gagging on something unpleasant.

"Into the Atom Age"
(Andy Partridge)

Andy had made a series of drawings experimenting with the pulsing effect that came from the frequency clash of green and red, inspiring the cover of the *3D EP*. One drawing was called "Into the Atom Age," as a childhood memory of his mother's love of futuristic fifties furnishings. "We had to have the palette-shaped coffee table, kitchen curtains (one, permanently hung inverted) with the jazzy, wirey-looking scenes of Paris life and wire poodles, plastic tiles in the kitchen that were gray with paint thrown on them like Jackson Pollock's. I was fascinated by that kind of kitschy future that everyone thought was going to exist. They thought that by 1977 everyone was going to be flying to work with their own personal jet pack, eating pills for lunch." Andy also wrote "The Fifties Kitchen Curtain," the piece of prose in the cover of *Go 2*, around this time.

Andy's passable impression of a Miro doodle. (CREDIT: ANDY PARTRIDGE)

"At one time I would have wanted this to have been a single," says Andy. "I just think it captured a lot of what I was into personally at the time. I read a book called *The Austerity Binge*, by Bevis Hillier, around that time and it was all about that 'kitschy sink' stuff. At one time, I wanted our music to have been like a musical version of a Miro painting, because Miro inadvertently designed the look of the fifties, just twenty years earlier. Lots of little, soft triangular things and shapes with holes in them and long jagged bits of wire with the odd chicken foot or a little roughly drawn star or splotty shapes. Although 'Into the Atom Age' was lyrically about that subject, the music of things like 'Cross Wires,' 'I'm Bugged,' the way we approached 'All Along the Watchtower'—they were probably closer to the Miro pictures."

In fact, "Into the Atom Age" was more a piece of overblown mid-seventies pomp rock, which Andy says he probably thought sounded like something Bowie would do at the time. He now admits it's more like Rush!

"I'll Set Myself On Fire"
(Colin Moulding)

Colin is no devil worshipper and is far too laid back to contemplate violent suicide, but the self-inflammatory concept of "I'll Set Myself On Fire" was taken rather too seriously by some fans, who would cover their hands in lighter fuel and ignite it at gigs.

Once again, Colin's interest in heavy rock flavored his writing, with demonic chord changes echoing Black Sabbath, a cheerful ditty by Black Widow called "Come to the Sabbat, Satan's There," and the mannered vocals of Arthur Brown's "Fire." "It was a big college hit around the time I met my missus in 1973 and so 'Fire' is very poignant for me." Throw in the manic laughter, which was a deliberate aping of Steve Bishop on the Sweet's "Blockbuster" and "Ballroom Blitz" and the song becomes a cocktail of influences. "These things tie up and make you write things you don't understand," Colin says. "There's some intense sloganeering on this track as well. There's an answering line, 'H_2O ain't good enough.' Like saying, there are many ways to commit suicide and my choice is setting myself on fire. Again, I think one of my half a dozen personalities was coming out in this song."

The sound of the match, by the way, is one match struck by roadie Jeff Fitches, edited onto the sound of six match heads igniting at once for greater effect.

"I'M BUGGED"
(Andy Partridge)

"I was big on American comics at the time," says Andy. " 'I'm Bugged' was written as a scenario from one of these old *Creepy Stories*. Sometimes you'd do these gigs and you'd look up from playing and virtually everyone in the audience, of all shapes and sizes, would have these cheap, plastic sunglasses on, stood there with their mouths open. It was like a little *Creepy Story* written around the audience looking like insects. Barry Andrews did a fantastic Egyptian keyboard part. I don't know where the hell that came from, but it seemed to fit my sort of 'ant guitar' perfectly. We'd had our first recording advance and we [each] got a new instrument. I got an Ibanez Artist guitar. You could put one of the pickups like right out of phase and it sounded like this funny, little scratchy praying mantis tone, just as if a praying mantis had a guitar. He'd be stood there, he'd finish praying, and he'd get his little insect green guitar out."

Live, the song was one of a number with very unpunk improvised middle sections which might drag on for several minutes, often without resolving back into the song. "It seemed to hypnotize the audience and it was one of those songs you could drag on for ages. It was a good crowd-pleaser," says Colin. In the studio, it was an excuse to give the roadies something to do. Says Andy, "We just sent both roadies out to the organ and said, 'Just play it how you want to play it. Just remember the song's "I'm

Mixing White Music *in The Manor.* (CREDIT: RICHARD COWARD)

Bugged." Jeff Fitches and Steve Warren both stood there nudging each other and trying to barge each other off the keyboard. I think they got into a fight about it. It was just them trying, in their roadielike way, to describe something insectlike."

"New Town Animal In a Furnished Cage"
(Andy Partridge)

After the war, German town planners would visit Britain to marvel at the rebuilding that had taken place in the former slums, cleared with the help of the Luftwaffe. Huge estates of bright new houses and tower blocks seemed a godsend. But for the first time, Britain had created itself an environment where people could get truly bored. Penhill Estate's worst example of this was

The Valley. There were no shops, pubs, restaurants, or clubs, and taxis and buses wouldn't stop there. It was no wonder people began to feel caged in. By the seventies, everyone realized the planners' dreams were the community's nightmare. Andy attempted to describe this in "New Town Animal." "I was trying to describe this kind of boredom of these places, where you desperately want to go out but there's nowhere to go. But it came out in a sort of quasi-Tamla feel. You had this four-beat snare going along which is a very infectious kind of rhythm but, of course, we probably spoilt it by all these jagged stabs and things that we put in."

"Spinning Top"
(Andy Partridge)

As one of the earliest songs on the album, "Spinning Top" was already well rehearsed as part of the set. Andy had written the "perverse little song" in 1975, while he was living with Linda Godwin. The two of them played the New York Dolls' first album and *The Rocky Horror Show* sound track till they were drummed into his head. "Spinning Top" and "She's So Square," he now realizes, were a result of those influences. "A lot of these songs sound like slices of 'Rocky Horror,' " he says. "It gets to be really 'Egyptians In Space.' The whole thing's meant to sound dizzy, so there are those semitone changes that have a dizzying effect, a bit like those on Tommy Roe's 'Dizzy.' "

"Spinning Top," "Neon Shuffle," and "Traffic Light Rock" were all get-rich-quick attempts by Andy to invent a dance craze. "I wasn't a good songwriter and I thought this was the path to instant glory." But as his audiences pointed out, a steady rhythm is the first rule of dance music. Something he would never grasp. XTC went on to create a number of undanceable dance records. The path to instant glory remains blocked.

"Neon Shuffle"

(Andy Partridge)

Another "stupid dance craze" from the Helium Kidz days, "Neon Shuffle" had been the epileptic ending to many a live set, with *Dan Dare* lyrics instructing the audience to dance themselves into a frenzy and no clear rhythm to help them do so. Midsong, the arrangement broke down to herald the Barry Andrews chaos that would end every gig. "He was so ramshackle it was unbelievable. He was always breaking keys on the organ and if it wasn't that, it was that bloody piano," says Colin. "It used to happen at every gig, because his fucking piano was on wheels and he'd get so carried away during that number, the thing would inevitably tip over. He'd end up standing on it, playing it laid on its back." Barry saw this end section as a track of its own and had it marked on the tape box as "The Complete and Utter Destruction of Berlin by Bombers."

IN THE SIDINGS . . .

"Hang On to the Night"

(Andy Partridge) (Single B side only)

Both Barry and his predecessor, Johnny Perkins, had hated playing "Hang On to the Night." They both felt that the Edwards Funfair keyboard sound demeaned their grand talents. Andy had made it a little less risible than in its original form as "Here Come the Saucers," but it was still very silly. "John Perkins hated playing this live because I got him to play this overtly bumper-cars keyboard and he wanted to be taken seriously—a Keith Emerson–type figure. I wanted him to be the Johnny and the Hurricanes thing. He 'abhorred its very womb,' as we say in school assembly. Good fun to play. Very moronic. I'm not even sure what it's about. It's a song about being out and drunk at night and you don't want it to end, basically." It's equally about the pleasure of laying in bed, curled up with his girlfriend with the lights out before dawn, something he probably was too young to do when he wrote "Here Come the Saucers." Either version was hardly the deepest of songs, and it only made it to the B side, though strangely, a performance video was made in the ITN sessions.

"Heatwave"
(Colin Moulding) (Single B side only)

A version of "Heatwave" was recorded during the *White Music* sessions at The Manor but was not released. The song was originally titled "Heatwave Mark II" and was resurrected for the sessions at Utopia with Mutt Lange in February 1978. "I think it's about sunbeds, personally, but it's intermingled with buzz words and squeaks and 'electricity can be fun' images," says Colin, who probably forgot why he wrote it because no *real* Swindon man would be found dead on a sunbed. "The Mark II Deluxe sounds a bit sunbeddy to me. But it's more of a relationship tune really," he says.

Although it was only a B side, the extra time spent on the Utopia sessions gave it a slicker feel than most of the album tracks. "The Lange version is once again supremely better than the outtake version," says Colin, drawing attention to the clavinet ideas of Barry Andrews and the clattering Partridge guitar. The guitar was always more inventive on Colin's songs because Andy didn't have to sing and the early recordings were true to the live arrangements. As Andy explains, "[If] I didn't have to sing the lead vocal I would have more fun, be able to relax, play more complex, difficult things."

"Traffic Light Rock"

(Andy Partridge) (Single B side, plus live version from Eric's Club, Liverpool, recorded by Manor Mobile and released on flexidisc)

"We were both very excited with the New York Dolls' 'Jet Boy' and were very impressed to know that the percussion noise was stack heels on a parquet floor. We kept thinking we'd have to make records with stack heels on a parquet floor. This is definitely influenced by the Dolls and glam and DC comics," reckons Colin. "It was just an inconsequential piece," says Andy. "I kept wanting to write a dance craze like the Hitchhiker or the Hullygully, but people had always complained, 'Your music's always stopping and going. Why don't you just bloody stick to it when you've got it?' So 'Traffic Light Rock' was describing the criticisms of the band in the form of a dance craze." The Hullygully's position in the "Dance Craze Hall of Fame" remains secure. However hard Andy tried, XTC would never be a dance band.

2

STRONG AND SILENT

1978

Take four young men, put them in a basement flat in the big city, allow them to convince themselves they are adults and rock stars, and stand well back! XTC's sessions for their second album, Go 2, *were turbulent and unhygienic.* White Music *hadn't rocked the world but*

(CREDIT: STORM THORGESON. BY PERMISSION OF VIRGIN RECORDS.)

it had given Virgin the confidence to continue and so, within months of its release, the company sent the four of them back into the studio. Abbey Road again. John Leckie again. After a short spell in Chunky's Red Brick Studios in Swindon, trying things out, they headed for St. John's Wood and the big studio by the zebra crossing.

Armed with Coco Pops and cases of beer, they settled into a large, rented basement in Belsize Park and proceeded to make their mark on the place. By the end of the six-week sessions they had almost destroyed the flat and the band.

Belsize Park is a sedate, leafy, Victorian part of London to the north of Regents Park and Primrose Hill. It nestles on the slopes leading up to the village of Hampstead and consists of large brick villas, built by wealthy merchants on the site of an old hunting park. In the late seventies it was a little worn at the edges but maintained an air of grandeur. Within the XTC flat there was more of an air of squalor. Dishes filled the sink, beer bottles and cans were scattered around, and the place stank of cigarettes, alcohol, unwashed sheets, socks, and bodies. In such an atmosphere of decadence, it is little surprise that the band did not get on. Andy's rant about the theft of his Coco Pops, which were at first a subject of ridicule, and then the focus of envy, became a running gag for months after. The thief was never exposed, but the lack of trust over breakfast cereals was symbolic of a problem in XTC itself.

Barry had started to write prolifically. His songs were simpler, based on more recognizable chord structures, with a Clash-like, urban quality to the lyics. There were no superhero comic book characters and spaceships here. His voice was more straightforward, as well. He didn't bark like a seal. He sang in a thinner, more boyish tone, with a near Cockney twang that betrayed his London origins and his devotion to the acceptable accent of punk. Neither Andy nor Colin liked Barry's songs or his voice and the fact they had twenty of their own to choose from made Barry's participation all the more irritating. But Barry was supposed to be an equal partner and they were obliged to record them.

Even though they were Barry's songs, Andy couldn't resist the urge to interfere with the recordings, making suggestions and criticisms midtake. He may have been trying to help but it wasn't taken that way. Andy didn't include diplomacy among his undoubted talents. As the sessions progressed, John Leckie had to act as mediator, keeping them out of each other's sessions. It made the album less live-sounding than *White Music* but it pushed them in the direction of the studio band they were to become. It was also the first time that Andy took a hand in the production, mixing one track while Leckie and assistant engineers, Haydn Bendall and Pete James, sat back and watched, bemused.

By late 1978, the singles charts were being deluged with disco. The fan base which chased XTC, the Boomtown Rats, and new bands like the Police and Dire Straits were just a small proportion of the record-buying public in Britain. The vast majority went to discos, run by leisure giants like Mecca, who had closed down dozens of cinemas to build bingo halls and sparkly nightspots. The "new wave," as it had been dubbed in an attempt to sound less negative than "postpunk," were stuck with sweaty pubs and clubs, risking maiming, electrocution, or drowning in phlegm. XTC was still getting spat at by its audiences, a sign of punkish affection not even the Sex Pistols had liked. This was beginning to upset Colin, who had never found a natural rapport with the crowd. He enjoyed touring and the excitement of visiting new cities, but it was taking over his life. Almost every song he wrote for *Go 2* was about gigs, touring, and the crowd.

XTC had toured constantly since finishing *White Music*. They were packing club-size British venues and had achieved some success around the Continent, supporting Talking Heads. They visited the great cities of Europe for the first time, hanging out with the Heads in the Amsterdam Hilton, posing for pictures in Hamburg, living the wild life of a band on tour, drunk, broke, filthy. After a brief respite from gigging, they took a hurried writing break. It was rushed, and the pressure they were feeling about too much work for not enough money showed through in the writing, giving the album a production-line theme.

Virgin was not happy with the rushed sound of what it saw as a single. So the band was sent to The Manor again, to work with Martin Rushent, who had found favor producing the Stranglers. It was a brief and rather odd session, but it produced "Are You Receiving Me?" and kept XTC in the public eye, though not surprisingly, without aiding sales of the album.

The choice of album title was a snappy way of saying this was the second album. Barry had suggested *Strong and Silent*, which was a contender for a while but *XTC's Go 2*, to give it its full title, was more straightforward and succinct. The cover artwork and complimentary "This is an advertisement . . ." publicity caused a lot of media discussion. The "This is a record sleeve . . ." block of white type was only found by a piece of luck and was chosen partly because so many progressive rock bands had refused it. To promote the record further, and to emphasize the band's love of dub, the first few thousand copies came with *Go+*, a free album of dub mixes. Journalists everywhere were taken with the concept and reviewed the album in the same functional style—"This is a record review. Its purpose is . . . , etc."

XTC'S GO 2

TALKING BETWEEN THE LINES

ON PRODUCERS

ANDY: *We asked Brian Eno to produce it originally.*

COLIN: *We liked what he'd done with Ultravox.*

ANDY: *He had been down to a few gigs, though he didn't talk to us. Dave Mattacks told me years later that, while he was drumming on "Before and After Science," Brian came in excitedly and said, "I saw this fantastic band last night called XTC and if I could join a band it would be that one." But we already had one balding mad professor of a keyboardist and we didn't need another. But we met him at Virgin's office and he spent twenty minutes talking himself out of a job saying, "You don't need a producer. All you need is an engineer just to capture what you do."*

COLIN: *So we went back to John Leckie. Anyway, working with anyone else felt like having an extramarital affair. Once again, Virgin wanted to use someone else for the single so we did "Are You Receiving Me?" with Martin Rushent. He'd made a load of money out of the Stranglers and was getting his own studio going. Once again, he cooked a pretty good groove out of us.*

ON ABBEY ROAD AGAIN

COLIN: *We did most of it in Studio Three but a few tracks we did in Studio Two, the Beatles' studio, at John Leckie's suggestion. It was pretty rundown and looked like a great big photographic studio. And all that trotting up and down stairs just to listen back to things was pretty exhausting.*

ANDY: *But it still had those Indian rugs on the floor and it was really nice to take your shoes off and sink your toes into them.*

COLIN: *It wasn't that special to me.*

ON LIVING TOGETHER IN BELSIZE PARK

COLIN: *We rented this poxy flat and had to fend for ourselves. It was like the "Young Ones."*

ANDY: *It wasn't the Monkees, I can tell you. I bet they didn't nick each other's Coco Pops.*

COLIN: *Somebody did gorge his Coco Pops but it wasn't me. It became part of XTC folklore, if we were looking for a place to stay it would be, "I'm not staying there. It'll be Coco Pops at dawn!"*

ANDY: *It was your usual bedsit fights and that probably came closer to breaking up the band than anything at the time. It got to the point where no one would clean up and it got really disgusting. Every flat surface was covered in beer cans, plates, sauce bottles, and piles of takeaway containers. Whoever's house it was, I feel sorry for them.*

ON BARRY AND ANDY

ANDY: *We fought tooth and nail and the atmosphere while making* Go 2 *was terrible because Barry was resenting my leadership. But I was desperate to make an impression on people. We were a new band in the public conscience and we had to be seen as doing a certain thing. Suddenly, he came up with seven songs and we already had twenty to go on. They sounded like they were coming from a different place and I thought they were a threat to the band's identity.*

COLIN: *They were just a different style and they did jar. It got so as Andy and Barry would go to the* *studio at different times. What got up Barry's nose was that, if he was doing an overdub in the studio, Andy, being Andy, would make it known that he didn't think something was right before Barry had finished. Barry would say, "Why don't you go away and wait till I've finished and then come back and tell me what you think." Which was fair enough really.*

ANDY: *Barry was desperately trying to get Colin and Terry on his side—taking them out for drinks, encouraging Terry, who couldn't sing if you threatened him with a loaded revolver, to sing backing vocals. I was the baddie in his eyes and vice versa. I like him a lot now.*

ON THE SLEEVE

ANDY: *We went to see Hipgnosis and, basically, we didn't like what they had done and it was all getting a bit embarrassing, really.*

COLIN: *We were edging toward the door and saying, "Look, we really need some time to think about this."*

ANDY: *Then, in the middle of this old fireplace in their office, we spotted this black piece of card with white type all over it, just describing what a record sleeve should be. They said, "That's the office joke, it's been turned down by everybody. They thought it was too undermining. Too blatant." So we said, "Great! We'll have it, then." I think they were relieved but a bit embarrassed because we bought the office joke.*

COLIN: *Inside the sleeve, democracy ruled and we each did something. I drew my map of Swindon, which took up most of the space. Andrews went 'round Park South Estate and took loads of photos, including him having a piss and the Chinese restaurant in the Devizes Road with Andy's future brother-in-law, Robbie Wyborn, in the queue, by pure coincidence. Andy wrote a poem, "The Fifties Kitchen Curtain."*

ANDY: *Terry didn't know what to add, but he had this old David Bedford record sleeve he used to dampen his snare drum in rehearsals. So I said, "Drum on that then." He drummed "Science Friction" and Hipgnosis ceremonially photographed the results to make Terry's enigmatic offering. There was also this idiot jigsaw where the inner sleeve fits against a gap on the print on the back cover and this time, in the photos of the band, Barry's can of beer wasn't airbrushed out. But it was Skol this time, so he was definitely going down in the world.*

ON THE RESULTS

COLIN: *I think I was reasonably happy with my stuff, but I thought it was an odd assortment. It had its problems and that worried me because the recording process was quite unhappy. It didn't seem as complete. At the time, I'd probably have said I was happy but it wasn't a wholesome experience.*

A FAN SPEAKS

DAVE GREGORY: *The first two XTC albums were the most intelligent punk records ever made, along with PIL's first and Elvis Costello's. I had thought punk was just another news story but when XTC did* Go 2, *I thought it was a real step forward.*

XTC'S GO 2

ON THE TRACKS

"MECCANIC DANCING (OH WE GO!)"
(Andy Partridge)

Through the late seventies, millions of young Brits would make weekly pilgrimages to Mecca. But their Mecca was an entertainment giant offering spiritual enlightenment through the Miss World Contest and dozens of ballrooms. These were the mosques for the disco generation, in which young girls shuffled 'round heaped handbags, while the lads plucked up and sucked down the Dutch courage to ask for a dance. Ian Reid, XTC's manager, owned similar clubs, like The Affair in Swindon, where XTC drank and smirked at the staggering of sozzled Swindonians, robotically dancing to Kraftwerk. "People would get drunk and then try and behave like a machine," says Andy. "The twentieth-century mating dance. Get drunk, go to nightclub, pick up girls, pretend to be a robot. I thought it was a subject worthy of a song. I suppose it's sort of on the pun of the Mecca club chain and people dancing to the new computer music."

The choppy keyboard- and rhythm-driven result opened many gigs and was as close as Andy felt *Go 2* got to a single, but Virgin felt it would only enhance XTC's name for oddballism. "We were being heavily criticized as being quirky and irky. All those adjectives were being thrown at us at the time so it probably wasn't a good idea for a single," says Colin.

"Battery Brides (or Andy Paints Brian)"
(Andy Partridge)

Even before the advent of laser-read bar codes, supermarket checkout girls seemed capable of punching prices while their minds wandered, unaware that they had served you. "They're dreaming of something, probably marriage, kids," says Andy. "Every generation seems to produce—like battery hens—endless streams of checkout girls who just sit there in a dream. 'Battery Brides' was meant to sound like the dream of a checkout girl."

Even before the advent of computer-driven music, Andy seemed capable of playing guitar while his mind wandered, unaware that the audience and the band were waiting for him to sing. "This bloody song always did drag on too long live," says Colin. "You know what Partsy's like—a bit of tendency to drag things out." "I'd sometimes get the most irate looks from Dave Gregory if he thought the intro had gone on too long," says Andy. "He'd be just glowering at me, 'Get on with the fucking song,' but I'd be sort of blissed out, just chiming away with harmonics and drones."

In the studio, the dream was enhanced by the slow acceleration

XTC on the streets of Hamburg, 1978. (CREDIT: JILL FURMANOVSKY. BY PERMISSION OF VIRGIN RECORDS.)

of the song's "Bjorn Borg" onomatopoeic bass line, Andy's low, quiet vocal, matrimonial keyboard references, and the sinisterly whispered, "Here Comes the Bride." The low vocal, which John Leckie saw in the mold of Brian Eno, offered a new color to the XTC palette, hence the alternative title. It was a hint of the future voice of Partridge—life beyond the seal's bark.

"Buzzcity Talking"

(Colin Moulding)

It was Virgin's Simon Draper who spotted that the chords to "Buzzcity Talking" were almost identical to "Green Tambourine" but even the plagiarist, Colin, hadn't considered it. For him this was just a hurriedly written song about the new life he was leading. For the first time ever, he had "gone abroad," crossing the narrow strip of water that protects Britain from any sense of community with Europe. Across the English Channel was another world, full of foreign things, many of them eager to see XTC. Colin and Andy would usually share hotel rooms in Europe's great cities, buzzing with excitement, unable to sleep. " 'Buzzcity Talking' was the closest I'd got to a road tune," he says. "The tour was virtually the first time we'd been out of the country. It was exciting but grueling with all the working and traveling and drinking and shagging and all that soaked up into my brain. It obviously had to come out. You almost forget who you are and what's gone before." "It's all drink-fueled and new and illicit and exciting and if you've never been out of England, which we hadn't, you just couldn't sleep. You'd be wide awake all the time," adds Andy.

"Crowded Room"

(Colin Moulding)

Although the punk era offered a point of entry for young, radical artists, their audiences were the same young, irrational, piss artists their parents had been—hordes of drunk, drugged-up, adrenaline-charged adolescents looking for an excuse to fight or get laid or both. A rabid herd mentality pervaded most sweaty punk gigs across Europe and Colin found himself an unwilling participant in the mayhem. Thus, "Crowded Room" and the David Byrne-ish panic in Colin's voice. "I think this is my paranoia about audiences coming through, along the same lines as 'The Audience,'" says Colin. "There's probably a bit of stage fright here. Musically it's a bit barbaric. It sort of goes along with the brutality of playing live and witnessing fights in the audience and not being sure if you were going to be roped in. It seemed quite a violent time, really."

"The Rhythm"

(Colin Moulding)

Occasionally during touring, the band would get a night off to see a movie. One night in Leeds, they saw *Saturday Night Fever*. They could never have guessed that the scriptwriter's daughter, Erica Wexler, who appears briefly in the film to refuse Travolta's lascivious advances, would one day make her own lascivious advances to Andy and inspire "Seagulls Screaming Kiss Her, Kiss Her" and "Another Satellite." Instead, Colin saw Travolta's character as one typical of the era. "The film's a real timepiece. I think this song springs from seeing that. It has a very similar sentiment to 'Meccanic Dancing.' The guy gets his kicks at night by dancing."

For the first time on record, XTC felt confident enough to discard the rock 'n' roll crutch of harmonic distortion for the subtleties of acoustic guitar. "I'd started to feel my own style at this time," says Colin. "I think this song sort of pointed a way for me. I enjoyed its melodic quality. For me, melody is still what lures people in. Words have become more important but melody is so deep rooted with me that it's impossible to escape." While it was recorded, Barry was kicking against Andy's leadership. "This was one of these days I was banned so that Barry could work without me chipping in," says Andy, giving a perfect example of why he was excluded. "I came in the next day and said, 'John, play me what you did with Barry yesterday.' I remember hearing the Liberace piano break in the middle, and I can remember thinking, Oh my God! It's so pompous. I was just appalled that this was on a record that had my name on it, but I can see it's totally and utterly campily attractive now."

"RED"
(Andy Partridge)

In contrast to the acoustic touches of "The Rhythm," Andy's pent-up frustration over the Abbey Road sessions and Barry and money and management exploded into the recording of "Red." Thanks to a foul-up over bookings, John Leckie had to shift camp into the cavernous Studio Two, home of the Beatles and the Abbey Road echo chamber. For a Beatles fan, the aura on entering the room is palpable, but XTC were stroppy young punks with no thoughts for sixties hippies, at least not that they were aware of. Instead, the big box of a studio offered ample space to make a screaming row. "Red" was to be that row, a rant on all the negative things associated with the color red—anger, blood, violence, communism, embarrassment, possibly even Watney's abominable Red Barrel beer.

"I wanted 'Red' to sound a mess, drenched in reverb. We pumped it out down the old echo chambers and really soaked it," says Andy. "Barry Andrews played saxophone, squealing and squeaking away at maximum violence. He could only play a couple of little riffs on it, but it was more for the Stooges' 'Funhouse' flavor. He sounds like he's been shoved into the air conditioner saxophone first." A position, no doubt, into which Andy would happily have inserted him. And having cranked the maximum unpleasantness out of the track, they did exactly what the Beatles did with the cacophonous "I Want You (She's So Heavy)," in the same room a decade before—they cut the end off the tape.

Years later, Colin admitted that he would rather the tape had been cut about three minutes earlier.

"Beatown"
(Andy Partridge)

The honeymoon period was ending. The gloss was already rubbing off being a signed rock band. Andy was beginning to discover that, more often than not, musicians were about the poorest famous people alive. His paranoia about being ripped off was just beginning to germinate and, although he didn't realize it, was influencing his songwriting. "I didn't know what 'Beatown' was about until I thought about it years later," says Andy. "I think I was trying to say a sort of 'Kids Are Alright' kind of thing. The band's in this place that they've made for themselves—this Beatown—and they can't be touched by the corrupt workings of the music business." But the creeping paranoia was souring the positive tone with acid phrases—"They use the head and not the fist"—showing the first spark of anger that would engulf him in later years.

The music masked this. By threading paper through the guitar strings, he played a cheerful banjoish rhythm and his pride in discovering the flash chorus chords helped him forget the substance of the song. Once more, the improvised intro was ripe for Partridgeal abuse on stage. While the rhythm section thumped and Barry doodled atonally, Andy would taunt the audience into a frenzy. It became the perfect show opener. "This used to start the shows for the *Go 2* tours," says Colin. " 'Radios In Motion' got put on the back burner so that Andy could whip up the audience doing an Iggy Pop while we were doing our stuff."

"Life Is Good In the Greenhouse"
(Andy Partridge)

"I've never thought deeply about this song. I'm sure there's a meaning behind it. It's one of those songs that was written and I didn't know what the hell it was about. I think it's just a song about being okay in my little space. I don't want to be made a fool of but I'd rather be thought of as a simpleton than be somebody who is thought of as intelligent but manipulated." So said Andy of his first ever mix. "Leckie got very stoned, and I was saying, 'John, do you think you could make it more sort of . . . ?' He said, 'Well, you do it, Andy. You do it.' Haydn Bendall just sat back and they let me mix the thing."

So Andy swamped everything in different reverbs and echoes, trying to create a strange tropical jungle of sounds. The soft *bong! bong!* in the bridge is Terry striking two metal lamp shades from the studio. The hissing noises are made by Andy. Vocals were harmonized an octave up to sound like manic Mickey Mice and Colin plays a strange almost harplike, strumming bass line. With the third-beat snare strike, the overall effect is vaguely dub.

"It's a very unusual-sounding record," says Colin. "Everything sounds as though it's far away. It reminds me of Roger Eagle's club, Eric's in Liverpool. Most of the gigs that we played there had this heavy dub warm-up music with deep basses and skanking guitars and little things drenched in echo." Eventually, the recording of "Greenhouse" would become just such a warm-up tape. By the time the band came on, audiences would be singing along on their own.

"Jumping In Gomorrah"
(Andy Partridge)

"Harlots if you're able, next stop Tower of Babel." Andy's irreligious sense of mischief would get him into trouble in later years, but the sheer banality of "Jumping In Gomorrah" helped it slip the attention of the Bible bashers. But Andy was more concerned at the reaction to his humor. "It's made us a lot of enemies over the years. People think XTC's a comedy group or that we don't take things seriously. I think if something's a little funny then let it come out. All my favorite people use humor in their music from time to time, so why not us. I thought, Let's take all these heavy phrases and almost do this idiot line dance thing with them. Just imagine people in long biblical robes carrying the ark of the covenant along and hula-hooping." So he yelled, "All aboard for Sodom!" down a toilet tissue tube and hurtled into a rock 'n' roll guitar solo. "This is Chuck begat Chuck begat Chuck begat son of Chuck guitar solo. Occasionally I like to slip back into that Chuck Berry sort of guitar solo thing. When you're stuck for anything to do, just go back to the year Chuck and start from there." The rest of the band hated it. "I think it was Barry's least favorite of Andy's songs and he let it be known he didn't want to play it live," says Colin. "It didn't connect with me, either. It's almost something Jonathan King would write."

"My Weapon"

(Barry Andrews)

"My Weapon" was to earn XTC their first hate mail. It was one of those wonderful moments of misread XTC irony and Barry caught all the flak. "This was very misunderstood, especially in the press," Andy says. "What he was trying to do was write from the idiot's point of view, thinking of his penis as this hurting thing. But I don't think Barry's like that. He may come off like a cross between Nosferatu and Joe Strummer but underneath I think he's a pretty sensitive little librarian." Barry had written about seven songs, including "Sargasso Bar," "Us Being Us," and "Things Fall to Bits," which were all recorded for the album. This one even featured the unlikely talents of Terry Chambers on backing vocals. But with the weight of competition, only this and "Supertuff" were contenders for the album.

Virgin predicted the trouble that would follow but, according to Colin, the song was accepted to keep Barry sweet. "We went to Simon Draper's office to decide what would go on the record. 'My Weapon' suggested that he was a male chauvinist pig, wanting to hurt women with his knob, but he says it was the complete

Strange signs in Hamburg. (CREDIT: JILL FURMANOVSKY. BY PERMISSION OF VIRGIN RECORDS.)

opposite and that he was being sarcastic. Virgin didn't see it that way. They didn't mind 'Supertuff,' but they didn't think it was wise to put it on the record." "It got on because we thought if it didn't, he would leave," says Andy. "He came in for a lot of stick over this and got hate mail from women. I didn't like it much at the time but I understood what he was trying to do and I did feel for him. It's a pretty good song, I have to say now." Colin disagrees, "I think it's totally odd. 'Supertuff' had a friend in 'Life Is Good In the Greenhouse,' but this stuck out. What with Andrews's voice, as well, it was a fish out of water. To carry a song like this you need a voice of some power."

"Supertuff"
(Barry Andrews)

Barry's devotion to the "principles" of punk led to some odd lyrical ideas. "Supertuff" was an ode to thuggery, weakened by the theatricality which always tinted Barry's music. His slant on punk was more Broadway, a little Rotten and Hammerstein. Combined with the thinness of his voice, the song never became the Clash clone it wanted to be. "It's a sort of *Clockwork Orange* scenario," says Andy. "Barry Andrews's thoughts on known hard men and the fear they can instill." The white reggae self-dubbery was recorded live, with very few overdubs. It was the only track of Barry's that Andy enjoyed playing and so the only one performed at gigs. The recording showed that enthusiasm with Barry's "Hammer Horror" dark-back-alley piano motif, Terry's deliberate aping of Steve Goulding's famous "Watching the Detectives" drum fill, and Andy's curious percussive guitar effects, created with a loosened E string pulled over a fret and twanged. But no amount of enthusiasm for the song could make it an XTC number. "This is the song where Barry shoved himself off and took his paddle and just rowed away saying, 'I'm off to find my own little island,' " says Andy. "I don't mind listening to it now," says Colin. "At the time I just thought, What! I think Andrews's voice was part of the problem because it was weak and so Cockney. But on reflection, it's not that bad. It's just different."

"I Am the Audience"
(Colin Moulding)

The news that Mick Jones of the Clash had had his guitar smashed during a stage invasion at Newcastle City Hall hit Colin quite hard. British audiences in the late seventies were getting more press than the bands themselves. At one point, Andy was threatened with a gang-beating after criticizing Newcastle's Angelic Upstarts on radio. "Ian Reid got hold of Mensy from the Upstarts and brought him backstage," says Colin. "Andy had to do a lot of explaining. In the end, he agreed not to beat him up."

Andy took most of the onstage risks. But Colin was extremely nervous. "We were just very frightened of being bottled off and having them invading the stage and beating us up. So I wrote this about violence at gigs." "It would be a book in itself; the stuff that was thrown at us on stage," says Andy. "Things like a mud-filled brassiere, a passport, full beer cans, biscuits, lighted cigarettes, broken glass, stones, coins, other members of the audience, you name it."

This was reflected in the record's yob chorus, with Barry and Terry joining in on backing vocals. John Leckie opened with some psychedelic tape phasing, running the same recording on two tape machines, recorded at different speeds. Andy played a "Watching the Detectives" guitar riff. Barry hammered out a very Jerry Harrison-ish, jerky clavinet. For some reason, whenever he was singing about something that made him nervous, he sounded like David Byrne. "David Byrne-ish? Well, aren't we all?" says Colin.

IN THE SIDINGS . . .

"Are You Receiving Me?"

(Andy Partridge) (Single, only on the French version of the album and subsequent CDs)

Andy never really got involved in the rock 'n' roll promiscuity that other band members might have enjoyed, but he wasn't squeaky clean. On just one occasion, he succumbed to the temptation of the flesh and spent several weeks burning in hell for his sins. After confessing to his future wife, Marianne Wyborn, that he had had a brief affair with one of the staff at Virgin Records, he became convinced that she was retaliating. "I was constantly paranoid that she was having an affair behind my back and I think that was starting to show in the song."

A version of the song was recorded with John Leckie during the Abbey Road sessions, but once Virgin saw it as a single, they decided to invest in a more expensive session, using Martin Rushent as producer. "He was disturbingly late," says Andy. "We were at The Manor at nine in the morning, gear all buzzing and ready to go, and Rushent turned up at something like six in the evening. We were incensed and I don't know if being angry at him made us play better, but we captured a blinder of a version. He did a pretty good mixing job, a more violent mixer than John Leckie, who was very amiable." "I think he cooked a pretty good groove out of us. I certainly changed the bass part on his version," says Colin.

"We did an appalling video with Russell Mulcahy who later went on to direct *Highlander*," says Andy. "It was complete and utter chaos actually, and I don't know what people will get watching that video. The song's about this paranoia of being double-timed and there you have our fat roadie, Steve Warren, doing sado-masochistic things to Marilyn Monroe look-alikes and then the British Army, telephone boxes full of exploding smokebombs, and whatever anyone had in the kind of props box," says Andy. "Needless to say, no bastard bought the single either!"

"Instant Tunes"

(Colin Moulding) (Single B side, not on album)

While Andy tried to write "oh-well-at-least-I'm-having-fun" songs about the band's poverty, Colin took a more cynical view. Andy still believes Colin wrote "Instant Tunes" about Viota cake mix. "I used to love Viota and so did he. As kids we were always hanging 'round our mothers when they were cooking them so we could lick the bowl. There was so much sugar in them. So this is Colin's paean to the Viota cake mix of 'anyone can write a song.' "

"Actually, I think it's probably got a connection with 'Only A Northern Song' by George Harrison," says Colin. "It was part of the 'product' concept that was part of the *Go 2* thing. We were getting a bit jaded by the business of writing tunes and getting nothing for it, whereas 'Instant tunes bring instant cash.' The cake thing comes in the idea of production line tunes made to order to bring in cash for everyone but us."

GO+

(Supplementary free minialbum supplied with early copies of Go 2*)*

The lucky few to buy early copies of *XTC's Go 2* got a free twelve-inch, 45 rpm, minialbum of six "dub" tracks called *Go+*. Only a limited number of copies were pressed, but it did appear later, on a CD called *Explode Together. The Dub Experiments 1978–80*.

XTC had been attracted to dub along with the whole punk fraternity, who saw it as an anarchic way of dismembering music. "Dub used to sit very well with punk," says Colin. "In the clubs, you'd have all these girls in fishnet tights and heavy makeup dancing to dub reggae, mechanical music from Europe and Televison and Talking Heads all together in one melting pot."

XTC played a warped kind of live dub as part of the live set and on album tracks such as "All Along the Watchtower," but this was not the mixing-desk-driven dub that was pouring out of Jamaica. True dub was the forerunner to a lot of the more industrial ideas of hip-hop. It contained odd "borrowed" snippets of other people's reggae records, masses of effects, and a ruthless creativity in the way the engineer would cut different sounds, layer echoes, and add other effects. This was using the mixing desk as a musical instrument and, as Andy had got the studio bug, he really wanted to try it. "I knew how they were doing it but there was this magic about it," says Andy. "I thought, If you can dub reggae, why not take any kind of music and make this new sculpture out of it?"

XTC's first attempt at real dub mixes came at the end of the *White Music* sessions. They recorded a number of tracks that didn't make the album, one of them being a rather botched version of the theme to the TV sci-fi puppet show "Fireball XL5." It didn't come out well but Andy suggested trying a dub mix for fun. John Leckie was always up for anything unusual and so they created "Fireball Dub," which was included on the first cassettes of the album sent to Virgin. "It didn't make it onto the record but it was very easy and it gave me a taster," says Andy. "I logged the idea away to do the same thing on the next album and see what we could do by dismantling the tracks on the mixing desk. I thought, naively (as always), that it would be nice to give away the dub mixes as a sort of supplement to the album."

So, over a couple of extremely long days and nights in The Manor, they attempted to dub the album. In the event, they managed only five tracks, partly because "Life Is Good In the Greenhouse" was already pretty "dubby" and partly because the others didn't work. The ones that made it were "Dance with Me, Germany" based on "Meccanic Dancing," "Beat the Bible" based on "Jumping In Gomorrah," "A Dictionary of Modern Marriage," an accelerated version of "Battery Brides," "Clap Clap Clap" based on "I Am the Audience," and "We Kill the Beast" based on "The Rhythm."

They came out so well that BBC Radio One "guru" DJ, John Peel, preferred to play *Go+* tracks to *Go* 2. "He made a terrible faux pas and played the whole of one side at 33 rpm one night and then made some excuse about preferring it that way," says Andy. Andy enjoyed the process so much that he wanted to do it again, but he would have to wait until the next album for that.

3

BOOM DADA BOOM!

1979

It doesn't take a degree in psychology to work out what went wrong between Andy Partridge and Barry Andrews. Although XTC had transformed Barry from a show band organist to a new wave icon, his presence had enhanced XTC's chances of signing a record deal and had raised their public profile. His one-man stage riots and the continual fear that he would electrocute himself made him the focus of many gigs. Andy was the band leader but Barry was the star, and he knew it. But he wanted to be taken more seriously by the band. The rejection of so many of his songs on the *Go 2* sessions had driven a wedge between him and Andy. Unless the other members of the band sided with him, he would have to leave. Andy wasn't going to let anyone wrest control of the band from him. Anyway, Colin and Terry had known Andy too long to shift loyalties and they were unlikely to forgive Barry for turning up for one tour with a saxophone instead of his organ.

For XTC, Barry's departure couldn't have come at a better time. The success of songwriters like Elvis Costello and Nick Lowe opened the doors for intelligent lyrics in the classic style. Devo, Ultravox, and even Gary Numan showed the demand for a bigger sound—*Star Wars* to Barry Andrews's *Dan Dare*. As Barry went on to better things with Restaurant for Dogs, Robert Fripp's League of Gentlemen, and Shriekback, XTC began a new phase of musicality.

Initially the fans were not so sanguine. Barry's leaving was a gargantuan shock to them. He was the perfect antihero: small, balding, pounding the guts out of his Crumar. To some fans, he was a vital part of XTCness and they left with him. But Andy already knew who he wanted in the band, reversing a decision from four years earlier.

Dave Gregory was the least likely-looking rock god. With a slight squint, a soft, gently lilting, husky voice, and terminal shyness, he was the antithesis of Barry. Andy and Colin had decided years earlier that he was too good to play in their band, which is probably as well. In 1977, attitude and image outweighed musicianship and Dave's fashion-unconsciousness would probably have scared off any fashion victim A&R scout. By 1979, the visual image was less important. XTC was an established recording band which needed to improve its musical capabilities. Dave's tweedy Fender Tremolo amp and identical Stratocasters might have earned him the nickname Squinty Two Strats, but at least his equipment worked

Dave Gregory's head replaces Barry's on the Swindon mural of XTC. Barry was added in again when Shriekback had success. (CREDIT: COLIN MOULDING)

and the band was in awe of his playing. Dave was the tight, slick, diligent fourth man Barry would never be. Dave could stand at the back of the stage, blissfully unaware of audience attention, laminating the songs with a rich, thick lacquer of sound. He was a guitarist, which avoided comparisons with Barry, though reluctantly he could play keys if required. His playing was as likely to pay homage to Joe Pass or Chet Atkins as Hendrix or Page. He was also a man who could write dots. He could score music. For the first time, XTC had a member who was a real musician. But Dave was not the gripping stage performer Barry had been. And perhaps the loss of an alternative onstage focus was a contributing factor to what would befall Andy Partridge in the next two years. Colin's songwriting had improved to the extent that he would take the lead on many songs, but Andy was the boss. The pressure was on him.

Nineteen seventy-nine was all change in other ways. Greater leaders showed less tenacity than Partridge. Callaghan, Trudeau, Somoza, the Shah, Amin, Bhutto were out. Thatcher, Khomeini,

Saddam, Ortega, Runcie, and Haughey were in. Three Mile Island's near meltdown almost sent Pennsylvania hurtling after Voyager and Pioneer, changing forever the world's attitude to nuclear power stations. Iran took sixty American hostages, encouraging America to side with Saddam Hussein for almost a decade. And the Soviets invaded Afghanistan, wrecking their chances of big syndication fees for the next Olympics.

XTC knew little of it. They were a touring machine, traveling the world in the discomfort of a cramped van, earning a measly £25 a week each. They were suspicious of their financial status but carried on regardless. Songwriting continued to be prolific, usually on dressing room toilet paper or motel notepads. Rehearsals and arranging took place onstage during sound checks. Colin had started composing late and been forced to air the dirty laundry of his early songs in the public glare of a signed band. But over two albums, he had begun to develop his own style. The new album was to shift the focus of Virgin's interest in XTC toward Colin.

DRUMS AND WIRES

TALKING BETWEEN THE LINES

NEVILLE: *So, when did Barry decide to depart?*

COLIN: *I was sharing a room with Barry at the Gramercy Park Hotel in New York and things were really at an all-time low. He said, "You know, I'm going to leave as soon as the time is right." And I said, "I should think so." And he was really surprised that I didn't want to leave, as well. He said I would be "Ken B Side" in this band, and I just thought, Well, it's okay to be Mr. A Side if you've got the talent.*

ANDY: *I knew something was up and I took the liberty of phoning Dave Gregory from a hotel in Boston. His brother answered and I said, "Tell Dave when he gets home, does he want to join a band?"*

DAVE: *I was dep-ing [standing in] on some country and western gig and when I got home, Ian said Andy had a very important message, so I thought maybe he was going to offer my band a support tour.*

ANDY: *Then when we got back, we were in Ian Reid's office and . . .*

COLIN: *Barry just threw in the towel. It was rather frightening, really. I thought, Well, here we are. We've made two records and we're having the time of our lives and it's all going to end.*

ANDY: *He just said, "See ya, chaps." Christ! It was traumatic. Barry's sound was really integral at that point.*

COLIN: *It just felt as though he stopped us from being ordinary.*

ANDY: *The first two albums are just dominated with that whizzing sense of frivolity—that nutty baroque space music on that whizzing organ.*

COLIN: *And he had an unusual way of playing piano.*

ANDY: *When he remembered the bloody piano.*

COLIN: *But he was the maverick. We'd fit these three parts together into what we thought was tight and*

Barry in Boston, that fateful night. (CREDIT: BY PERMISSION OF VIRGIN RECORDS.)

professional and then he'd come and scribble all over it.

ANDY: *He was the piece of the jigsaw that didn't fit.*

DAVE: *I can understand Barry leaving, though. Anyone trying to present songs to Andy is in for a very hard time indeed. Colin, he tolerated because he'd grown up in Andy's shadow and had been nurtured by him. I remember Colin as being very shy. He was just there in the band. It was years before I heard him speak, and in the early days he had so much hair you couldn't see his face.*

ANDY: *I used to go and see Dave Gregory playing in bands like Pink Warmth. He always seemed much older, but he just started playing earlier and was much more talented. On Saturdays, I would go into Kempster's Music Store or the unfortunately titled John Holmes Organ Centre run by this quasireligious guy we called The Vicar. Dave would sit there and noodle on a guitar and I would try to jam along and get tips until we'd get thrown out. He could play all the standards of the day note perfect.*

DAVE: *The Helium Kidz were rotten. They couldn't play and everyone looked down on them. But there was something about Andy I liked, something that set him apart. When he started writing songs, I thought they had something.*

COLIN: *I met Dave at Hook Village Hall when we were rehearsing. I think he heard the row and just popped in to check us out.*

DAVE: *They played "Adrenalin" and for the first time I started getting worried because Andy clearly had more talent than I did. Every time I saw them after that, I felt more threatened.*

ANDY: *I'd think, Well I'm a stumbling idiot compared to Dave, so when I asked him to join I was really trying to impress him with all the work we had.*

DAVE: *I didn't know he was going to ask. I didn't know Barry was leaving and I would have thought they'd wanted another keyboardist.*

ANDY: *Thomas Dolby had asked to join but we didn't want yet another balding mad professor keyboardist. We did hold auditions, though.*

COLIN: *That was a horror.*

ANDY: *It was an excruciating couple of days. The few that could play they were just bedroom victims. So we said, "Let's just get Dave."*

DAVE: *I drove through two feet of snow to get there and I remember Andy stopping proceedings halfway through and telling me to stop "Ernying." I said, "You what?" And he said, "Stop going erny, erny, erny!" It was just one of my guitar clichés.*

ANDY: *So we sat outside afterward and said, "You're in."*

COLIN: *I think his first comment was, "You'll have to cover my mortgage."*

DAVE: *Yeah, well, I'd just bought a place with my brother.*

ANDY: *They were the Liam and Noel of Swindon. Always fighting.*

DAVE: *We did a radio session with the BBC first, I hadn't really left Dean Gabber and His Gabberdines and they weren't very happy. But that was my real audition. I remember sitting outside Ian Reid's office hearing it on a crackly radio and by the time it had been broadcast, I had been inducted. I didn't think I'd last more than a couple of weeks because I didn't think the fans would put up with a guitarist.*

ANDY: *The first gig was at Roots Club in Exeter, in April 1979, and I was pretty worried about how he was going to go down.*

COLIN: *I remember he was frighteningly louder than everyone else.*

ANDY: *Such a mild-mannered character and he comes on like ten Pete Townshends.*

DAVE: *I got bollocked, but I wasn't that loud.*

ANDY: *He was painfully loud.*

COLIN: *And he always had biscuits on the top of his amp.*

DAVE: *That was for emergencies with my diabetes.*

COLIN: *And the last vestiges of flared trousers. Our trousers were somewhat narrower than his.*

NEVILLE: *But he could play better than any of you. So what about the album?*

COLIN: *We thought about Nick Lowe producing us because I liked "I Love the Sound of Breaking Glass," but then Steve Lillywhite came down to our manager's club and we seemed to hit it off.*

ANDY: *We liked the drum sound he'd made on the Siouxsie and the Banshees record.*

COLIN: *And he'd also worked with Eno on the Ultravox thing.*

ANDY: *He came connected to Hugh Padgham, the Virgin engineer, who seemed to do a lot of the donkey work for him. Hugh had spent months working on this new drum sound with the Townhouse stone room ambience gated through an SSL console. It was the brand-new, violent sound of the late seventies.*

COLIN: *We were supposed to go to the Townhouse for* Go 2, *but it wasn't finished.*

ANDY: *Virgin said, "Go and work in our new studio, it's brilliant," but when we got there all these builders said, "It's not finished, so piss off!"*

COLIN: *But this time we worked there, starting with "Life Begins At the Hop" in Studio One.*

ANDY: *The session was sort of a tryout for Steve and Hugh. They were both incredibly young and Steve didn't really make any musical decisions. He was just Mister Vibey. Jethro Tull was in the next room and Terry's drums were coming through on their mandolin overdub, so Ian Anderson came in to gently complain. We were quite chuffed that someone like him would complain and gave him a credit.*

COLIN: *The arrangements were just our live ones. If it was one of my songs, Dave played the meat and two veg stuff and Andy added the icing on top.*

NEVILLE: *Iced meat and two veg! Mmmmm!*

ANDY: *That's because I'm crap at learning songs, so unless I've got a lot of time to learn, I just improvise all the stuff on top. The thing with Dave is he allowed us to be more ourselves. With Barry, I kept writing with a whizzy keyboard in mind. So when he left it was "Phew! I don't have to do that anymore."*

COLIN: *I never wrote anything with anyone in mind so it didn't bother me.*

NEVILLE: *So why choose* Drums and Wires?

ANDY: *I was reading a lot about Dadaism at the time and wanted something with Dada in it. I saw this brilliant picture in* The Beano *(a British kids funny paper) with Gnasher the dog playing drums and the words "*BOOM DADA BOOM!*" above him. I thought,*

Brilliant! We'll cut out the frame and use that but it was a silly idea and "Drums and Wires" seemed to suit the sound of the record. All drums and guitar strings.

DAVE: *I don't think I took my role in XTC seriously right up to* English Settlement. Drums and Wires *was just great fun for me. I'd always dreamt about doing this. We were just there for two or three weeks. The songs were brand new. The studio was brand new. The band was brand new and I'd never heard of Steve or Hugh. The next thing we knew we were getting four-star reviews in all the papers. How did that happen?*

The new XTC on tour in Tokyo. And Andy thought Dave was unfashionable!

(CREDIT: THE ANDY PARTRIDGE COLLECTION)

DRUMS AND WIRES

ON THE TRACKS

"LIFE BEGINS AT THE HOP"

(Colin Moulding) (Not on European album, single only)

Up to this point, Colin Moulding's songwriting had consisted largely of thumping out a bass riff and creating some sort of melody around catchphrases. "Life Begins At the Hop" was a departure. First, it was clearly about something real in Colin's life. Second, he wrote it on his new acoustic guitar, which he had gotten from Ian Reid in exchange for his entire one percent shareholding in XTC's production company, Allydor. It was the first time he had written the chords to a song. The midweek youth club hops at St. Peters church hall in Penhill, Swindon, were among the first opportunities Colin and Andy had to see live music. "It was about going down to the hop and seeing amateur bands like Oozy," says Colin. "O-o-z-y. Not so much the machine gun as a weeping boil," adds Andy. This was where adult life on the Penhill Estate had its painful birth and Colin wanted to capture that in the song. The Tamla-ish beat, mimicking the records played at the hop, set the tone for a friendlier XTC. "Any kinship with punk went completely out at that point," says Colin. "It was easier to allow up our influences by then," says Andy. "It was an excuse to start again. It was okay to say, 'Yeah, it's like a Motown record.' " The song charted in the U.K. and found them attracting daytime national radio play. "It was our first demihit," says Colin. "We even played on 'Top of the Pops' . . . and it went down."

The band was happy with the single, but the American label decided that a re-recording was in order to suit their market. Cameron Allen was recruited for the sessions at Wessex Studios. Even Sting and his then wife, Frances Tomelty, were dragged in from the next studio to add handclaps, but it was a humorless disaster. "I really felt sorry for him. He just couldn't get anything different out of it that was going to please us," says Andy. The version remains in the vaults.

"Making Plans for Nigel"

(Colin Moulding) (Single and album track)

At last a hit! And of all things, about a mollycoddled kid being forced into a life of servitude by his parents—a perfect subject for the underdog-loving Brits. It was a simple song with no intended controversy. The name Nigel and the choice of British Steel for the boy's career were coincidences. "Nigel sprang from my subconscious for no reason other than the fact that I knew a few boys at school called Nigel and they all seemed to be rather put upon. Nigel is the sort of guy who stays with his mum till his forties and keeps pornographic magazines under the floorboards," says Colin. "I chose British Steel because I wanted something corporate." It was great timing. A month after the album was released, 100,000 steelworkers went on strike. The union even called him

Arrrgh! *Boston, Mass., 1979.* (CREDIT: BY PERMISSION OF VIRGIN RECORDS.)

to ask his opinion of their plight—he didn't have one. British Steel was so annoyed, it found four Nigels in its Sheffield plant to appear in *Steel News*, saying how good their prospects were. Anyone who's seen the film *The Full Monty* knows how good Sheffield steelworkers' prospects turned out to be.

Andy was convinced that Virgin Records was grooming Colin for stardom around this time. "I was incredibly jealous that everything Colin did was getting all the attention," says Andy. "He was the handsome sod and I was the egghead. You could see Virgin's reasoning. He looked like a cross between Chrissie Hynde and Nureyev. The thing that really annoyed me was that once they had decided this was the single, they devoted about a third of the studio time for the whole album to this."

"I don't think it was much to write home about musically, but it probably has some merit for the drum pattern and I think credit should go to Terry Chambers," Colin suggests. The unusual, Devo-influenced drum pattern was suggested by Partridge during rehearsals, according to Dave. "Andy stepped straight in and started changing things. He had a lot to do with the arrangement," he says. "I reckon Andy might be right that it took a long time. Lillywhite was under pressure to come up with a hit and that was the track they chose, so I suppose it worked."

Virgin was so convinced that "Nigel" would turn into a hit that it took out an insurance policy against it becoming one. If it did succeed in the U.K., it might mean canceling an Australian tour. So a Lloyd's assessor listened to the song to estimate its chances. It was a hit. "Making Plans for Nigel" took XTC out of the credible power-pop genre into mass appeal. It reached number 17 on the U.K. charts. They mimed to the song on children's TV shows and on BBC TV's "Crackerjack," the aging comic star Peter Glaze sang it to the kids.

The video, directed by Russell Mulcahy, featured a mad-looking Nigel (an actor often mistaken for a band member) in a strait-jacket, while Andy pranced around, dressed as the joker on a giant game board. In the middle of the song, a huge Styrofoam dice was thrown on to the set and Andy dived into it with his guitar. "Once I was in I couldn't get out. There I was for the rest of the song. It was one of our great Spinal Tap moments."

"It was the first time I realized that it was all right to write songs about something small. I suppose it opened a door for songs like 'Bungalow,'" says Colin. "The biggest thrill for me came up years later when I opened up one of the national newspapers and the headline read 'Making Plans for Nigel' on an article about the Chancellor of the Exchequer, Nigel Lawson. To have sunk that far into the consciousness of the nation is really special to me."

"HELICOPTER"

(Andy Partridge)

This whole song stems from Andy's memory of a Lego ad in the sixties "educational" comic *Look and Learn*. "It had always stuck in my mind. There was this scene of these two kids flying around on jet packs over this vast Legoland," says Andy. "And the sound of a tremolo guitar reminded me of a helicopter. So the idea came to me about this girl who's flying around out of reach with her own helicopter pack."

"It was our first venture into disco," says Colin. "We had a thing about disco then." "With its 'Peasoup! Peasoup!' drumbeat," adds Andy. "It's the same rhythm as 'Generals and Majors' actually," says Colin.

Dave Gregory had already discovered rap through the Sugarhill Gang's "Rapper's Delight" and Colin and Terry liked Chic and *Saturday Night Fever*, but the link between disco and XTC remained a tenuous one. Certainly, the fans who would go nuts for "Helicopter" at gigs would have been appalled at the idea of it being a disco record. "It went down phenomenally well live, which annoyed me after a while because it's no great piece of art," says Andy. It was no great piece of singing either. The track was recorded almost live and Andy's voice was shot to pieces.

"Day In Day Out"
(Colin Moulding)

Many of Colin's songs have been inspired by a phrase. Strumming away on his new acoustic guitar, riffs would sound like phrases and the phrase would become the hookline of the song. So it was with "Day In Day Out," a song on a subject of which he knew nothing—the daily grind of factory work. "I've never worked in a factory so I don't know how it came about. In fact, I've never had a job that I didn't like. But basically, it's a bit of musical Mike Leigh."

Years later, Colin admitted that there may be a hint of his brother in the song. "Graham's always worked in a factory and as far as my mother's concerned he can do no wrong. But she still doesn't think I've got a real job."

"It has a pleasing depression to it," says Andy. "All the instruments sound like factory parts. We bought a little monophonic Korg synth and the moaning noise at the start is that sort of groaning 'morning' at the start of the week's work."

"When You're Near Me I Have Difficulty"

(Andy Partridge)

"This is actually about an early schoolgirl crush, called Vanessa Kearley," admits Andy. "She really did have that effect on me. I'd get within a certain radius of her and I couldn't function. My legs would go all wobbly and I couldn't talk. I held her hand one evening and walked her home from the Deers Leap off-license [liquor store] and I was in transports of delight for weeks after. I used to fantasize about her. I knew she was really into 'The Man from U.N.C.L.E.' and I used to try to get myself to look like Ilya Kuriakin. I had my hair cut to look like his and wore dark rollnecks whenever possible and I remember making us these triangle badges in my best smudgy Biro." The song was recorded quite quickly and some surprising errors got through, including the awful out-of-tune intro. Virgin considered it with "Real by Reel" for a single release and the band spent a few days with Steve Lillywhite in DJM Studios trying to improve it, but the idea was dropped.

"Ten Feet Tall"

(Colin Moulding) (Album track and first U.S. single, electric version)

XTC's first attempt at an acoustic song was born out of Colin's admiration for Nick Lowe's "Cruel to Be Kind." It gave Colin his starting point and the resulting song sounded so unXTC that Dave thought Colin should release it as a solo single. But if the sound of the song broadened the spectrum in which XTC could be seen to work, the lyric was simply another word association idea which stemmed from an attractive phrase. "I just thought that if I wrote too much about myself, it didn't have any ambiguity and didn't sound so good. It wasn't till much later that I could write from personal experience."

More telling of his personality at the time was his naughty

schoolboy alternative lyric. "I feel like I'm walking 'round with Ten Foot's tool" referred to the council groundsman Colin had assisted in earlier years. "He was known as 'Ten Foot' because the girls at the school had seen the bulge in his trousers and knew he was a bit of a star in that department. They'd shout, 'Come on, Ten Foot, you show us yours and we'll show you ours.' "

Touring, I love it. Australia, 1979. (CREDIT: BY PERMISSION OF VIRGIN RECORDS.)

An electric version of the song was recorded later as part of the "Wait Till Your Boat Goes Down" sessions as the first, if atypical, U.S. single. Andy wrote an extra vocal section for the middle section but wasn't happy. "It lost some of its charm but it was more robust," says Andy. "It was just a shame that our first American single didn't sound like us."

"Roads Girdle the Globe"
(Andy Partridge)

Andy had never liked motor vehicles. The only one he ever drove was a moped, as a teenager, and that scared the life out of him. So he had been trying, without success, to write a lament to the sacrifice of Britain on the altar of the motor car. "I stayed up late one night and watched a Scandinavian film called *Petrol In Their Veins*, which was sort of a forebear of *Crash* about a couple who were besotted with all things mechanical," says Andy. "That tipped me over the edge to finish this song. The sarcasm of it lies in this religious chant to the car and naturally it had to be clamorous and grinding.

It's really ugly." The ugliness was fantastic and the song remarkable, attracting a cover by Dave Stewart and Barbara Gaskin.

"If ours sounded like a car crash, theirs was more like the velveteen interior," says Andy. "It's such an improbable song," says Dave. "I remember Andy bringing this up with 'Homo Safari' and 'Pulsing Pulsing.' I just thought, You cannot be serious! It was just twisted metal-made music. Then we got into the stone room at Townhouse with that loud drum sound and these wirey guitars and I thought, Well, fucking hell! This is a great track!"

"This song is the epitome of the sound of *Drums and Wires* for me," says Andy. "The guitars sound like someone cutting the string on a bale of barbed wire." The clamor was increased by recruiting roadie, Steve Warren, Al Clark (Virgin's A&R director), Laurie Dunn (Virgin's head of International), and Hugh Padgham to sing backing vocals on the record, indicating that it must have been recorded in the evening—label managers only turn up at dinnertime.

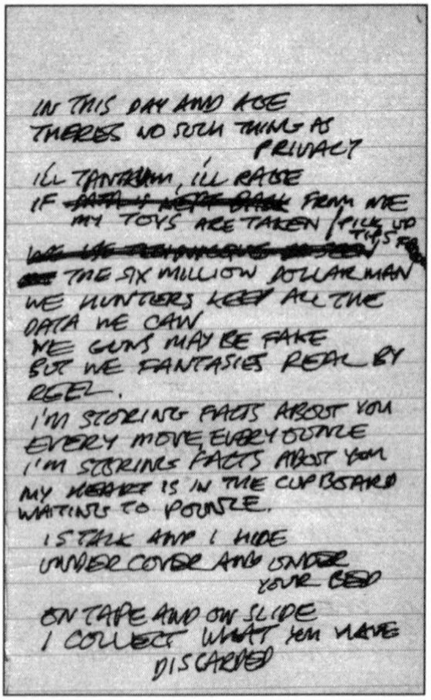

Unused ideas for "Real by Reel" from Andy's notes. (CREDIT: ANDY PARTRIDGE)

"Real by Reel"

(Andy Partridge)

Now Margaret Thatcher had her feet under the table, she could get down to creating the police state she wanted Sleepy Britain to be. Walking out in front of increasingly large crowds, the noisy "Real by Reel" was a very public way of expressing Andy's need for privacy. "The song is just a piece of slick paranoia. I don't like the thought of people prying and spying on me and because 1984 was on the horizon and you were starting to see security cameras around, I was becoming professionally paranoid about being watched."

"Millions"
(Andy Partridge)

In the days before the Tiananmen Square massacre, Andy was obsessed with all things Chinese when he wrote this naive love letter to the Chinese multitude. He wore Chinese slippers and jackets, ate Chinese food off Chinese crockery, watched Chinese films and, as the song says, really believed that China's time was coming. The song even borrowed the idea that the Chinese were chosen people. "I read an old Chinese proverb that said when God baked the first batch of humans, he underdid them and they came out white," says Andy. "So the next time he left them in a bit longer but he overbaked them and they came out black. But by the time he did the Chinese he'd got it worked out and they came out golden brown and just right." As the lyric says, "Bake you golden like the Yangtze mud."

Musically, however, any attempt to sound Chinese was less complimentary. "I'm afraid there's something rather condescending in that 'ying tong,' Widow Twanky guitar figure, a bit 'I'm a Yangtze Doodle Dandy.' " It was actually written for the Barry Andrews song "Things Fall to Bits" where he had asked Andy for something that sounded "Made In Hong Kong," but it wasn't used. Dave played this riff on the record but thought the mix ruined it. "I liked 'Millions' but I thought the mix was lousy," says Dave. "The guitars disappeared. They were more interested in getting an atmosphere to the sound."

"That Is the Way"
(Colin Moulding)

Colin became a parent very young, and was always worried that he should not talk to his kids the way his parents did to him. But he probably did. "That Is the Way" was written around a list of such parental phrases. It reflected Colin's concerns about the way parents relate to children. To this day, Andy's and Colin's mothers are wondering when they will get proper jobs. Even after they'd had a couple of hits, Vera Moulding thought she was being helpful when she suggested Colin audition for the Harmonics, who earned "proper money" getting regular bookings at workingmen's clubs in the area. Dave and Andy tell of a night in the village hall at Lydiatt Millicent, in 1970, when Andy's dad dragged him out of a local teenage jam session. "Andy was having the time of his life playing real music and showing off to all his friends after all those years playing in his bedroom on a stolen guitar," says Dave. "Suddenly there was this silhouette standing in the doorway, wearing a police coat and holding a flashlight," says Andy, who was up on stage while his friends lay around on the floor. They thought it was a raid, but it wasn't. "He flashed his light around and then said, 'Andy! Where are you? Your mother's worried sick and you're coming home right now.' Andy was incredibly embarrassed," says Dave.

"That Is the Way" was the first time XTC swallowed their pride and hired a session musician. "I had two lots of everything on the song and we needed something to lift it in the middle," says Colin. "Steve Lillywhite had worked with Dick Cuthell on the Members' 'Offshore Banking Business' and I think Dick was on call. So we virtually gave him a free rein and so he came up with all these flügelhorn riffs."

"Outside World"

(Andy Partridge)

"He has two Strats lying in their cases," ran Andy's alternative lyrics at gigs, in reference to Dave's identical guitars. But the real words were daft enough, alliterative tongue twisters concealing Andy's personal fears of the horrors of world events. "The lyrical content is a lot of wordplay to fit the machine gun rhythm," says Andy. "I thought it would be good to write a song about the modern world in this nursery rhyme fashion. To be honest, I think the 'she' is actually me not wanting to know about the horrors of the outside world with all these noises stopping me from hearing what's going on."

Andy took a long time to piece together the lyrics and is nonplussed when Colin draws some parallels to Elvis Costello's "Pump It Up," especially in the line, "Bad black and white men, standing in their pigpen/Selling guns to simpletons to shoot them in the abdomen." "I never knew what the lyrics to Costello's song were, but maybe it sunk in," he says. Onstage, this would be played at lightning speed, depending on Dave's dexterity, his foot stomping the stage as he tackled the complex riff that rocketed through the song. "We used to save this for an encore, didn't we?" says Colin. "Well, you'd do yourself in playing this in the middle of the set," says Andy. "I can still see Dave stamping his foot while he was playing that riff."

It was a riff he had transformed in the studio, adding inversions that Andy admits did much for the song. "That's Dave's musical expertise finding those intervals. Colin and I were still pretty naive technically."

"Scissor Man"
(Andy Partridge)

For over a century, millions of children have been terrorized by the book of *Struwwel Peter*, a horrific lesson to children on the virtues of personal hygiene. It is pure Victoriana, but it still strikes home a century on. Tim Burton's film *Edward Scissorhands* showed the Struwwel influence and Andy's "Scissor Man" was based around the Struwwel story. "It used to scare the shit out of me as a kid. He wouldn't cut his hair and wouldn't wash. His nails grew really long and in the end all his fingers are cut off. I used to wonder who this bogeyman was who crept in to snip off your fingers."

The period look of the book also influenced the music, most of which was pure Victorian music hall music. "You could almost imagine Danny Kaye singing it in *Hans Christian Andersen*," says

Andy. The song was recorded very quickly with the band playing live to capture the living dub section at the end. "The bit at the end grew into a bit of a monster live. I couldn't wait to get to that bit," says Andy. "It was like, 'Okay, permission to improvise, now!' " Dave would often make sure they got there quickly, setting a breakneck pace. "We used to play it so fast, Gregsy would start it off and play it faster and faster each night. He'd go off the scale," says Andy. "He would think the speed was fine but something that was okay for his part would make parts that we played sound ridiculous," says Colin. The studio version of this section gave Lillywhite the chance to exercise his own passion for dub, switching mute buttons in and out on the desk, though careful listening will pick out a few missed beats.

"Complicated Game"

(Andy Partridge)

If anyone's ever wondered what the irritating grinding buzz is running all the way through this track, it's Colin Moulding's electric shaver held against a microphone. Everything that the band could find was dumped onto tape to build "Complicated Game" to a gargantuan racket. The song is a lament to the futility of choice, from the quiet verse debating which side to part one's hair, through the choice of left or right in politics to a deity's perplexing dilemma over planetary placement. "It's one of those 'you get born and it doesn't matter and then you die' songs. It's terribly futile and dark," says Andy. Colin doesn't remember the shaver, but Andy says it was out of tune and needed slowing down on the tape to get the right drone. From then on, the tension begins to mount. "It's just built on those droning chords in G and starts off incredibly quietly and ends horribly noisy," says Andy. "Short of hiring in an orchestra, we had to make the giant orgasm at the end on guitars."

"I loved Andy's guitar solo at the end," says Dave. "It really shows the difference in his style and mine. I could never have done that. It was recorded in one or two takes and I think this is the first take." "I had my amp right up and my flanger set on metallic overkill," says Andy. "I played it without hearing the backing track to stop me getting trapped into the rhythm. Steve just pointed when he was recording and I played. I didn't hear it with the track till it was recorded."

IN THE SIDINGS . . .

"HOMO SAFARI"

(Andy Partridge) (Single B side only, not on album)

"This was sort of insane incidental music I had written around a riff I had at home," says Andy, who had offered this for the first recording session because nothing else was sufficiently rehearsed. "It was knocked out during the 'Life Begins At the Hop' sessions, basically to stop the record from warping." The chunky instrumental had very Devo-sounding drums and once again showed the disparate nature of XTC's influences. The title was more camp for the safari idea than for the homo one. Andy lifted the safari idea from the German bandleader Bert Kaempfert's "Swingin' Safari," though the comparison ends there. The homo aspect was a reference to the Latin for "man," not in any way an allusion to homosexuality, though of course people assumed it must be. This track actually set a trend in XTC instrumentals and was to be followed by a series of sequels.

"CHAIN OF COMMAND"

(Andy Partridge) (One of two giveaway single tracks supplied with early copies of the album)

From the start, the band was aware that this would be a filler track at best. Recorded almost live in the same session as "Pulsing Pulsing," it was completed quickly and leaves little impression. "As a teenager, I was constantly making battle games and strategical games," says Andy. "Though, funnily enough, I never learned to play chess. And I was fascinated by the wars that go on in your body, armies of microbes fighting off invading diseases and so forth. It fascinated me from *Fantastic Voyage* onward. Really, it's just what people do in war, microbes laying down their lives to save the greater country."

"Limelight"

(Colin Moulding) (One of two giveaway single tracks supplied with early copies of the album)

Although this song was never expected to become more than a B side, Andy is surprised at how strong "Limelight" sounds today. Mark Fisher published a fanzine named *Limelight* after this, his favorite XTC song. It is also notable for establishing the two-guitar, left-right, skanking sound that opened "Wake Up" on *The Big Express*. "It was probably about fame," says Colin. "With what little fame we'd had at the time, it was probably about where we'd come from and how people there treated you. The relationship changes. They go all coy on you."

"That horrible chord at the front, the worst chord in the world, was edited on because Dave had to retune his guitar again and again until he found it. It's kind of a waker-upper," says Andy. "But listening to those backing vocals, 'Ha ha, he's in there now. Ha ha, he's holy cow,' still make me smile. They're obviously about what people were thinking 'round Swindon: 'Look at him. He thinks he's really famous now.' "

"Pulsing Pulsing"

(Andy Partridge) (B side only, not on album)

"This was a funny little unfinished, stillborn idea," says Andy about the second song in these sessions on the subject of anatomy. "It's a sort of sister piece to 'Chain of Command,' a song about the pulse of life. It's such a small thing but it's life itself." It was a little song, but it gave the chance to experiment. The increased emphasis on the drums caused by Terry's cymbal-less playing was a trick Lillywhite and Padgham were to use to good effect on the Peter Gabriel *Melt* album they produced soon after. Andy's Fender Bronco guitar is also unusual, as it wasn't plugged in, just held to a microphone and strummed in a thin, stringy sound. Something XTC would use a lot on later recordings.

"Bushman President" (Homo Safari #2)

(Andy Partridge) (B side only, not on album)

Andy recorded and produced this strange little instrumental while the rest of the team were having dinner at the Townhouse. "I said to Steve, 'Just leave the tape on and plug up that Korg synth with a little reverb, would you?' and I just necked my dinner down quick and came running back and knocked this thing up. I overdubbed all the parts using the monophonic synth."

Andy already had the title, which led to its slightly African undertones. It became the introduction tape at gigs. "It was like a fanfare for the band," says Colin. "And the signal for the band to go on stage was when someone said, 'It's galloping.' If you weren't ready to go on stage and Terry heard it, he'd go, 'Moulding! Where are you? It's bloody galloping!' "

"TAKEAWAY"/"THE LURE OF SALVAGE"

(RELEASED BY THE ARTIST MR. PARTRIDGE)

It was October 1979. A thick fog shrouded the dank streets around London's Regents Park. Deep in the bowels of Regents Park Recording Studios, Andy "Frankenstein" Partridge and John "Igor" Leckie carried out crude experiments on the flesh and bones of *Drums and Wires*. Andy's "dub" bug had inspired Andy to reconstruct XTC's music into a new album, to take odd bits and pieces from *Drums and Wires* and other multitracks, chop them up, turn them around, and add to them. This was heading further into dub territory than *Go+*, but bore little resemblance to the dub reggae that inspired it. Leckie was a willing assistant for this frenzy of musical prosthetic surgery and Andy wanted him because he was good for this type of work, and because he felt guilty about him not producing *Drums and Wires*. "I suspect I wanted to offer him a little compensation, which is a terrible thing to say," but he says it anyway.

The week's work of long days, interspersed with late-night horror movies in London's West End, brought forth a collage of noises and poetry. Marianne was dragged in to record handclaps and noises and a viewing of *Alien* inspiring excessive use of hissing noises on the album. "It was fun to pull all this stuff apart. It's like taking a welding torch to a perfectly good car, cutting it up and sticking it together in a different order to create something good and new out of it."

Initially, Andy had wanted to call it "Takeaway" and was going to package it in a brown paper bag with Chinese symbols on it—he was consuming quantities of Chinese food at the time in a fit of Sinophilia. But "The Lure of Salvage" was such a delicious phrase and the discovery of a photo of Jayne Mansfield floating in a pool full of Mansfield look-alike hot water bottles changed his mind. Clumsily, he combined the two names and scribbled out a few of the hot water bottles to represent the holes in dub music. It was a quirky album and the press was perverse in its reaction. "I remember the *New Musical Express* saying that I was the wrong color to be messing around with dub; which is great coming from a supposedly PC newspaper!" he says. Still available with *Go+* on the CD *Explode Together—The Dub Experiments 1978–1980*. The tracks were as follows:

"COMMERCIALITY"
(Andy Partridge)

"Refrigeration Blues" was another faller at the last fence of *White Music* but the bass and drums, combined with blocky guitar and buzzing synth noises, formed a backing track for Andy's poem "Commerciality," an earlier work; probably a by-product of the production-line theme that flavored *Go 2*. "I improvised and yelled it in probably one take," he says. Funny. You'd never know.

"THE DAY THEY PULLED DOWN THE NORTH POLE"
(Andy Partridge/Colin Moulding)

Butchering Mutt Lange's production of "Heatwave" and slowing it down created a contradictory, chilly-sounding piece. "So I came up with a suitably frosty title and added a little echoey, cod-eskimo keyboard." I'm sure the Inuits would be honored to be so treated.

"THE FORGOTTEN LANGUAGE OF LIGHT"
(Andy Partridge)

"The Forgotten Language" was actually gibberish, a totally scat lyric over the drums and bass of "Millions" from *Drums and Wires*. "It had an exuberance, which I quite liked, so I put it on the record. Japanese fans have told me that some of the words are Japanese things that they can understand! And talking of gibberish, Japanese record companies insist on writing their own lyric sheets if you do not supply them. I've seen the lyrics for this and they are surreal!"

"STEAM FIST FUTURIST"
(Andy Partridge)

Andy and John rushed back from a bowel-evacuating screening of *Alien*, leapt to the controls of the "Nostromo" mixing desk, and dubbed the hell out of "Real by Reel," liberally smothered with Ridley Scott–type steam blasts to create "Steam Fist Futurist."

"Another 1950, Shoreleave Ornithology"

(Andy Partridge)

In 1977, outside the earshot of his fellow punks, Andy would listen subversively to Charlie Parker records. One night, while doing so, he penned a rambling little poem about nothing in particular. Two years later, he recited it over the looped bass and drums of "Pulsing Pulsing" and, voilà!, "Shoreleave Ornithology."

"Cairo"

(Andy Partridge)

As "Homo Safari" was already an instrumental, it was an easy dub mix to turn into one of Andy's ridiculous "dance crazes," in this case to be called "The Cairo." Marianne added clapping and, as usual, it became a dance craze nowhere other than in Andy's head.

"The Rotary"

(Andy Partridge)

Terry's ferocious drumming on "Helicopter" was a perfect target for Partridge/Leckie "dubbery." "There was this Neanderthal aggression that Terry put into this track that was just brilliant," says Andy. "I put a no-key rhythm guitar over the top. These spikes of sound. These sheets of chords. And then sang this mad improvised vocal," which Andy admits was inspired by Beefheart's "Blimp," itself a tribute to the legendary Hindenburg disaster radio commentary. From zeppelins to helicopters in one bizarre hit.

"Madhattan"
(Andy Partridge/Colin Moulding)

The chopped and shaped remains of "That Is the Way" from *Drums and Wires* resulted in "Madhattan," including slivers of Dick Cuthell's flügelhorn. "We really went to town on the dub techniques here, with harmonized drums and stuff," says Andy, though whether the town he took it to was New York or Swindon remains a mystery.

"I Sit In the Snow"
(Andy Partridge)

The four line poem "I Sit In the Snow" was a piece of haiku which Andy had written in an idle moment and had dug out of his notebook for "*Takeaway*." Repeated over the looped middle section of "Roads Girdle the Globe" with sleighbells and other frosty sounds, it became one of the most successful tracks on the album, in Andy's opinon.

"Work Away Tokyo Day"
(Andy Partridge/Colin Moulding)

The sun rises over Tokyo to the sound of a fake bamboo flute played on Andy's little Korg. "But the peace is shattered by adding all Barry Andrews's sax overdubs from 'Red' to create a traffic jam." Laid over a turbocharged version of the backing track of Colin's "Day In Day Out," this traffic jam racket sparked the idea that became Andy's multilayered sax solo on "It's Nearly Africa" a couple of years on.

"New Broom"
(Andy Partridge/Colin Moulding)

"*Takeaway*" was one of the few occasions where writing credits to Moulding and Partridge combined, though Colin had little say in the dissection of his tracks or the way in which "Making Plans for Nigel" became a song about "Mr. A," the Steve Ditko comic character. Mr. A was a zero-tolerance kind of hero who saw things very simply. "I used to use him to clear my head about things," says Andy. "But it's also just the sort of thing ultra-right-wing idiots could abuse." It was unlikely that any such misguided folks would hear his poem based on Mr. A, "New Broom," which he yelled over the ponderously slowed-down backing track of "Nigel."

"Takeaway"/"The Lure of Salvage" finally cleared Andy's system of his dub obsession. "It was a huge buzz to sit in front of a massive mixing desk, sending things down a thousand miles of echo and adding a million tons of reverb. It was like crewing Fireball XL5 but I got the dub thing out of my system. It was like working in a laboratory and I don't feel the need to do that now. We didn't have any programming or sampling then, so most of it was done live at the desk and sounds very rough and ragged. These days, I think a lot of it doesn't work for me, but some of it is a charming period piece." Charming might not be the ideal adjective, but *"Takeaway"* was an interesting diversion.

4

TERRY AND THE LOVE MEN

1980

"Making Plans for Nigel" was a hit, but not such a major hit that Virgin had to cancel the Australian tour and put a claim into Lloyd's. The idea of flying to Australia made them nervous. The whole band was terrified of flying. DC-10s had been dropping out of the skies in

recent years and although they were in a 747, they were convinced that the longer they were in the air the more likely they would crash. The four gibbering wrecks drank their way around the world and arrived without a scratch.

Once they were there, Dave Gregory was happy. He'd never played much farther from Pig Hill than London clubs and here he was, traveling the world, playing unusual places, sharing hotel rooms with its ugliest bugs—and Andy! Despite a suspect layered haircut, flared jeans, and extra puppy fat, the fans seemed to like the new member.

Andy, on the other hand, was miserable and couldn't wait to get home. Someone had stolen his guitar in New Zealand and he was missing his woman, having to make do with the unusual comforts offered by the latex orifice of a rubber shark! Early one morning, while sharing a hotel room with Dave, he dragged the phone under his sheets and called Marianne. Trying not to wake Dave, he asked her to marry him. He promised to do it as soon as he returned from the Japanese leg of the tour. She agreed and he gently placed the telephone back on the bedside table and slid back under the blankets. "Congratulations," moaned Dave, and drifted back to sleep.

When they finished in Japan they needed a rest. Dave, Colin, and Terry decided they liked Japan and wanted to stay on to test the delights of the bathhouses. But Andy was in a hurry and raced home on the next plane, an empty one barring the flatulent Japanese businessman who insisted on sitting next to him. Two days later, Andy married Marianne, without the presence of the band.

By the second half of 1979, XTC was back in the U.K. touring theaters. They were now minor stars, even if their bank balances and the comments of fellow Swindonians suggested otherwise. Steve Lillywhite asked Dave to play on Peter Gabriel's third album. Thomas Dolby asked Andy to produce him and Virgin indulged Andy in funding the recording of Mr. Partridge's "*Takeaway*"/ "*The Lure of Salvage*." Then it was more touring around Britain and Europe and yet more touring until somebody pointed out that there was a U.S. tour coming and there wasn't any product to sell.

The nature of the charts was changing dramatically. The Police had scored two number ones with their second album. Blondie was up there with them. Perhaps XTC could make it, too. So they chose a hit producer, Phil Wainman, who had earned fortunes with and for the Sweet and the Bay City Rollers, to produce "Wait Till Your Boat Goes Down," a single which sank without a trace. It was the start of a new decade and to celebrate, XTC spent two months touring the United States. The tour was a success. They weren't selling many records there but everybody wanted to see them play. They had overcome the loss of Barry Andrews and Squinty Two Strats was hailed a new hero. To trumpet the end of the tour, Mount St. Helens erupted and the British Steel workers were given a 15.5 percent pay raise, and Andy and Colin wrote one of the best albums of their careers.

Andy and Marianne, the happy couple, without band or rubber shark.

(CREDIT: THE ANDY PARTRIDGE COLLECTION)

Messrs. Lillywhite and Padgham were brought back to produce and the whole thing was reeled out in about six weeks. But these were not happy times for Gregsy. His health, due to his diabetes and possibly aggravated by the exhaustion of touring, was very poor. This lowered his tolerance for Andy's vaudevillian despotism. When Andy wanted his way, he would laugh you into submission, but Dave wasn't laughing. He'd realized that he was unlikely to become a contributor to the writing in the band, and felt outside the clique. He wouldn't be able to listen to the album for over fifteen years. Colin was also showing an interest in matters outside the band, rushing straight back into the studios with producer Mick Glossop and a bunch of friends to record the "Colonel" sessions. The only member of XTC involved was Terry.

Black Sea would have been called *Terry and the Love Men* had Chambers not refused to wear a Lurex tuxedo on the cover. It was even promoted as *Terry and the Love Men* in Japan. At the last moment that was changed to *Work Under Pressure*, a hint at the band's mood at the time. They had a set designed by Swindon artist Ken White and dressed in diving suits. But after the photo session, Ian Reid vetoed the title, and the less specific *Black Sea* was reluctantly adopted. It spawned four singles, the worst of which was Andy's biggest hit to date. They attracted critical acclaim and reasonable sales, though how you pigeonhole a band who could record "Sgt. Rock" and "Travels In Nihilon" on the same album was a hard one for the marketing department, so they split the publicity campaign between the serious national media, the independent music press, and schoolgirl magazines. XTC awareness was at an all-time high in the U.K.

BLACK SEA

TALKING BETWEEN THE LINES

NEVILLE: *So let me guess . . . you spent the year touring?*

ANDY: *We didn't come off the road except for a few weeks off to write the album and most of that was written on tour, on that yellow notepaper or that very hard, truck stop toilet paper. We spent months in America and got the record for cramming the Whisky in L.A. three nights in a row.*

COLIN: *Didn't Todd Rundgren turn up there?*

ANDY: *No, that was Chicago. Someone screwed up our backstage requirements and all we had was bread, trays of Wonder [bread], nothing else. Like* One Day In the Life of Ivan

Denisovich, *"Da! Must haf brod." And Todd stuck his head 'round the door, scraping his head on the ceiling, and said, "Hey guys, great rider!"*

COLIN: *So who was it in L.A.?*

ANDY: *It was that little woman from "Dallas," Charlene Tilton.*

COLIN: *Small woman, big boobs.*

ANDY: *Just right for standing your beer on her head. Sorry, Charlene.*

COLIN: *Dave had a bit of a thing about her.*

ANDY: *I remember the minutiae of touring but missed all the news and the charts. You get this three-month popular culture amnesia.*

COLIN: *When we were in Italy in 1982, Spandau Ballet became big and when I got back I thought, Who are these upstarts?*

ANDY: *Tablecloths were in by then. But we almost missed the Falklands War altogether.*

COLIN: *And the Chernobyl disaster.*

ANDY: *Yeah, we took a detour and didn't play the Chernobyl Workingmen's Club that night. Something to do with the P.A. melting.*

COLIN: *I think I missed the upbringing of my kids at that point, too. They were about three and five.*

ANDY: *I was jealous of you having kids. I wanted some and you had a set but you can't loan them out, can you?*

Colin playing "Towers of London." (CREDIT: FRAN SOIR)

COLIN: *Still I suppose we'll remember the camaraderie, like our dads in the navy.*

NEVILLE: *Was your dad in the navy?*

COLIN: *No.*

ANDY: *But he remembers his time in the navy with some confusion.*

NEVILLE: *Which is as appropriate a moment as possible to mention "Wait Till Your Boat Goes Down."*

COLIN: *Virgin thought we needed a follow-up to "Nigel" before we started work on the album and of the ones we rehearsed in Tootsie's garage, "I Overheard," "Don't Lose Your Temper," "Officer Blue," and "Wait Till Your Boat Goes Down," only the one was deemed worthy of a single release.*

ANDY: *They chose Phil Wainman to produce, who reminded me of a Mediterranean waiter with his open shirt and tanned complexion. I kept waiting for my pasta to arrive.*

COLIN: *But he was Cockney.*

NEVILLE: *Not very Cockney.*

ANDY: *Anything's very Cockney to us. We're the living Troggs tapes, mate.*

NEVILLE: *Anyway, the boat sank, didn't it?*

ANDY: *We only got to hear the mix on tour and he did a good job, but it didn't communicate with the audience.*

NEVILLE: *So on to* Black Sea*?*

ANDY: *I was certain we were going to call it* Tigers In Tune World *and I went into Chunky's Red Brick Studios under Swindon Town Hall to noodle a few tunes. "Walking to Work" was a theme to the supermarket soap opera that Marianne never wrote. "Spy In Space" became "Living In Another Cuba" and "Jumping the Gap" became "Travels In Nihilon."*

NEVILLE: *And then back with Messrs. Lillywhite and Padgham.*

DAVE: *They'd been off doing Peter Gabriel's album and we wondered if they'd want to come back to us but, surprisingly, they did.*

COLIN: *Before the album, Andy was asked to do stuff for* Times Square.

ANDY: *Appalling movie, but it gave us the chance to see how Steve and Hugh had progressed working with*

Peter. I think they developed a few interesting new techniques and there was a new toughness to our recordings. Partly because Hugh had been working on that gated, ambient drum sound.

DAVE: *Partly because we'd spent eighteen months promoting* Drums and Wires *and we'd beefed up our performance muscles.*

NEVILLE: *I bet you had.*

DAVE: *Plus we had some great new songs.*

ANDY: *But we had great camaraderie with them. They were our age and had the same sense of humor.*

NEVILLE: *God help us all!*

COLIN: *We lived above the Townhouse Studios because Virgin owned the whole block. Real luxury—bare box rooms with a bed and carpet.*

ANDY: *And exquisite cigarette burns. The food situation was very weird because the outside caterers locked the fridge at night to stop us snacking. One night, after Scotland had lost badly to England at soccer, we found Jack Bruce, legless, trying to jemmy the padlock off the fridge door. He looked at us desperately and one of us asked, "D'you see the match, Jack?" And he snarled, "What fuckin' match?"*

COLIN: *We had six weeks there, longer than* Drums and Wires. *But we still recorded most of it live.*

ANDY: *We hadn't progressed that much. I was still terrified of the red light coming on. I even asked Steve if he could disable it so I wouldn't know we were recording. We would try to stand where we could see each other so we could nod or shout cues. I used to wonder what all the shouting was on other records, like the Beatles'* White Album, *but now I know. It's just musicians shouting, "Here comes the chorus."*

DAVE: *I didn't enjoy making* Black Sea. *Partly because I had trouble with my health but also because of Andy. He's not a very giving musician when it's his song you're recording. And I was disappointed because I wasn't contributing any songs of my own. I had thought when I joined that I would be writing, but there wasn't room for me. I'd probably been lying to my-*

self that I was a songwriter. I was incredibly frustrated during the sessions and then it was just tour, tour, tour. The album came out to critical acclaim and enhanced our reputation, but I felt no better than two years earlier. It was just another job.

ANDY: *All of us were feeling the pressure. In fact, the diving suit photo on the cover was because we were going to call the album* Work Under Pressure. *But Ian Reid felt it showed him in a poor light and told us to pick another name. So it became* Black Sea.

BLACK SEA

ON THE TRACKS

"RESPECTABLE STREET"

(Andy Partridge) (Single and album track)

Stuck for a scratched record sound to enhance the misleading, Noël Cowardish introduction to the album, Steve Lillywhite calmly sacrificed his test pressing of *Peter Gabriel 3*. It was just the sort of neighborly act between musicians that "Respectable Street" deserved.

The song was a vehement attack on the hypocrisy of snobbish neighbors. "At 46 Kingshill Road, we had an amazing neighbor we called Mrs. Washing because she was always washing everything," says Andy. "You could look into her backyard any day and she'd hang out carpets, mats, shoes, children's toys; just everything. They'd occasionally thump on the wall if I was getting a bit noisy and yet they were just as noisy. The song was about the hypocrisy of living in a so-called respectable neighborhood. It's all talk behind twitching curtains. It's all Alan Bennett land." "Respectable Street" marked a distinct change in Andy's lyrical work. Images were less obscure, and his powers of observation were becoming sharpened in the mold of Ray Davies. "With Dave having been in the band for a while, he was starting to exert his sixties influence on us," says Colin. "With Partsy it rekindled an interest in a lot of bands from the sixties like the Kinks."

The single version found Andy rerecording the vocal because the new A&R manager, Jeremy Lascelles, felt Andy's observations were too sharp for broadcast. *Sex position* became *proposition*, *abortion* became *absorption*, *contraception* became *child prevention* and *retching* became *stretching*. It was mixed in short time by Steve Lillywhite and partway through, they noticed a strange backing vocal at the end of the song. "It was Terry Chambers yelling in annoyance at having got that far through the song and thinking he'd made a mistake," says Andy. "His moan bent the note until it got to the key of the song. It sounded great, so we overdubbed some more of it."

To promote the single, a video was recorded depicting XTC playing the respectable neighbors as a string quartet in their living room while a family of aged punks kicked up a row next door. "In fact, the old fella they hired as Mr. Punk was teetotal," says Andy. "But they'd given him beer and said, 'Come on, swig this beer to look like a punk' and he was totally out of his skull. He couldn't stand."

"Generals and Majors"

(Colin Moulding) (Single and album track)

As is so often the case with Colin's songs, the music suggests a phrase and the phrase suggests the lyric. "Generals and Majors" sounded slightly military even when he first demostrated the simple F-chord progression on his acoustic guitar at rehearsals. Once Terry had added his "Peasoup! Peasoup!" disco drum goose step, the song had become a march. "I really only had one verse and so it was more or less created in the studio," says Colin. It was almost killed in the studio, as well, had it not been for Andy discovering the opening guitar riff.

"It was definitely going to be a song about the military, but from the pompous, slightly humorous side rather than an antiwar song," says Colin. "We'd been talking about the TV series 'The Great War,' and I was thinking about all these pompous generals, like Haig. So it came out of that." The simple chord structure opened up endless possibilities for melodic hooks, starting with Andy's jangling opening riff and going on to Dave's low guitar motif, the whistling, and the catchy chorus. "We had more hooks than a fishing tackle shop," says Colin. There was even a catchy bass humming vocal line, sung by Townhouse Studios' Scottish chef, Step.

The song was guaranteed a good reception at gigs and high levels of airplay on radio ensured its familiarity to the public. It was lightweight and a minor hit.

The video was also lightweight. Virgin had originally wanted "Towers of London" as the first single and a video had been finished. But "Generals and Majors" came out so well they changed their minds and, as the budget had been spent, it looked as though there would be no video for the new MTV. During the filming of a BBC documentary on a staged rerecording of "Towers of London" at The Manor, Virgin's Richard Branson used the publicity value by throwing a huge rock 'n' roll party in the grounds. The band explained to Branson that they were worried about "Generals and Majors." Branson slipped a few notes in the right direction, rented some uniforms and, hey—presto, a video. "The idea was that Branson and his next-door neighbors in Oxfordshire were all the generals and we were their waiters, mocking them," says Andy. "Intercut with Branson dicking around in the lake and us on go-carts and a half-deflated bouncy castle and there you go, that's your video."

"Living Through Another Cuba"

(Andy Partridge)

"Spy In Space" was a failed demo idea, which Andy had scribbled in Swindon's Red Brick Studios before starting work on *Black Sea*.

It was ditched but it did yield the riff which developed into "Living Through Another Cuba." It was Andy's opportunity to express his fear of nuclear war. "Until very recently, I'd been paranoid about the possibility of a third world war. I was a fifties child and my parents genuinely expected it to happen. So I wanted to write a Dylanesque protest song in the form of a list." This came out of it instead, with references to Russia, America, and little Britain, a toothless bulldog sitting on the fence.

Musically it was manic, with dub echoes everywhere on vocal "whoops" and drums. Terry's Sniper drum synth was cranked up to whistle every couple of bars and a fake Space Invaders machine on the fade placed the song firmly in 1980. Would that Andy's sense of history was so accurate. The Cuban missile crisis was not in 1961, weakening the whole point of the lyric!

"Love At First Sight"

(Colin Moulding) (Album track and Canadian single)

Some rehearsals for the album were made in Terry "Fatty" Alderton's Tudor Studios in Swindon and "Love At First Sight" developed there. Colin had the sneering schoolyard melody and a riff which sounded like a fanfare, especially once Dave had suggested an alternative tuning. It was this fanfare which heralded the lyrical idea of a game of love.

The song was full of borrowed ideas. The pinch-nosed voice on the chorus tugged its forelock in the direction of current hits "Video Killed the Radio Star" and "Pop Musik" and the middle section melody smacks of Andy Williams's "Can't Get Used to Losing You."

Andy admits that he was short of ideas for the solo in the middle. "It was sort of a panic really, so I just did this steam train chopping thing. I really enjoyed doing it. We'd got plenty of little musical ideas so we just needed some more row at that point."

It wasn't an international hit, but Polygram Canada thought it could be with a little tweaking. "They said they wanted to make a couple of alterations," says Colin. "We left them to get on with it and they sped it up!"

"Rocket from a Bottle"

(Andy Partridge)

On November 5, 1605, a group of well-to-do Roman Catholic terrorists attempted to blow up the Protestant King James I along with his entire parliament. Guy Fawkes was caught trying to light the gunpowder and was burned at the stake. Ever since, the British have celebrated the rather perverse Guy Fawkes Night with the ritual Guy effigy burning and fireworks, paid for by kids displaying their Guy-constructing skills in exchange for donations. " 'Penny for the Guy' was really big 'round Penhill," says Colin. "You'd have about twenty of them lined up outside the shops." "It looked like a massacre 'round there," says Andy. The next day, Penhill would be strewn with burned-out rockets and blackened milk bottle rocket launchers.

That is the link to rockets and bottles, but the meaning of the song is just a jolly, optimistic, happy-go-lucky song about being in love. "I was a big fireworks fan and so that was the connection. When you're in love you feel like you could go off like a firework," says Andy. Once again, Dave was forced to play a fat-fingers piano, like the Velvet Underground's "Waiting for the Man." But he also came up with a very interesting guitar solo. "He went away and worked this out in his inimitable style," says Andy. "Again, it's a type of fanfare. I think a lot of Gregsy's guitar playing sounds like fanfares."

"No Language In Our Lungs"

(Andy Partridge)

There is general consensus that this is one of XTC's finest moments. " 'No Language In Our Lungs' was one of our best things ever," says Dave. "All the guitar parts had a marked purpose." "It's also one of my favorites and going back to the album, you pick this one out. There's so much air in it," says Colin. "You can almost get your hands into the recording and get 'round the back of the instruments." "The weird thing is that this is about the fallibility of language and that you can't say what you mean. Yet it was one of the few songs where I actually said what I wanted to say. I was really proud of the line, 'I would have made this instrumental but the words got in the way.' That's the essence of the song."

The recording was filled with effects, including the voice of Alan Whicker recorded from the television in the studio. "You'd have to be a right Whicker wanker to guess which program," says Andy. But the power of the song lay in the guitars and simple bass line. "The guitars remind me of 'Rain'-period Beatles," says Andy, who now admits the similarity of the slow arpeggio guitar sound of the Beatles' "I Want You (She's So Heavy)." "I didn't realize it at the time, but it sounds just like it."

"Towers of London"

(Andy Partridge) (Single and album track)

"*Clank!*" Terry tests the combined strike of plate and fire extinguisher.

"Okay?" he asks.

"Take 103!" answers Steve Lillywhite, exaggerating, in a muffled imitation of Ian Reid.

Andy grunts a dirty chuckle.

"One, two, three, four," counts Terry and kicks in one of the best riffs ever written.

Dave Gregory describes "Towers of London" as "a great single." "With half-assed lyrics," says Andy. "I think I was trying to rewrite 'Waterloo Sunset' to be honest. I'm fascinated with history and I wanted to look at the way Victorian London grew from the point of view of all the workmen, the people who died cutting all the tunnels of London, but 'Tunnels of London' didn't sound right. The lyrics didn't really say what I wanted. I wanted to say something sympathetic about the people that died to build the Victorian showcase. I tried to write a Kinks–type song but I got a little bit out of my depth. That backing vocal line 'La, La, Londinium' is desperate."

Musically, however, it's one of his most memorable songs. A mass of different movements with guitars, synthesizers, and voices overlayed in the most complex collection of hook lines. The song was chosen to be the first single and a video was made around the city. "We did part of it on a boat going up the Thames," says Colin. "It was a particularly breezy day and our barnets were blowing all over the place." (Barnet fair = hair in Cockney rhyming slang.) "And then they phoned us up and said they weren't going to release it yet." The BBC also made a documentary of the making of "Towers of London," though the whole thing was faked at The Manor, some time after the album was finished.

"The night after Lennon was shot we were playing a gig in Liverpool and seeing as the end of 'Towers of London' could easily mutate over the chord at the end, I went into 'Rain,' " says Andy. "I remember becoming really emotional at that point. I thought, Bloody hell, we're in Liverpool on the night John Lennon's been shot and we're playing a Beatles song. I had tears rolling down my cheeks."

"Paper and Iron (Notes and Coins)"
(Andy Partridge)

There is hardly an XTC album that doesn't have some complaint about shortage of cash. Over the years, being broke has provided a rich seam of lyrical material. "I think I've always been besotted with the subject of not making enough money to live on," says Andy. "There are a lot of songs on the subject. This song is about the little humiliations you have to go through to earn your wage. I had a job painting posters in McIlroy's department store, which was quite a nice job but there were these people who felt they had the right to humiliate you just because they were your bosses."

It hadn't always been about money. The original song was called "Moebius Mood" after M. C. Escher's perspective-perplexing engraving "Ants On a Moebius Strip." But money was a more pressing subject than ants.

The song was hell to sing on stage and even the recording proved to be too much for Colin. "You sent me and Gregsy in to sing those backing vocals and it was so fast, with no breaths; we were almost passing out by the end," says Colin to Andy. Once more, a piece of studio kitchenware bit the dust on the recording—the high-sounding drum rolls under the solo are played by Terry on a metal tray clamped to a drum stand.

"Burning with Optimism's Flames"
(Andy Partridge)

Luckily, when they played this live, Andy didn't have to play guitar while he sang the rapid triplets. Onstage and in studio, Andy could barely muster enough breath to sing a whole line. "This was a self-cheering-up song and when I talk about 'she,' I'm really talking about me," says Andy. "I really enjoyed playing it, especially when we got to the big-sounding middle eight. It sounds like something from the film *The Big Country*."

The version on the album is somewhat shorter than was recorded. "Steve Lillywhite said, 'I'm really worried that this is too long. Let's get rid of a verse and a chorus.' I was horrified as he pulled out all this tape and took out a razor blade and cut a chunk off. He stuck the ends together and played and it did sound better."

The line "In like Flint and styling" refers to the movie *In Like Flint*, which Andy only saw because he liked the way the movie poster artist drew James Coburn's immaculately pressed trousers! "We always used to think that Dave was rather stingy with the money when he joined the band," says Colin. "So we used to sing 'Our man skinflint.' "

"Sgt. Rock (Is Going to Help Me)"

(Andy Partridge) (Single and album track)

It's always the way. You write a song you don't like and everybody wants to buy it. Then they listen closely and misunderstand it and threaten you with violence. It was on "Sgt. Rock," the album's fourth single and biggest hit, that Andy got his first taste of the hatred Barry had suffered with "My Weapon."

"I gently detest this song. It's such a light piece of inconsequential fluff and then suddenly it's a single. I wanted it to lay in the corner of the album for a bit of fun. I actually got hate mail from feminists who thought I was advocating beating women up. I wasn't, at all. It's the song of a nerdy kid who has this funny little fantasy that if he could be like Sgt. Rock and be the tough guy, women would respect him. Obviously he's got it wrong. I wish I hadn't written it. I died of embarrassment the moment it came out. They just didn't get the humor of the situation. I was also really mad at Alex Harvey writing 'Give My Regards to Sgt. Fury' because I'd always wanted to write a song about him. So I had to change my allegiance from Jack Kirby's Marvel hero to the Joe Kubert–drawn DC hero instead."

"Travels In Nihilon"

(Andy Partridge)

Alan Sillitoe's book *Travels In Nihilon* had made a big impact on Andy. The strange story of a group of travel writers who visit a newly opened Eastern European state described an amazing view of anarchy. With an inkblot for a flag and dangerous living considered an optional extra, it seemed the perfect metaphor for punk to Andy. He had felt betrayed by the false promises of punk and now he expressed them in song. "The whole song is about the incredible sense of disappointment I felt with the whole punk movement," he says. "This is our 'Tomorrow Never Knows.' 'There's no youth culture, just masks they let you rent.' Punk had started out as this honesty thing and I was sickened by the hypocrisy. I believed it when Iggy sang it but it all came to nil." "I don't think any of us were untouched by punk because we were all so young," says Colin. "Andrews was always going on about it. He thought Joe Strummer was a god. Perhaps Johnny Rotten was the mayor of Nihilon."

"Travels In Nylons," as it became, was based on the bass riff salvaged from "Jumping the Gap" with one of Terry Chambers's cyclical drum patterns creating a frantic, manic, doom-laden rhythm track. "It was one of those things that only took off in the studio," says Colin. "It was a really brave journey into a new musical area," says Dave. "As a structure, the thing just piled on and piled on like a juggernaut," says Andy. Though the power of the imagery was undermined by the sad impression of rain, recorded in Steve Lillywhite's shower at the studio. It is not, contrary to some fans' conjecture, a reference to Hitchcock's *Psycho*.

IN THE SIDINGS . . .

"Wait Till Your Boat Goes Down"
(Andy Partridge) (Single only)

Andy had written "Wait Till Your Boat Goes Down" late one night, lying in bed while Marianne tried to sleep. "I just lay there, stark bollock naked with my acoustic and my notepad and thought, 'What a great melody. Perhaps it's even a single.' I couldn't get to sleep that night."

The song was a snideswipe at the upper-class girls who had looked down on Swindon's working-class lads, girls that Colin called "Westlecott Road types," who lived in the nicer part of town and looked down their noses at boys like Andy. "People say only write what you know, but this was a fantasy about women who treat you haughtily. What did I know about such women?" says Andy. But he'd been snubbed by a few.

Virgin suggested working with producer Phil Wainman. Terry was intimidated because he was a drummer and seemed to want to play on the record. Though Andy thought he looked like a Mediterranean waiter with his open shirt and dark coloring, he is quite complimentary: "He did a pretty good job, although we had a slow half-time rhythm and he put this heavy dub delay on it, possibly at our suggestion. I think it made the rhythm rather awkward. If anything, he decommercialized it." That ensured nonhit status. Phil also crammed in an American-tinted mix of "Ten Feet Tall" during the sessions and a rerecording of "Officer Blue," also aimed at America.

"OFFICER BLUE"

(Colin Moulding) (Single B side only, not on album)

"This is the worst B side we ever made—the splinters scraped from the bottom of the barrel," says Colin of his tribute to the police officers who would occasionally catch him heading home in the early morning, in the wrong place and the wrong state of mind. "I think what inspired me was all those policemen that would pop up in *Yellow Submarine*."

"I don't know how we got away with this mix," says Andy, who mixed it with Colin. "Parts of it are completely out of tune and the Korg solo is in the wrong key." Though this had never bothered Andy before.

"TAKE THIS TOWN"

(Andy Partridge) (Sound track song from the movie Times Square, *released as a joint single with the Ruts' "Babylon's Burning")*

Andy was so honored to have been asked to write music for a movie that it didn't occur to him that it would be rubbish. It was, but by then XTC had submitted "Take This Town," "Love At First Sight," and "Rocket from a Bottle." Luckily, the only one used was

"Take This Town" and then only playing on a transistor radio behind a screaming woman in an ambulance.

"I was really flattered to be asked but it turned out to be the turkey that ate New York. The song was the most rockist song we'd ever done," says Andy. " I read the script and tried to project into the minds of these young girls growing up and finding themselves. There's a bit of Thin Lizzy in there and the middle section is pure Tom Petty and the Heartbreakers. Also, I really loved the sailors' chorus in *South Pacific* and always wanted a bit of that sound in something. So the backing vocals have this really Broadway thing." There is also a hint of Bernstein's "Maria" hidden in the melody, though how it got there, Andy cannot say.

Andy went to the premiere party of the film in America and schmoozed with the Hollywood set. It was there that he was introduced to a young fan named Erica Wexler.

"STRANGE TALES, STRANGE TAILS"

(Andy Partridge) (Single B side only, not on album)

Although this was produced by John Leckie at Matrix Studios for the *Go* 2 sessions, it laid dormant until pressure for output forced Andy and Colin to remix it. "It just wasn't fit for human consumption," says Andy. "It was a health hazard," agrees Colin. The original version included Barry but Andy replaced him. "We didn't want people to indentify us with the Barry Andrews sound so I played his on the Korg and the solo was replaced with a guitar recorded backward."

The song is merely a play on words based around Andy's and Colin's love of the American "Strange Tales" comics, but its only questionable lyrical merit lies in shoehorning a rhyme out of *uniform* and Babylonian *cuneiform*. "It was a pretty tough time for us," says Colin about the barrel scraping that went on in reviving this and "Officer Blue." "It was a little bit of panic stations coming up with tracks."

"Smokeless Zone"

(Colin Moulding) (Single B side, not on album)

"This is just a light complaint about pollution. It's just a list of grumbles and it was pretty apt that Andy picked up the mouth organ and started wheezing through it. If there can be a light dig at pollution, this was it," says Colin.

"Smokeless Zone" was not a popular song with the band and was destined for the B bag pretty early on. "We took it as far as we could take it until I got fed up with it, so I just fucked off to bed and left the guys to try to get a good take of it."

"Terry tried something different on this and played all the drums separately," says Andy. "Steve Lillywhite had pointed out that the Banshees' drummer couldn't play a decent take on the full kit but he could get a great sound playing things separately in different takes. But Terry couldn't grasp it so he never did it again. You can hear on the track that some of the cymbal crashes are out of sync. Everyone asks what the silly bit of Mickey Mouse vocal is at the front. Steve Lillywhite was messing around with a harmonizer at the time, and he would sometimes switch it on when you weren't expecting it. You were trying to sing and your voice would come back all high and sped up. It was a joke that lasted about two goes, but he left a bit of it on the tape."

"Don't Lose Your Temper"

(Andy Partridge) (Single B side, not on album)

In another instance of misunderstanding, Andy wrote "Don't Lose Your Temper" as meaning don't lose your ability to lose your temper. "It means don't lose your ability to get wild and get angry. It's sort of about the way people become tamed once they get into a relationship and they lose something of what made them exciting. I suppose it's aimed at Marianne, really."

The song was recorded very quickly and is notable for the presence of Rick Buckler, drummer with the Jam, who drifted in from the next studio, armed with a bottle of Bull's Blood wine to see what was going on. He was drafted in to add handclaps.

"The Somnambulist"

(Andy Partridge) (Single B side, not on album)

The U.K. Musicians Union had some strict rules about the recording of tracks for lip-synched TV performance and when XTC was invited to play "Nigel" on "Top of the Pops," they were supposed to rerecord it. So they showed up for a fake session at Olympic Studios. "The record company executive came down with the union chap to check that we had started recording and were playing on it," says Colin. "Then he would take the union man off and buy him the fattest lunch possible and they'd come back an hour later and miraculously the recording had been finished and we'd get on 'Top of the Pops.' "

"Of course nobody rerecorded anything. It was all a complete sham. The union knew it and the record industry knew it," says Andy. "As soon as they'd gone, everyone said, 'Let's go to the pub.' But we still had about an hour and a half left of studio time booked and I thought studio time was incredibly precious. So I said to Terry, 'Before you go to the pub, just play *thump thump* on your bass drum.' " Engineer Laurence Burridge made a three-foot tape loop with the drum on it and ran it from the tape spool and 'round a mic stand. By the time they returned from the pub, Andy had written, recorded, and mixed the track.

The idea for the song stems from a meeting with a member of Virgin's New York staff a couple of years earlier. "I had been in the Perry Street offices and there was this Irish secretary there who played me some of her songs. The one thing that stuck in my mind was this line about sleepwalking being like deep sea diving. I thought this was a brilliant idea and thought I could write a whole song around it."

"History of Rock and Roll"

(Andy Partridge) (Solo track released on Miniatures *by Morgan Fisher)*

IN A COUPLE OF PAYMENTS IT
MAY EVEN BE MINE
A DAY IN A BOX
OPEN UNIVERSITY
SWAT UP AT HOME
KITCHENETTE COWBOYS
FROM CARDIFF TO ROME
MILK ON THE DOORSTEP
NEWS ON THE MAT
NO REASONABLE REASON
FOR LEAVING THE FLAT
A DAY IN A BOX
A PEG IN A HOLE

YOU BROKE THE CIRCLE
YOU CALLED ME A SQUARE
YOU SAID YOU'D DESIGNS
TO GET YOU SOMEWHERE

"Day In the Box," an unused song for the Black Sea *sessions from Andy's notebook.*

(CREDIT: ANDY PARTRIDGE)

"Morgan Fisher of Mott the Hoople rang me up and asked would I contribute to this project that was great works of art condensed to sixty seconds. So I thought I'd try the history of rock 'n' roll. It was actually recorded during the *Black Sea* sessions and covers each decade of rock 'n' roll in one sound—the fifties hiccup, the sixties fuzzy guitar, and the eighties farting synth in thirty seconds. He loved it and I probably made about £6.75." In that sixty seconds, Andy summed up what was steadily turning XTC from a stroppy punk band into one of the richest music wellsprings Britain was to produce.

5

ROGUE SOUP

1982

Andy Partridge jumped out of the van and sank up to his knees into the snow. The band huddled in the van as he trudged out into the field and relieved himself against a tree. It was upstate New York in December 1980, but it could have been another time and another planet. Else-

where, Poland's dockworkers were fighting for independence, dozens of American diplomatic staff were awaiting release from Iran, Ronald Reagan was settling into the Oval Office, and the British police were closing in on Peter Sutcliffe, the Yorkshire Ripper. Standing in the middle of the monochromatic landscape beneath leaden skies, Andy looked down to zip up his fly and lost himself. The exhaustion flooded through his mind like a tidal wave and swept all memory before it. He looked around, not knowing where he was, when it was, why he was there, who he was. The soft snow and low clouds suffocated all sound and distorted his sense of perspective. There was no point of reference, nothing to focus on except the van and the faces peering out at him. He shuffled toward it through the snow. Silently, he climbed in, curled up in the fetal position, and convulsed in uncontrollable sobbing.

All bands become ground down by touring. But XTC hardly seemed to leave the road, spending days with no other human contact before being thrust in front of thousands of screaming fans. And for what? They were playing the same gigs as the Police and were selling similar numbers of tickets but nothing was coming back. The Police were traveling in style, sleeping in style, and worrying about nothing but playing. XTC had a van, two roadies, cheap motels, and enough money per diem to feed a small rodent at Calcutta prices. This was gnawing at Andy—their paltry income, not the small rodent—and when these things eat at him, it affects his health and the well-being of anyone within spitting distance. He had already missed one gig in Canada through gastroenteritis, leaving the band to busk a set of Colin's songs. Now he was feeling emotionally sick. He decided to himself that he wouldn't tour after the next album.

The rest of the band were aware that Andy was unhappy; well, you would be with someone sobbing all over your stage gear. But they thought it was just a phase. They were enjoying touring, despite the discomfort. Dave was only just beginning to grasp that this was a full-time career and despite his apparent indifference to audiences, he loved playing. Colin balanced his natural shyness with a desire to show off and, anyway, assumed that touring went with the territory. Terry treated touring as a nonstop party. Touring was an opportunity to see the world and drink it dry. Only on tour could he hold equal status with the rest of the band.

Back in Swindon, he was just good old Terry Chambers. So when it was announced that there would be a two-month break in touring to write for the next album, he took the opportunity to sign on at a building site to make some beer money. This was spent rapidly, usually with his mate, Dave Simpson, a man with a Rod Stewart haircut and a Ford Capri, which he was always crashing. Andy thought Simpson had a permanently broken leg. But this didn't impede him or Terry in their wild nights.

While Terry played, Colin and Andy wrote on their cassette decks. Like Lennon and McCartney before him, Andy was balancing his hatred of tours with a passion for the studio. He became a session whore, recording with or producing Joan Armatrading, the Residents, Riuichi Sakamoto, and Thomas Dolby. The rest of the time was devoted to writing new material on his new acoustic guitar—generous to a fault, on a BBC TV show where artists would give away T-shirts, he had given his guitar and Colin had donated a gold disc.

The new acoustic guitar pushed him toward acoustic arrangements, surreptitiously undermining the band's ability to play them live. Colin heard the direction in which Andy was heading and bought a mellow-sounding Ibanez fretless bass. Over the weeks, they created an album that took them away from the loud, violent, exuberant naivete of XTC past and into XTC pastoral.

After rehearsing in Swindon, they made an abortive attempt at recording with Clive Langer and Alan Winstanley. It galvanized their thoughts toward producing themselves—after all, how hard could producing be? They booked The Manor for a couple of months in the autumn and asked Hugh Padgham if he would mind engineering without Steve Lillywhite.

Recording was rushed, between tournaments of conkers, an English children's game involving threading string through conkers, the horse chestnuts that were falling in autumnal Oxfordshire, and swinging them to attempt to conquer, or smash, your opponent's chestnut. As they played they toyed with names: *Rogue Soup, Motorcycle Landscape, World Colour Banner, Explosion of Flowers, Knights On Fire.*

They settled on *English Settlement.* It was a double album, every marketing man's nightmare, so the American label insisted on a single disc and removed a couple of tracks. The fifteen songs rambled on for up to six-and-a-half minutes and covered every area of XTC's musical interests. It was a beautiful, if whimsical, album and three tracks into it lay one of Andy Partridge's finest moments, the Top Ten U.K. hit "Senses Working Overtime." It was to be their biggest hit to date, and it was to be the catalyst that drove Andy to near madness. With a hit like that, there was no way the band couldn't tour again.

ENGLISH SETTLEMENT

TALKING BETWEEN THE LINES

NEVILLE: *And yet more touring!*

COLIN: *Insensitive management.*

ANDY: *Kept us touring.*

COLIN: *Kept us on low per diems.*

ANDY: *Sent to claim back the colonies for Britain.*

COLIN: *The Vasco da Gamas as we were then known.*

ANDY: *The Vasectomy da Gamas. Playing these cattle sheds across the Midwest and thinking, Everyone in here is wearing a ten-gallon hat. And I'm not! Are they going to look on what we do favorably?*

NEVILLE: *Probably not, if they could have heard some of the things you were saying. Still, you have to take the rough with the smooth and you could always have fun in the studio.*

ANDY: *Virgin had an idea that we should work with the hit producers, the Madness producers, Clive Langer and Alan Winstanley, to make a single. We went into the Townhouse with "Ball and Chain," "Punch and Judy," and a little instrumental idea, and the first day Clive walked out saying, "You don't need me, then, so I'm off." We finished the session at AIR Studios with Alan but we only kept "Thebes In a Box."*

NEVILLE: *Clive couldn't handle the aroma of "Eau De Swindon," I suppose.*

ANDY: *We spent the summer of 1981 writing and rehearsing in Fatty Alderton's Tudor Rehearsal Studio and it was very sweaty. No air-conditioning and all the Swindon heavy rock bands would rehearse there, drink their cider, and piss in the corner.*

NEVILLE: *Talking of "Eau De Swindon."*

ANDY: *Terry had forgotten how to drum. He spent the early summer working on building sites and when he set up his drum kit it was more like scaffolding. He was just useless. He said, "Give me a couple of hours and I'll get back into it." Hod carrying had put him in a different frame of mind and he'd been off on some wild binge to Brighton. There were tales of people crashing through glass roofs from second-floor balconies and of leaving huge turds in the urinals. Chambers would be a bit of a yob on the quiet. It was 'round about this time that he and a mate broke into the Chinese fish and chip shop by the Whitehouse bridges. They were really pissed and, naively, they thought there would be cash bursting out of the till.*

COLIN: *But there was just chips.*

ANDY: *All they found was an enamel bath full of precut chips. So, disgusted, they both pissed in the bath and left. I'll have it known we don't condone such behavior.*

NEVILLE: *You were still short of cash, then?*

ANDY: *We all bought new instruments. Like an idiot, I gave away my old acoustic guitar on the BBC Saturday Morning "Swap Shop," so I had to buy another one.*

DAVE: *It just sold in a rock memorabilia auction for £600, I think, which isn't bad for an Antoria.*

ANDY: *It was worth about £20.*

COLIN: *I bought a fretless bass.*

ANDY: *It horrified us when you bought that.*

COLIN: *I thought I was doing the right thing, that it would fit in with the acoustic stuff we were writing, but it was impossible on tour. You have to have a flair for playing something without frets and I haven't. As soon as the lights went out . . . the rest is history.*

ANDY: *And Dave bought the twelve-string Rickenbacker that's all over* English Settlement.

DAVE: *I'd always dreamed about owning one but it had seemed like a bit of frivolous folly until now. I fell totally in love with the sound.*

NEVILLE: *True love at last.*

ANDY: *I forced Terry to buy a couple of drums, a new snare, and a timbale and I bought a Yamaha acoustic. When you get a new instrument you cannot prize it from your hands, snigger, snigger. It forced me to give myself permission to write songs on acoustic but not make the conversion to electric. I thought, Wouldn't it be nice not to*

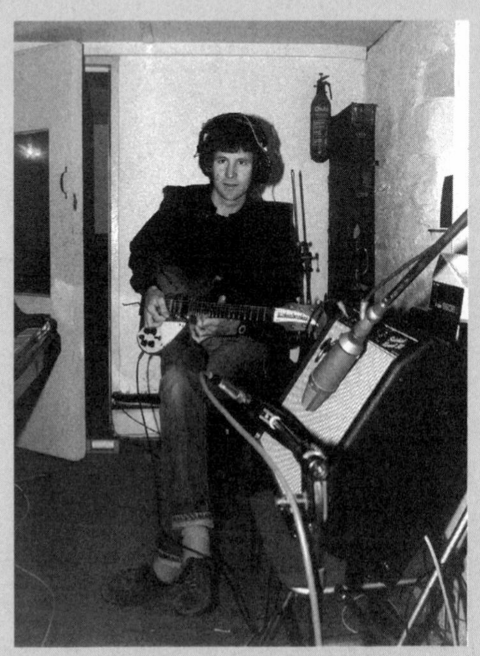

Dave on Rickenbacker. (CREDIT: COLIN MOULDING)

worry about touring. It opened up possibilities for new sounds where the live arrangement mattered less. I'd become unhinged a couple of times on tour and wanted a break. I mentioned it to Colin, who seemed confused.

COLIN: *I just thought you weren't a real band if you didn't tour.*

ANDY: *And Dave was a real schoolmaster and said, "You'll buck up. Get out there and show 'em what you can do." I didn't ask Terry because I knew he'd be hostile. He just lived to get on that plane and start drinking.*

DAVE: *The touring experience was only just beginning to pay off. But I realized that Andy was just really tired. I thought he might change his mind when we finished the album, but I'd just got used to the idea that this was a career and thought, Well, maybe this is the start of our* Pepper *period. Our nontouring phase. It's a shame, because this is the album that would have done it for us.*

NEVILLE: *It did for Hugh Padgham.*

ANDY: *We thought, foolishly, that we could save a few quid and just have Hugh. He'd always done the donkey work for Steve Lillywhite, anyway.*

COLIN: *And we wanted to be in charge for a change.*

ANDY: *We thought, It's only a matter of twiddling a few knobs.*

COLIN: *And Hugh could handle that while we made the musical decisions.*

ANDY: *Perhaps it wasn't such a good idea because for me the album sounds unfinished.*

DAVE: *We just didn't have enough time.*

NEVILLE: *Trying to record twenty-five songs in six weeks isn't that smart, is it?*

ANDY: *We did lose a few along the way, but we could have lost more.*

COLIN: *But if you haven't got a producer figure, the band gets self-indulgent.*

DAVE: *There weren't too many songs. Just not enough time.*

ANDY: *Hugh did make some musical decisions, like cutting two minutes out of the middle of "Melt the Guns," but he's not that argumentative, just quietly insistent.*

COLIN: *He indulges your whim.*

ANDY: *And then probably does what he wants while your back's turned.*

DAVE: *I just wish we'd had more time. And as a band we were playing the best we'd ever played. We were a pretty well-oiled outfit.*

NEVILLE: *Especially Terry, by the sounds of it.*

ANDY: *We had a visit from our fat, Dutch friend, Hans de Vente, while we were there. We'd won the Edison award for best album in Holland and he asked if he could collect it for us. Then he wanted to keep it. I said it didn't have his name on it so no, and he said something like "Shove it up your ass!" and stuck it head down in a flower bed.*

NEVILLE: *And what of the "duck" on the cover of the record?*

ANDY: *I don't know where the name came from.*

NEVILLE: *Possibly your determination to take root in England and leave the touring world behind?*

ANDY: *I think it was just that we were fascinated with the Uffington Horse. It's kind of a local badge. Colin's even got it on his license plate.*

COLIN: *Only because it's the symbol of the car dealer. It's not some vanity thing.*

ANDY: *Yeah, sure! The American label thought it was a duck. It's a very primitive depiction of a horse, but it doesn't matter. But it's a boundary marker for the tribes, a boundary that says, "Swindon starts here."*

NEVILLE: *"Beware! Here there be monsters." And what opinion of the album?*

DAVE: *It was a watershed record for us. We'd made a couple of raunchy guitar records and then this acoustic side came out. It was definitely a progression. The first side sounded like a collection of well-honed songs, but gradually it felt there was more work needed.*

ANDY: *Big, empty, unfinished landscape. A journey from "Runaways" to "Snowman," a journey of unnaiving. With hindsight, I like the unfinished nature of it. It makes it sound bigger, more open.*

ENGLISH SETTLEMENT

ON THE TRACKS

"RUNAWAYS"

(Colin Moulding)

The child ran on through the dark, along the hard shoulder of the motorway, from one pool of sodium light to the next, as oblivious to the late traffic as it was to him. This is how Andy pictures "Runaways." Like most kids, he had run away, getting as far as the footbridge that marked the boundary of Penhill. He waited there for half an hour and then wandered home to find his mother hadn't missed him.

Colin had never run away, so this first escape from the three-minute pop hit format was the product of his imagination. "My home was pretty settled, really," says Colin. "If my mum and dad ever did have a row, it wasn't until after I'd gone to bed. They weren't very demonstrative." As the opening track of the album, "Runaways" crept up on the listener as a mass of jangling guitars appearing over the horizon, driven by a booming, one-drop, reggae bass drum beat. This was a very different XTC. A very different way to open an album. "I thought it was a nice way of getting into such a mass of songs," says Andy. "It was just like walking toward a forest; getting bigger and bigger until suddenly you're in it and fighting your way through."

"BALL AND CHAIN"

(Colin Moulding) (Single and album track)

Swindon hadn't been called pretty for 150 years, but the devastation that passed for slum clearance in the sixties and seventies ripped the heart out of the community. The misery of the demolition site was fertile ground for germinating songs. But Colin wrote the lyric with all the subtlety of its namesake and has re-

Nonstop gigging. Boston, 1981. (CREDIT: C. VANARIA. BY PERMISSION OF VIRGIN RECORDS.)

gretted it ever since. "I cringe a bit when I hear it these days. It's far too overstated. Just too in your face." It was pretty unsubtle musically, as well. "We were all bullying Padgham, shouting, 'More violent! Louder! It's got to sound more aggressive,' " says Andy. "And the poor devil had mics all over the studio trying to get ambience on drums and guitar speaker cabinets and stuff. The raucous drunken chorus was like a bunch of Boy Scouts drunk on cider."

Of course, it's always the songs the writer likes least that get picked as singles—"Sgt. Rock" and "Dear God" go into this pot, along with "Ball and Chain." It was beautifully packaged in a sad picture sleeve of the last home owner holding out against demolition in Westcott Street, one of Swindon's Victorian terraces, but Colin still wasn't happy. "It should be tucked away somewhere down on side two," says Colin. "It got too much attention." "It really is a brave new Swindon," says Andy. "Mind you, I love the sentiment. I wish I'd written a song about it."

"Senses Working Overtime"
(Andy Partridge) (Single and album track)

Despite the bouts of depression that had kept him on Valium since childhood, Andy would often write celebratory songs on the sheer joy of living. "The Wonderment" was going to be such a song, but it wasn't going well. Sitting in his writing room at 46 Kingshill Road, he chopped up the song for scrap. The main riff was reconditioned to form the chassis of "Tissue Tigers" and the lyric? "A couple of weeks earlier, the Canadian label had asked to release a five-track EP and in trying to find a good name for a collection of five songs, I had called it *The Five Senses* EP. So I thought that five senses working overtime was the way in which you experience wonderment at the joy of being alive."

The song grew and grew, with Chaucerian plainsong verses with a few scattered rooks to get us in touch with the earth, a thumping middle eight to remind us that even bullies can be beautiful. Add jangling guitars and the perfect hook line chorus and—hey, presto! "Andy Partridge, the Valium king, presents a medieval frolic featuring the Bootleg Byrds playing 'Serf Music.' "

"I thought, Christ! How's this going to go down at Virgin? Because it was like something Genesis or Queen would have done, and these were the bands that were openly mocked two years before," says Colin. Dave immediately spotted similarities with the Beatles' "It's All Too Much," which Andy accepts is possible. "I suppose I must have been rewriting the idea, though I didn't realize it at the time. I can see the similarities." But he was actually making one of his regular attempts to write an "Autumn Almanac"-style of Ray Davies song, with movements. This time it worked and became XTC's only U.K. Top Ten hit. "Initially I thought the hook line made it sound like a single," says Andy. "But when it was finished I thought it was too bitty. Virgin said they thought it was a single, and I thought, No way! But I was very wrong there."

"Jason and the Argonauts"
(Andy Partridge)

Andy was born on the Mediterranean island of Malta, a naval stronghold since medieval times. His father had been in the navy and although the Partridges returned to Swindon when Andy was barely three, he loved his father's seafaring stories of far-off places. "I had always wanted to join the navy like my dad but luckily I joined a band instead and saw more of the world without the spit and polish. With us doing so much traveling and having our eyes opened by what we saw, I thought I could write a song in the form of a quest," says Andy. "The lyrics are a grab bag of bits and pieces that had gone in on tour."

Cream's "Tales of Brave Ulysses" had piqued Andy's interest in incorporating Greek mythology into a song and with a little imagination, he could see a simile between on-tour adventures and those of Jason and the Argonauts. "It was like a journey of life song," says Colin.

The music embellished this theme with a continuous cyclical riff of guitars representing the wheel of life with various other noises and melodies grinding against it, like events along the way. "I loved it. It appealed to my psychedelic leanings and showed that Andy was starting to get into areas that I loved," says Dave. But the romance was kicked out of it by its nickname "Chintzy," after "Jason and Chintzy," a rather bizarre couple, featured in a porn mag that was kept in the tour van because Jason had a traffic-light-colored penis.

"No Thugs In Our House"
(Andy Partridge) (Single and album track)

The National Front, a so-called "political" party which specialized in terrorizing nonwhite Brits, was a serious problem in the early eighties. Andy wrote "No Thugs In Our House" as a morality tale about one such politically motivated moron, called Graham, not realizing Colin's brother bore the same name. "I didn't know that at the time because his brother is a figure of mystery," says Andy. "I wanted to write a threepenny opera with each verse as a little scene." Graham hands out his neo-Nazi leaflets. Then, "bravely," he and his gang beat up an Asian youth, accidentally dropping his wallet at the scene. When the police come 'round to arrest him, his parents can't believe it of their little angel, though, as the father is a high court judge, he will make sure he fixes the boy's release.

"It's like violent Tamla–Motown meets Johnny Winter," says Andy. " I get to do my best rebel yell in this, which also gave me a chance to artistically clear my throat at gigs. Though, funnily enough, in my head I heard my guitar part as being more like 'Summertime Blues.' "

Andy continued the theatrical theme with the single sleeve, which is especially collectible, consisting of a paper Pollock's drama theater with a cut-out cast to act out the scenes.

"Yacht Dance"

(Andy Partridge)

"This was a brave move for us," says Dave. "It was our first fully acoustic song since 'Ten Feet Tall.' " But it was almost a completely different song. "Collecting Honey for the Queen" was, as Andy called it, "a ludicrous song about being a bee," adding insects to Andy's popular subjects of cash shortage, factory work, ancient rituals, seafaring, war, comic characters, and Swindon life. But "Collecting Honey" was not destined for greatness and we would have to wait for "Ladybird" and "Across the Antheap" before our insectophilia would be satisfied.

Slowed down, the music was worthy of conversion into the more memorable "Yacht Dance." "The music sort of sounded like boats on a lake to me, a sort of bastard son of 'Messing About On the River,' " says Andy. "It's a love song about how two fragile beings bobbing about on a sea of uncertainty while all this stuff tries to pull you down, look to the future and try to stay afloat."

Although Andy reckons Dave "Arpeggios R Us" Gregory got the nylon-stringed acoustic Anglo-flamenco style part for live performance purposes, it is as likely that Dave was just better at it than Andy. "I ended up playing Colin's little gut-stringed acoustic," says Dave. "It sounds difficult but it wasn't. I just worked out these little phrases that sounded like what the song needed." The song was performed live on the BBC's "Old Grey Whistle Test," though in that version it didn't feature the watery-sounding Indonesian anklung that they found lying around at The Manor. They didn't know how to play it but just shaking it sounded like a babbling brook.

"All of a Sudden"
(Andy Partridge)

Andy was beginning to feel older. His energy had been sapped by touring. He had raced through three years and "All of a Sudden," his youth was gone. Of course it wasn't, but everyone has the right to be a miserable bastard from time to time. "It's a big, miserable song," says Andy. "It just says you're not aware of things you have till they're gone—your weight, your age, your looks, your love. The song all came from finding this D chord but using G-flat and D-flat as its roots, so there's this confusion about which mood you're in. Just finding that chord change brought out this song. Sometimes that happens just on the flavor of a chord change."

It was one of the songs on the album that, with retrospect, Andy would have shortened but its rambling nature added to the effect. "It's a great song," says Dave. "And it was a great way to end side one of the album." The American label agreed with him, seeing it as a single. A video was made for "All of a Sudden," but because Terry was in Australia at the time, the shadowy figure of the drummer is actually Dave's brother, Ian Gregory, alias E.I.E.I. Owen of the Dukes of Stratosphear.

"MELT THE GUNS"
(Andy Partridge)

The instigation of "Melt the Guns" was a Steve Ditko sci-fi comic strip about a man who is considered contaminated because he carries a gun. But the message was about gun problems now, especially in America. "We couldn't really tour this one in the States," says Colin. "Before we'd finished they'd be loading up," says Andy. "I just really abhor guns. They are for one thing—killing. They're not for shooting targets, that's just to keep you in practice to make you more efficient at killing.

"I realized I was getting up on my soapbox a bit and that's why there's the Reverend Kinky Partridge in the middle shouting through my guitar amp." This middle section was taken from an earlier poem of Andy's and is a venomous attack on U.S. gun lovers, though the later massacre in Hungerford, ten minutes from Swindon, brought the subject closer to home. "America's love of guns still disgusts me. I am the anti–Ted Nugent," he says. "But it's not anti-American, it's anti-guns. I like Americans a lot. I think they've got much better manners than the English and that politeness is grounded in compassion." The Justice League of America, mentioned in this rant, is a comic book and the writers were so pleased with the mention that they actually gave Andy a cameo role in one issue, at the controls of a space ship.

The opening riff of "Melt the Guns" was the point of entry for Andy writing the song, and was "borrowed" a few years on for a rap record, called "Peace On You." The whole song was underpinned by an incessant ticking, counting out the time to our destruction and driving Terry bananas. He would never normally record to a click. Equally bananas was Andy's outro vocal scat, a hybrid of two Partridge heroes, Damo Suzuki of Can and Yoda of *Star Wars*.

"Leisure"

(Andy Partridge) (Not on all CD versions)

Andy on saxophone is not a pretty sound and his "wounded dog on a motorway" solo probably helped consign "Leisure" to the Dumpster on the U.S. version of the album. But the sentiment was an interesting one. The wicked witch Thatcher was, by this time, well on the way to putting all non-Tory voters on the dole and Swindon was badly hit. The song approached the subject by focusing on the unemployed's inability to occupy their enforced leisure time. "All they teach you at school is how to get a job," says Andy. "They don't prepare you for the idea of not having a job and as a result people don't know how to deal with their leisure time. So they come awfully unstuck and end up drinking and glue sniffing."

Birthday boy Andy gets a special cake at the English Settlement *sessions.* (CREDIT: DAVE GREGORY)

"There's something of the Groundhogs' 'Thank Christ for the Bomb' here," says Colin, who spots Andy's influences more readily than Andy. "Not to me," says Andy, affronted. "I thought it was more English music hall. The Groundhogs were the last thing on my mind."

"It's Nearly Africa"

(Andy Partridge)

Andy's lackluster sax playing wouldn't even compete with a U.S. president, but if Andy couldn't play a decent solo, he could multitrack lots of single notes. In "It's Nearly Africa," this sounded like a goose drive through rush-hour Lagos. "I wanted to be Charlie Parker and ended up like Dorothy Parker," he admits.

The song was an equally awkward cuss for Terry to record. He banished everyone from the studio because the drum pattern required concentration. Though, as Colin says, "You always got the feeling Terry wasn't playing with you. He was off on his own somewhere." "A lot of his playing was very inventive," says Andy. "Because he was unencumbered by musical convention."

"It's Nearly Africa" was another approach to one of Andy's pet subjects, that of the fear of losing one's innocence. "I thought a good metaphor for attractive primitivism was Africa," he said. "For years I had these chord changes knocking around and we'd even kick this thing around in sound checks with Barry Andrews. It was called 'It's Primitive Now,' then 'Jazz Love—Drum and Wire,' but in the end it provided the foundation for this. It's just saying, Wouldn't it be nice to get back to our naive selves. Because it seemed that this album was about gaining knowledge and losing naivete, this thing is going back the other way." The African flavor was increased with the "It's Nearly Afrikaan" Dutch of the pacified Hans de Vente on backing vocals.

"Knuckle Down"
(Andy Partridge)

There are a few films with outtakes stripped under the end credits, *Being There*, for instance. But this was the first song by XTC with outtakes in the outro. Dave had such a hard time finding a worthy solo that it was edited out and the debris used to decorate the fade of the track. Sharp ears will hear the edit point as the music rises to meet the missing virtuosity.

It was a simple song about not fighting, "Put your knuckles down, boys" referring to fisticuffs but inspired by Andy's inability to knuckle down and work. The sporadic percussive sounds include Andy impersonating a frog to save cash on a rented percussion box. The warped "Steptoe and Son" introduction was suggested by Dave, having lifted it from the middle. "It's just a bit of music hall. With different instrumentation, you could hear Max Miller playing this," says Andy.

"Fly On the Wall"

(Colin Moulding)

When Virgin's Simon Draper heard the demo of "Fly On the Wall," he thought it was a single. When he heard the final version with tremolo guitar, buzzing morse code synthesizer, and distorted vocals, he called it a travesty. Colin was pleased. He didn't want this getting the same unnecessary attention as Andy's "Sgt. Rock." "It's still a good song but if you give it too much pressure it will crumble."

The song was about Big Brother watching you, spurred on by the spate of "fly on the wall" documentaries that were appearing on British television at the time. But once he'd written it, Colin wasn't so happy about the content. "I think Andy's morse code buzzy-fly sound added a lot to the credibility of the song because it made the music sound funnier and gave an ambiguity to the song. You didn't know whether I was taking the piss or not."

"I was embarrassed when I brought the buzzing noise up," says Andy. "But there was no room for my guitar on the song because Dave's part filled it out. I felt locked out." "We had to find something for him to do," says Colin. "But I think it was a master stroke. The best thing about it is that with Dave's tremolo guitar, the heavy compressed drum beat, and the buzzy synth, there are no two bars the same. There is definitely an element of busking there."

"Down In the Cockpit"

(Andy Partridge) (Not on some versions of the album)

This, to Andy, is the weakest track on the album, being a clumsy "Volaré"-esque attempt at telling men to wake up to women's superiority and the fact that they will become extinct if they're not careful. "They used to roam in great herds—some say they used to be called men," run the lyrics. "It might have been taken from some sixties easy-listening tape," says Colin. "It's a very clean song but it lacks atmosphere." Andy plays a cool and jazzy solo in the middle of the track. "I'm also doing something I should never do, which is speak on record," he says. Though fifty years ago a voice like that would have been useful for voiceovers on smuggling movies.

"English Roundabout"

(Colin Moulding)

Had Terry not become locked into a bluebeat/ska rhythm, the pretty and folksy "English Roundabout" with its rapidly accelerating carousel ending would have achieved the easy-listening heaven Colin was seeking—a retired punk with pipe and slippers. It was certainly nothing to do with the famous multiisland traffic junction in Swindon, as many fans assumed. It was a gentle look at bustling English city life, influenced by a Pentangle track called, "Lightflight," the theme to the British TV series "Take Three Girls." "The area I was trying to work in was a light theme for a TV show. Noël Coward always said light music should be taken seriously and I have always liked light music," says Colin, unashamed. "It probably points the way toward what I want to do now. Something lighter and less in earnest. The authors I'm aspiring to are more like Cole Porter and Noël Coward. It did come out with a more bluebeat, ska sort of feel. I hadn't planned it that way but once Terry got into a rhythm it was very hard to stop him." "The word *pub* sometimes worked," Andy suggests.

"Snowman"

(Andy Partridge)

The journey of enlightenment that was *English Settlement* ended in the snow. A mandolin track on Eberhard Weber's "Fluid Rustle"

DOWN BY THE CANAL
LEATHER WEEDS
RUST PRAM BABY BATTER
SCULPTURES
MOTORCYCLE HOMO PUBIC GREY
GRASS
CEMENT BAG SKIRT
PLASTIC NURSE BOTTLE AND DOLL
ARM IN SCUM
ARM IN ARM
MOLESTER GALLERY AND
ELECTRICAL STORES REAR
BLOOD EYE BERRIES
AND AGEING COUPLES, MINNOWS
AND CONTRACEPTIVES
TRODDEN OUT LIFE
GYPSY SNOT AND TORN OUT
GENITAL SIGARETTE BURN
BEAUTIES
BECKON YOU INTO BROWN

Unused lyric for "Motorcycle Landscape," a rejected possible title track for the album.

(CREDIT: ANDY PARTRIDGE)

and the chilly atmosphere in Andy's marriage inspired "Snowman," though it took years for Andy to acknowledge the latter. "I started the song really not knowing what it was about. But I can see now that it's about my marriage which was getting rather cold."

Dave particularly related to the line "People will always be tempted to wipe their feet on anything with 'welcome' written on it," and reckons it's probably the best line Andy ever wrote, though Andy reckons the overall subject was more accurately described in "Always Winter, Never Christmas." It was Dave who played the opening piano, which was recorded onto a loop of tape run out from the tape machine and around a microphone stand.

"This was the first song Andy brought in after *Black Sea* and I guess it was pretty well rehearsed on the road," says Colin. "That's probably why it sounds so tight on the album," says Andy. "It's a desolate little tune but I loved playing it. I thought it was a nice way to leave the album."

IN THE SIDINGS . . .

"BLAME THE WEATHER"

(Colin Moulding) (B side only, not on album)

Had Dave not rescued "Blame the Weather," Colin would have dumped it one late night at The Manor. Dave added a middle section and breathed life into the song. "Together we knocked it up just before it was going to be recorded," says Colin. "I think the tune was inspired by a line from Chrissie Hynde's 'Message of Love.' But the title came from the measure of the melody. It's a 'don't moan' of a song."

"TISSUE TIGERS" (ALSO KNOWN AS "THE ARGUERS")

(Andy Partridge) (B side only, not on album)

At the height of XTC's U.K. fame, Marianne Partridge wouldn't answer the front door without hearing Andy's code: the two-note "Tissue Tigers" riff played on the doorbell. But the song was, unbeknownst to her, about the stormier side of her relationship with Andy.

Originally, the underlying riff had been part of "The Wonderment," which was split up to form this and "Senses Working Overtime." The melody line of "It's all hot air" was originally sung as "The Wonderment." But the final version of "Tissue Tigers" was more musically allied to "Scissor Man" in its gothic nursery rhyme/melodrama tone.

"It's a song about arguing," says Andy. "I suppose I just felt more confident in arguments than I had, realizing, 'all your arguments are paper tigers.' I suppose in a cartoon way this is about me and Marianne arguing."

Andy and Colin agree that the mix was probably a disaster, with its Phil Collinsish middle eight trying to counter the pantomime Widow Twankey atmosphere of the arrangement. "It was all done in a bit of a rush," says Colin. "That's probably why we let it run out with Gregsy's nerdy noise at the end."

"PUNCH AND JUDY"

(Andy Partridge) (B side only, not on album)

"I think Terry thought this was about him because of the line 'He's a drinker not a thinker.' He used to get pretty morose about it, but he was wrong," says Andy. "It's about that common syndrome when people have kids. Dad thinks the kid's getting more attention than him and starts taking it out on the child. It happened to me in a small way, although I didn't take it out on the kids, I just took it out on myself by drinking more. Musically it's not that adventurous but the lyric stands up on its own."

Of the two versions, Andy reckons the unused Langer/Winstanley one was the better one. "Their version was tighter and this was more flaccid, but because we were working with Hugh we thought we'd stay with our mate. It's stupid, really, because we should have just used the best version." "Though sometimes there are other reasons for choosing a different version," says Colin, obliquely.

"Heaven Is Paved with Broken Glass"

(Andy Partridge) (B side only, not on album)

Mixed by the band because they didn't think Hugh's rushed mix had done the song justice, "Heaven Is Paved with Broken Glass" is crazy paved with weird sound effects—drums played through a midget Archer amplifier speaker and synthesized cherub choirs. "It's just a song about disappointment and 'heaven becomes hell,' as the slowed down voice at the beginning says. There's something a bit Talking Heads about it which is a bit uncomfortable for me. It's not one of my better things in retrospect," says Andy. "I don't know whether there's too much of me or not enough of me in it. I can't decide."

"Egyptian Solution" or "Thebes In a Box" ("Homo Safari #3")

(Andy Partridge) (B side only, not on album)

Virgin gambled that Langer and Winstanley would bring the same chart-topping magic to XTC that they had with Madness, doyennes of the British ska revolution. But it was not to be. Clive

Langer walked out early in the session and all that survived of Alan Winstanley's work was a little improvisation for the "Homo Safari" file, written around a beat-box drum rhythm. "It was just a little noodle and any little noodle we came up with was put in the 'Homo Safari' box. It was like an orphanage for lost noodles, really," says Andy. "It's actually me drumming because I think Chambers was in the pub." "And it's Dave on bass," says Colin. "I was probably in the pub with Chambers."

"Mantis On Parole" ("Homo Safari #4")

(Andy Partridge) (B side only, not on album)

Once again, a Musicians Union pacifying session bore fruit in the name of "Mantis On Parole," another instrumental for the "Homo Safari" box. It was recorded in what should have been a "Top of the Pops" session for "Senses Working Overtime" and was based around a Charlie Parker-ish riff Andy had played for years. "Ian Gregory sat in on drums and we knocked it up before the man from the MU got back from lunch," says Andy.

"Over Rusty Water"

(XTC) (B side only, not on album)

"Over Rusty Water" was not so much written as discovered. Colin and Andy were trying to build an aural collage of outtakes as a B side. Sitting in The Townhouse studios they searched through tapes for suitable offcuts but it didn't seem to be working. "It was too personal," says Andy. "We understood it but nobody else would. But we were listening to the multitrack of the middle eight of 'Roads Girdle the Globe,' which I used for 'I Sit In the Snow,' and I pushed up all the faders at once. It created this wonderful, ethereal, soupy sound and that became 'Over Rusty Water.' I suppose it's the last vestiges of a dub mix."

6

OFF THE RAILS

1982

People take XTC too seriously. Barely a day goes by without a letter arriving from a fan, exposing the inner meanings of XTC songs. But they are invariably wrong. There are no hidden meanings, barring the odd spiked remark. Play the records backward and the most you will find is the way a guitar solo was actually played. For the most part, XTC songs are cameos, an oblique look at life, an idea, a feeling. XTC is neither the font of spiritual enlightenment nor a hotbed of political ideology. It is the humor of the band that makes it exceptional, especially that of Andy Partridge. Colin can see the hilarious in something and become engulfed in infectious giggles. Dave Gregory has a dry humor, tinged with cynicism. But Andy Partridge is a goon, or a Monty Python, or a Pete and Dud clone, accidentally filed under Music.

So why isn't a book about XTC one big laugh? Well, the humor in the story is soured by the misery that pervaded parts of their career. Even when Andy tells the story, woven with quips and puns, there is pain. To an extent, it was Andy that brought this misery upon them. He makes a pretty good tortured genius. He hates to offend or dominate but he does it effortlessly. He is very loyal and generous but frighteningly strong-willed. Only the easy nature of Colin and Dave have kept the band from shedding blood. Had Andy not held the reins so tightly, XTC would have been a lesser band, but the story might have been a happier one.

Andy's will is oft-misguided by the internal conflict between loyalty and intuition. He will trust the wrong people, choose the wrong singles, sign the wrong contracts, employ the wrong producers, and he will stick to his decisions until teetering on the brink of disaster.

So it was with touring. *English Settlement* had won international acclaim. Touring the songs would take them to that next step toward stardom. Loyalty told him to continue but intuition directed him away from touring. Mentally, he was tearing himself apart and in the middle of the *English Settlement* tour, he went to pieces. It transformed XTC's career, and is best told in their own words:

ANDY: *I couldn't take any more touring. It was really getting to me. I'd sort of set in my little brain that I didn't want to take* English Settlement *on* *the road other than a few one-off gigs. I wanted a normal life and there's no way on earth that being on the road is normal.*

COLIN: *But this whole business is not having a normal life.*

ANDY: *But especially the touring bit. You wake up in the same orange hotel rooms and think, What town am I in? I've actually had to ring down to reception on a couple of tours and they must think you're on drugs when you ring down and ask what town you're in. They say, "Oh you're in Raccoon Pancreas, Nebraska," and it's exactly the same as Moose Knob, Wyoming, the night before. I was vegetarian, and going on the road vegetarian you hardly eat anything. Free peanuts off the bar or a cheese sandwich, maybe. You really neglect your health. We did some gigs in Italy and I started to get more nervy before each night, with stomach pains before the gigs. I couldn't work out what it was. Some doctors came to see me and said, "Oh, it's a stomach ulcer," or "It's food poisoning," but they couldn't work it out. But the pains were real enough to me. And it got trickier and trickier to go onstage and I got very shell shocked because I was going against my deepest wishes to go out on the road again.*

By the time we got to Paris, I was feeling really weird, as though everything was in a dream. I remember doing an interview one afternoon for this TV station and they shoved me in this old woman's house, for some reason. I'm sat there with her and the chenille tablecloth and a bird in a cage and a cup of coffee doing this interview, and I thought, What the hell am I doing here? This is so stupid. It was like a really weird dream.

And then we did the sound check and I thought, This doesn't feel right. Stop the world I want to get off. That night, we rushed onto the stage and in the intro of "Respectable Street," I had a huge panic attack. I thought I was going to die. The room started spinning and I was overwhelmed with fear. I felt like such an ass and I thought, Am I going mad? Is my brain coming unhinged? Somebody called an ambulance because they thought it was appendicitis. And it was a big gig, Le Palais. It was a televised simulcast and it was sold out.

DAVE: *Andy ran offstage and the promoter ran out and promised the audience that he would put on another show the following night, to make up for it. But when Andy heard about it, he ran.*

COLIN: *They naturally believed that Andy would be well enough in himself to do the second night.*
ANDY: *They were adamant. The record company got really vicious and I felt really stupid. I was distraught. Somebody called an ambulance but someone else said, "Oh the traffic's really bad, you'll have to call the fire brigade to lead the way for the ambulance." So I'm laid in the corner in a fetal ball with Ian Reid going, "Come on! Pull yourself together!" Which was just what I didn't want, and suddenly all these firemen burst in the room.*
COLIN: *It sounds like a Russell Mulcahy video.*
ANDY: *Either that or a Beatles lyric, "Then the fireman rushes in." And they're looking 'round for the fire and there's me lying in a sobbing mess clutching my stomach.*

Some doctor said, "Oh, you just need some rest. Take these tablets and maybe we'll look at you tomorrow."
DAVE: *Frankie Enfield, the tour manager, said the only way Andy was going to get out of playing was to leave town.*
ANDY: *The French record company got wind of this and said, "You must stay. You must not leave. You must play the gig." I just thought, You insensitive buggers. This is incredible. You're holding me to ransom. I'm virtually a hostage. I sneaked out in a taxi the next morning and got out on a plane. I was in a state of high tension. If someone had said "Er,* boo*!" to me I'd have gone* aaargh*. I was over . . .*
COLIN: *Oversensitized.*
ANDY: *Overwhelmed by everything. I got back and we canceled the English leg of the tour so I could go and get some advice. I thought it was stage fright and that if it was, it might not happen again. So I agreed, somewhat foolishly, to go on this American tour which was kicking off in Los Angeles.*
COLIN: *San Diego.*
ANDY: *Ah yes. San Diego and then it went on to Los Angeles. Anyway, we did this gig in San Diego and I was very, very wound up. I played the whole gig with this incredible pain in my stomach and it was just unbearable. It was just basically my body and my subconscious saying, "Look, you've got to stop doing this, this is not right. This is not what you want. This is not a normal life, you haven't got kids, you haven't got a house. Where is all the*

money from these shows?" My subconscious was making me ill to force me to stop. I played this show in San Diego feeling like death and then the next show was in . . . er . . .

COLIN: *The Palladium.*

ANDY: *In Los Angeles. I think that was sold out and I remember laying on my bed. We were all supposed to meet in the cafe up the road.*

COLIN: *Ben Frank's.*

ANDY: *That's it. And then go on from Ben Frank's diner to the gig. I lay on my hotel bed and I was petrified. I couldn't move my legs. They were turned to jelly and I couldn't function. I was laid on the bed for ages, thinking, I can't do it! I can't do it! I can't even get off the bed to walk to Ben Frank's. But I did get off the bed and I walked there painfully slowly. I was scared to death and I just remember saying, "I don't want to do this gig."*

DAVE: *Ian Reid was there and Frankie Enfield and we were having a post-sound check dinner. Andy came in looking white as a sheet. We already knew something was up because he'd been moaning about touring all day. But when he said it, we just sat there and thought, So that really is it then. I thought, Fuck me! We've spent thousands on shipping all this gear, a big PA, paying roadies, the bus, lights, and it's all wasted. How are we ever going to pay to get it back?*

ANDY: *Chambers looked daggers at me. He just looked at me like he was a knife thrower with malintent. And Reid said, "Well that's it then. You're going to get your legs broken by the promoter. You'd better have a real illness. We'd better take you to hospital else you'll never get out of the place alive." I thought, This is crazy. I just want to go to sleep and for the rest of the world to disappear and now I've got to go to hospital and pretend to be ill.*

It was really humiliating. I have to go to hospital and I'm laid on this casualty ward bed and the person next to me has got gunshot wounds, bleeding everywhere. Another person on the other side of me is having a fit. And I'm laid there thinking, I just want to go home. Then a doctor came up and looked at my clipboard and said, "Partridge! What's wrong?" and I said, "Um . . . er . . . pains in the stomach." And he said, "Right, bend over!" and so I bent over and he shoved his finger up my ass, wiggled it around a bit, wrote something on a piece of paper, and said, "Right! You can leave!" And that was it.

COLIN: *What was the verdict?*
ANDY: *I've no idea.*
COLIN: *Perhaps he got some pleasure from it.*
ANDY: *Perhaps he wasn't even a doctor.*
NEVILLE: *Perhaps he had tickets for the gig.*
COLIN: *"I will have satisfaction!"*
ANDY: *I think he was the bloke topping up the coffee machine. This was very disturbing to me at the time and I'm trying to make light of it because it gets me very miserable when I think about it.*

The next day I think you and I decided to fly home first and we had to fly to New York to get a connection to fly back to England.
COLIN: *We were three days getting home.*
ANDY: *Three days, because we were snowed in in New York. But I remember feeling like a mad person waiting to check in for the flight and there was a real mad person there. There was this red Indian who was drawing nuclear missiles raining down onto this city in a bubble on this big piece of paper. I said, "Er, what are you drawing?" and he said, "I am an authentic Indian chief of the so-and-so tribe and my name is so-and-so and I am drawing my invention, a magic shield which can protect cities from nuclear attack. But the Pentagon isn't interested." I just thought, Well, this is bloody typical. I'm feeling like a loony standing here with this real loony. When I got back I went to a hypnotherapist and, supposedly, relived a lot of stressful goings-on onstage. I don't know if it was any help to me, but I kind of learnt to relax a bit more. I guess it was just a mental problem causing a physical problem, which they can do. All the other tests didn't show anything.*

We had just moved to this house and it was in a terrible state. I spent a lot of time sat in the garden just writing poetry and songs and strumming on the acoustic guitar. Quite a lot of songs came out: "Beating of Hearts," "Ladybird," "Desert Island." But I was obviously unhinged badly because I couldn't leave the house. If I touched the front door latch I was overcome with tremors and felt nauseous and couldn't move. I knew that people would see me and I'd be on display and they'd be expecting me to give them some sort of performance.
COLIN: *I think the whole period was a combination of pressures. Sooner or later, if a band is continually on the road, something's going to snap. If you don't overplay your hand you can go on for quite a long time touring but*

our management at the time just overplayed the golden goose, to mix metaphors, for about five years.

ANDY: *And there were no luxuries on the tour, were there? No comforts.*

COLIN: *The irony of it was that on the aborted tour, we had a whole coach to ourselves. It was like we'd finally arrived, luxury-wise.*

DAVE: *For the first time there was the thrill of being four lads from Swindon, playing full-size stages, with roadies and a big PA system. It was exciting.*

ANDY: *But you'd have to fight for everything. We were kept in this continual poverty. It was beginning to unhinge me badly that this money was being scooped up and we just never saw it. So like Colin says, if you get kept on the treadmill, something's going to snap and I was in danger of snapping very badly.*

Slowly it died down and I could leave the house. I went for more hypnotherapy and was writing songs in the meantime, but I felt like a real casualty. I just thought, Oh my God! This is just going to relegate me to the Syd Barrett thing, I suppose. Just being this dribbling rock casualty.

COLIN: *Living with his mum.*

ANDY: *No! I wasn't that bad. But it was a very tough time for me.*

COLIN: *We certainly had a few lean years around this time. We weren't earning any money from the gigs anyway, so it didn't make any difference whether we toured or not financially. But at one point we weren't going to get our gear back from America.*

DAVE: *Entec impounded our gear because we couldn't pay them for the PA and we had to go cap in hand to Virgin to pay the bills.*

COLIN: *And there were lots of rumblings about promoters suing us, although that didn't come to anything. But it was more the drop off in interest from the record company that mattered. Jeremy Lascelles took over about this time.*

ANDY: *And that was very bad for us. He was not supportive. He was just critical.*

COLIN: *I think we realized that the only way out of the mess was to write some decent material.*

ANDY: *We just had to make another album. It wasn't going to put the thing right, but the only thing to do was to do what we do best, which is making records.*

Terry disliked it all, intensely.

COLIN: *I can only speak for myself, but if there's something out of my control I don't worry about things that I can't change, and if someone says we're not touring anymore I just think, Well, what can we do? Okay, we'll make records then.*

ANDY: *You must have been disappointed though?*

COLIN: *No, not really.*

ANDY: *Well, that's very warming, because I felt like I was just public enemy number one. Certainly from Terry. I mean, Terry wasn't ultrafriendly before then. Terry and I weren't like great buddies. It was a kind of pal-y working relationship, but after this incident I really felt that I'd opened the fridge door every time there were any dealings with Terry. I was spoiling his round-the-world carousing.*

COLIN: *I realized that our passage wasn't going to be an easy one, but it wasn't the end of the world. I don't worry about anything that I can't change. I thought, Well, we'll either fold or we'll go on and make another record. So that's it. I tend to accept things like that. Life's too short for "what if?," isn't it?*

DAVE: *It wasn't a conscious decision made out of spite, so I felt sorry for you. It was something you didn't understand yourself. It was making all our lives difficult because of it. I was disappointed but I thought you'd think about it and that after the next album, you'd feel better and that penury would twist your arm into touring again. But it didn't. It was a shame because the tour was the best we'd ever done. At the Italian, German, and French gigs, the audiences were going nuts. They'd never been like that before in those countries.*

ANDY: *I think everyone thought, We'll do this album and then he'll want to go back on the road. But I think that I'd been severely physically and mentally dented by the continual touring process and what was happening on the business side. It wasn't so much stage fright as panic attacks about being onstage. And onstage is one of the safest places to be. The audience loves you, you're having fun. I used to love playing live but as the years went on, it became this mobile prison sentence. I still have bad dreams about it now. Only two nights ago, we were onstage in something like the Canterbury Odeon and there were just half a dozen people in the audience, nobody could remember how to play the songs, and all the house lights were on. There was no atmosphere and somebody was cooking hot dogs at the front of the stage and handing them out. I still* *do have bad dreams about being onstage because, to be brutal, I don't think I was cut out for it. Certainly I wasn't cut out to be the front man but it sort of fell to me by default.*

COLIN: *But I think you were always going to be the front man because you wrote most of the songs.*

ANDY: *But I would rather have had someone else be the singer and take the majority of the limelight. I know that when Colin was singing onstage, I felt more relaxed. The light wasn't on me. I have to be brutally honest, I don't think I was cut out for pop stardom, even though at one stage you could write off to* Melody Maker *and buy lamp shades with my face on. Why lamp shades, I don't know. I suppose the idea was that you could have my beautiful cheeseburger face grinning at you as you dozed off. Something for them to comfort them as they lay in the ward, strapped in their beds. But I wasn't really cut out for pop lamp shadedom.*

From this time, until at least the date of publication, XTC did not play live before an audience again, barring a couple of TV appearances, including *Letterman* in the U.S. and *The Late Show* on BBC. Even though large sums of money have been laid on the table, Andy, in particular, has resisted temptation. Dave has played live on numerous occasions and Colin is not against the idea. And in recent years, Andy has said that he might just play, under certain strict conditions. But until they do, the only way to see just how good XTC was live is to seek out the few rare video performances available.

7

FRUITS FALLEN FROM GOD'S GARDEN

1983

At yuletide in Merrie Olde England, in days when door-to-door entertainers didn't have to compete with The Sound of Music *and* Raiders of the Lost Bloody Ark, *troupes of mummers would travel around the villages performing* George and the Dragon and other fave plays in dumb show. The word *mum* came from the same origins as the pan-European word *mumble*, except that mumbling wasn't an absolute. To keep mum was to keep absolute silence, to say nothing. Therefore, mummers were mimers, and were derided for it, just as people would laugh at David Bowie's invisible wall mime in future centuries.

Andy Partridge was little above mumbling. For much of 1982, he sat like an old widow, huddled in a shawl in the back garden of his recently purchased, old and gutted house in the posh Old Town of Swindon. It was only a terraced house, with three smallish bedrooms and a lean-to kitchen. But it was his home and it had a small patch of ground at the back in which to warm his weary bones. He was frail and feeble, but there's nothing like a little emotional turmoil to turn on the creative tap.

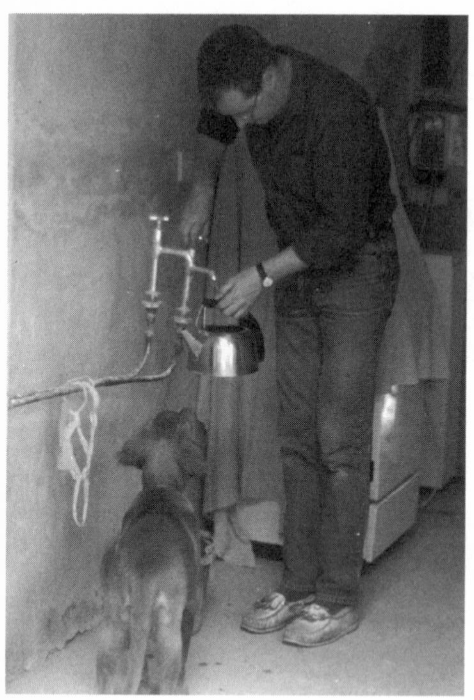

New home, new dog, no touring.

(CREDIT: THE ANDY PARTRIDGE COLLECTION)

Always the fatalist, Colin Moulding regarded his enforced retirement from touring as an opportunity to make better records and to spend more time with his family. But the experience must have had an impact. Despite the luxury of a five-month writing break, the Muse wasn't with him. Colin was to write just three songs for the next album.

Andy, "the victim," was actually on a creative roll. The breakdown had been costly to his health, but he had got what he wanted. XTC wouldn't tour again. He could devote himself to writing and recording and producing. He wrote and recorded the sound track to *Ocean's Daughter*, a Mike Portelli movie, with a theme initially titled "The Garden of Earthly Delights," though this name was dropped. For a couple of weeks in August, and for the first of a number of occasions, he worked with producer David Lord in his Crescent Studios. But for the most part, he led a sedentary life for the first time in half a decade.

XTC's turmoil had been nothing compared to the changes in the world. Argentina decided to invade the British-owned Falkland Islands, giving Maggie Thatcher a winnable little war to boost national pride before the next election. The pope decided to make friends with the Brits for the first time since Henry the Eighth had given the Vatican the finger 450 years earlier. In similarly generous mood, Queen Liz agreed to give Canada independent sovereignty—not that she had much choice, of course, as she probably told Michael Fagan, when he turned up in her bedroom one night. It was a momentous year.

Music was changing, too. Raw was out, polished in. The most coveted album of the year had been Japan's *Tin Drum*, a supremely shiny work of art by a band of glam rockers led by the twice-voted Most Beautiful Man in the World, David Sylvian. The album was a sumptuous production and the producer was Steve Nye.

Having chosen him to produce the next album, provisionally titled *Fruits Fallen from God's Garden*, XTC started recording in September 1982 in the rustic, rural recording residency of their former producer Martin Rushent. Despite a shaky start, tracking continued in The Manor through November and mixing transferred to AIR Studios, in Oxford Street, London. It was there that Nye had studied under Beatles' producer George Martin. But all was not well between Partridge and Nye. Much of the album was remixed at Virgin's behest, and Andy received the ultimate snub from his new A&R manager: the album, now named *Mummer*, was rejected.

MUMMER

TALKING BETWEEN THE LINES

COLIN: *Everyone was into this beautifully clean production around 1982. People like Green from Scritti Politti and Japan's* Tin Drum. *A little mechanical but beautifully polished.*

ANDY: *And I asked Virgin who produced it, which is how we found Steve Nye.*

DAVE: *But Japan was a very different group from us. They were keyboard driven. It was a very beautiful record, but Steve wasn't right for us.*

ANDY: *But Virgin wanted a single and we wanted a change from Hugh, so we got Steve in to record "Wonderland," "Beating of Hearts," and something for a B side.*

COLIN: *We'd been writing for about five months over the summer.*

ANDY: *A luxury after five years of constant touring.*

COLIN: *But not much by our standards now.*

ANDY: *We went to Genetic Studios in Pangbourne, Martin Rushent's complex up in the woods. It was like a group of huts in the woods.*

COLIN: *Like a holiday camp.*

ANDY: *So we set up the gear and waited. But Steve didn't turn up till late afternoon, ambling in in his cricket jumper [sweater] and baggy pants. It wasn't, "Hi, you must be Steve Nye." It was more, "Where the bloody hell have you been?" And he seemed so unconcerned.*

DAVE: *We weren't in the best of moods, but I thought he was genuinely sorry.*

COLIN: *Well, I didn't take to the guy.*

ANDY: *It didn't help that he was so grumpy. He would say the occasional very funny thing but it wasn't till the album that we experienced the full spectrum of his grumposity.*

DAVE: *That's a bit unfair. Steve had a very, very dry sense of humor. He doesn't join in the japes but I got on with him fine and found him very funny. You've got to respect people for having their own ways and sometimes Andy does not.*

COLIN: *He was a good farter.*

ANDY: *He could fart to order.*

COLIN: *And he knew some good curry houses.*

ANDY: *And we tasted the results the following morning.*

NEVILLE: *Which might be the reason Terry left the band after those sessions.*

ANDY: *We were rehearsing the album proper in the old Mechanics Institute theater scenery store in Swindon when he left. Terry didn't like the fact that we weren't touring and he was having problems with his Australian girlfriend.*

COLIN: *Who was pregnant.*

ANDY: *And not happy about being brought from sunny Newcastle to a soggy estate in Swindon.*

NEVILLE: *I can't imagine why.*

ANDY: *We were working on "Love On a Farmboy's Wages" one lunchtime, and he put his sticks down, picked up his keys and cigarettes, and said, "I'm off then, chaps. I'm leaving the group, so . . . er . . . see ya!" And that was it, cymbals swinging on their stands.*

COLIN: *He didn't think much of the new material and Andy was trying to show him the drum pattern to the track and he couldn't get it.*

ANDY: *I think he thought we were compromising him into a position where he'd leave, but we weren't. Luckily, Dave saved the day by remembering Pete Phipps, who'd supported us in Random Hold.*

DAVE: *He'd been the drummer with Gary Glitter and I thought it would be fun to have someone like him replace Terry. He was this great, loud drummer.*

ANDY: *So we called him up and two days later, he was in.*

Terry Chambers drums himself out of the band. (CREDIT: THE ANDY PARTRIDGE COLLECTION)

DAVE: *But as Andy had decided to make such a change in the sound of the band, he turned out to be an odd choice. Still, he's one of the few musicians we've asked back to work with us again.*

NEVILLE: *You asked Steve Nye back to do the album, despite the complaints.*

ANDY: *The results of the first sessions sounded good so we thought, Why not let him do the album?*

COLIN: *I think we were probably enamored of the fact that he was a protegé of George Martin and AIR Studios. But we did remix most of his stuff.*

ANDY: *"Wonderland" had to be remixed by the late Alex Sadkin and Phil Thornally, and the noisier ones were redone by Phil at Rak Studios, so we overspent badly. But Steve's quieter mixes sounded really nice. He was a great engineer.*

NEVILLE: *And how did Virgin react to all this expense?*

ANDY: *Jeremy Lascelles said, "No, I don't like it. Go away and write another album."*

NEVILLE: *How encouraging.*

ANDY: *I was totally crestfallen.*

COLIN: *We thought it was a good album with lots of singles. It might not have been as consistent as* Black Sea *but it was very hurtful to hear all this criticism.*

DAVE: *He may have had some justification. It sounded really good when we were making it but on listening back, it lacked sparkle.*

COLIN: *We thought, As he's thirty-fifth in line for the throne, he must be right.*

NEVILLE: *Watch the sarcasm, now.*

ANDY: *As his ass was going to be on the stamps one day, we'd better listen to him.*

NEVILLE: *His ass?*

ANDY: *If I was the queen, I'd have my ass on the stamps so they really knew what they were licking.*

NEVILLE: *So you wrote another album?*

ANDY: *Just two tracks, "Gold" and "Great Fire" and Jeremy liked "Great Fire."*

DAVE: *They brought in Bob Sargeant to produce it. Nice chap. Did Haircut 100 and the English Beat.*

ANDY: *We did it in Odyssey Studios in London and Virgin accepted the record. We had wanted to call it* Fruits Fallen from God's Garden *and I'd got Dave Dragon from the Design Clinic to draw up a sleeve in which we had fruit for our heads, sitting outside an old country estate. But they didn't want us seen as fruits and the mention of God in the title induced panic amongst the marketing bods [people]. I still liked the title* Fallen from the Garden, *but in the end we picked* Mummer.

MUMMER

ON THE TRACKS

"BEATING OF HEARTS"

(Andy Partridge)

Long hair and a fake buckskin jacket had never made a hippie of teenage Partridge. It was just in his bones. In 1982, when he discovered that the Glitter Band's one-note guitar tuning could make a guitar sound Indian, the hippie just poured out of him. Sadly, the mock-tablas and sleighbells of "Beating of Hearts" sounded as fake as his buckskin jacket, and true psychedelia remained out of reach. But as he barred his fingers up and down the multiple E strings, and the old prostate-troubled, seal's bark voice came thundering back, the message was as valid as anything strummed at Woodstock.

"It's just saying that the affairs of the heart are preferable to acts of war. Whenever I see that piece of film of the Chinese student standing in front of the line of tanks, I think that this expresses the sentiment that I meant to convey in this song. That the heart is stronger than tanks and bombs and screaming war planes."

Although the track didn't warrant a video budget, Channel 4 television asked XTC to make a program for their "Play At Home" series. "Beating of Hearts" was one that the band filmed, performing seated in Swindon's Wyvern Theater, wearing white shirts, projected with war scenes and flowers.

"WONDERLAND"

(Colin Moulding) (Single and album track)

"Wonderland" was the mutant offspring of a cheap echo unit and a schoolgirl called Jennifer Skirton. "I started messing around with this cheap reverb and the Korg synth and created this echo going

Partridge at eighteen and clearly a hippie. (CREDIT: THE ANDY PARTRIDGE COLLECTION)

down the scale," says Colin. "It sounded like some *Alice In Wonderland* music played in a deep grotto. I think what inspired me to write this was a girl I knew at school, called Jennifer Skirton. She was one of these girls that you mustn't touch because she was so wonderful but she would put you down at the drop of a hat. I did get to sit next to her at school and that seemed like the happiest day of my life at the time. But she went out with older boys and there was the rub." The recording, at Genetic Studios, featured some funky drumming from Terry. "He nabbed the end section from 'Don't Stop the Music' by Sly and Robbie," says Andy. "Hans de Vente brought this tape into the studio and we thought it was the funkiest thing going."

Although Andy hardly played on the record, he did feature with Dave Gregory in the video, as a gardener tending roses at the Tudor mansion, Hatfield House. "It was appalling," says Andy. "It would have been passable if they hadn't got in these five male dancers in suits. Everyone thinks they're us." "I would have chosen a film of Jennifer Skirton swimming underwater," says Colin.

"Love On a Farmboy's Wages"

(Andy Partridge) (Single and album track)

After discharging from the navy, Johnny Partridge had a series of odd jobs. He often took young Andrew on the Latton Creamery truck, down deeply hedged Wiltshire lanes, gathering milk churns from the ancient stone farms around Swindon.

Although this was as close as young Andy ever got to a farm, the image offered a romantic, Thomas Hardy angle for another song on the perils of poverty. But "Love On the Piss Poor Wages," as it became known, was full of snippets of his own life. " 'People say that I'm no good/Painting pictures and carving wood,' was Marianne's parents telling me what a 'jumped-up tu'penny ha'penny ticket writer' I was. I painted posters in McIlroy's department store when I met her and this was their stinging comment on that. They were very angry at me because she was just about to get married to this teacher and move to the south coast."

Enhancing the English folkiness of the lyric, the song was built around a Bert Jantsch-ish guitar run, tuned normally but awkwardly fingered, the clattering clay pot drum pattern that had pushed Terry over the edge, and an unintentionally cowlike bass by Colin. "If I'd known Andy wanted a cow, I'd have really turned on the ointment," he says.

It wasn't an obvious single, though it was a favorite of Dave's and of Radio One DJ Mike Read, who used to try playing it on the guitar on air. "He always got it wrong," says Andy. "I suppose that's why he was sacked."

The single sleeve was made from a photo of Andy's own wallet, which was gold blocked with "XTC—Love On a Farmboy's Wages." He had to throw it away in the end because he was too embarrassed to show it in the pub.

"Great Fire"

(Andy Partridge) (Album track and single)

Rising out of adversity, "Great Fire" was written literally moments after Jeremy Lascelles of Virgin rejected the first version of *Mummer*. "I put down the phone and sat with my head in my hands and thought, Now what am I going to do? I was just staring blankly at this chocolate box full of pens which had scenes of old York 'round the edge. I thought it looked like London around the time of the Great Fire of 1666." This train of thought carried him from great fires to great love and the song was completed in about ten minutes, all thanks to Terry's chocolate box.

Bob Sargeant produced the song at Odyssey Studios and, for the first time on an XTC record, real strings were used, including Nigel Warren-Greene and Gavin Wright, who had played on "Eleanor Rigby." Short of an ending, they lifted an idea from the Monkees' "Pleasant Valley Sunday" and allowed the entire mix to disappear into a wash of reverb. "I thought Bob did a good job and it was a good song," says Dave. "The first time I heard the single on the radio I thought, This sounds like a hit, we should be hearing a lot of this. But it wasn't." BBC Radio One played it . . . once!

"Deliver Us from the Elements"
(Colin Moulding)

One night, Colin sat in his bay window staring up at the stars. He always had a passion for astronomy, unlike the astrophobic Andy. Colin liked the feeling of insignificance astronomy's vastness gave to little Earth and its littler people. Strumming a couple of chords he tried to portray this power. "I wanted to write a song about how insignificant we are down here, but I knew I couldn't write in astronomical terms," he says. "Sort of 'Making Plans for Rigel'?" says Andy. "So I felt it was better to carry that sentiment through on a more earthly level," Colin continues. The song remained a two-chord wonder until the rehearsal stage, when they added the Mellotron "desert storm" choir sound and Andy's synthesized pulse. Suddenly it became the vast song he had wanted.

In the studio, Dave added a real Jew's harp and almost split his lip when it flicked him in the teeth. The moment of impact is recorded as a *ping!* in the introduction, though the subsequent swearing was edited out. The reversed sound effects and the excessive ending hinted at the Dukes that were to come. "You can see we were gagging to become psychedelic by 1983," says Andy.

"Human Alchemy"
(Andy Partridge)

One day, during the mixing in AIR Studios, Andy opened the door to step out for a moment and Japan fell in—the band, not the country. They had been working in the next studio and having heard that their heroes, XTC, were recording with their old producer, Steve Nye, they had been listening at the door. The song Steve was mixing was "Human Alchemy," a difficult song to write. Originally, it had been an instrumental dub jam called "Jacobs Ladder," played in the urine stench of Fatty's rehearsal studios. But it deserved a strong lyric. "I wanted to write a song about slavery but it's not a subject I know about. Being a white man, it is something I still feel guilty about and this provided the perfect vehicle for the subject. I didn't want to sing anything crass about how awful slavery was. It needed a new approach and, liking the Third Ear Band album *Alchemy*, I thought slavery was like a human alchemy where black human beings were being converted into gold for other people.

"I hope the lyric didn't come off pretentious, because the nearest I got to slavery was having a black great-great-grandfather. I don't think I saw a black person till I was about eleven and he was a dustman. I followed him for hours around our estate."

"Ladybird"
(Andy Partridge)

Sitting in his hotel room on a rainy day in Italy, Andy watched a spider making its web in the rain. In his head, spiders led to insects and the tragic story of "Ladybird Ladybird." He noted the idea down for future reference. The song was another completed in the back garden in Swindon, unwittingly weaving in his thoughts about a woman called Erica, who he met at a film premiere. It came out as a cross between McCartney's "Your Mother Should Know" and a Dave Brubeck jazz tune, embellished with George Harrison–style picking which Steve Nye insisted on keeping, finally kicking out Andy's insistence on trying to sound unique.

The whole band liked the song. "It's got this off-the-cuff feel about it. We skimmed the atmosphere of the planet Jazz here and it was quite exciting to do that," says Andy. Colin disagrees. "Jazz is by its very nature exploratory and the tunes I played on this were very set." But he likes the song. "Some songs have a sort of bass *thrumm* to them that I like and this is one of those. It's also really well recorded. Pete Phipps does the most exploratory thing with his scurrying insect sound."

"In Loving Memory of a Name"
(Colin Moulding)

"This is probably one of my least favorite of my songs ever," says Colin, to Andy's surprise. "It's just about moping 'round a graveyard and just remembering the lives of the people there. It doesn't spring from personal experience or my imagination. I like to write about things that are part of me. It's just borne out of melody. I think I had a bit of 'Martha, My Dear' in my head at the time. It has that ploddy piano." It also has a middle eight that sounds like a straight lift from Bernstein's "Maria," but it is a much better song than Colin thinks.

Dave Gregory played the piano, as usual, though Colin wrote it on the upright at home. "I think Dave plays most of the instruments on this," says Andy. "I don't remember playing anything."

"Me and the Wind"
(Andy Partridge)

"A fan wrote to me and said, 'Ah! I know what this is about. This is about your relationship with Terry Chambers and all the clues are in there, aren't they?' There are 'snares,' 'sitting on your stool,' 'while you crack the whip,' 'imprisoned in your drum beat.' "

Andy is bemused by the suggested association with Terry's departure. "Me and the Wind" was just the bittersweet feeling at the end of a relationship, as the sound track to a scene from *Whistle Down the Wind* or *Billy Liar,* standing on a windswept hill, looking out over the landscape. But was it Terry? It even had the sort of tumbling drum pattern Terry would hate. "Maybe it was a subconscious thing, knowing Terry was going to leave, but I don't think so," he says.

The song started on guitar with a pianoish sound, but Andy decided it was better to strain Dave's wrists playing a real piano. Steve Nye recorded through an autopanner, so it whizzed around the stereo image and Andy added to the wind effects by blowing through a flute. "I think it sounds like the music you hear when the Romans are coming," says Colin. "It could have been a theme to something like *I, Claudius.*" Andy looks even more bemused.

"Funk Pop a Roll"

(Andy Partridge)

Andy was quite convinced that his career was on the rocks by now. The album was almost completed but Virgin seemed indifferent. Giving up touring had made him no friends and he had even banned Ian Reid, their longtime manager, from the sessions. But there was nothing like a good dose of venom to inspire him. "Funk Pop a Roll" was no pastoral *Mummer* song. It was XTC power pop in full flight, biting hard into the hand that fed them—the record industry. In such a laidback recording, the violent "Funk Pop a Roll" stuck out like a sore thumb. "It's an oddball, this one," says Colin. "It probably belongs more with *The Big Express.*" It was a blatant song about the music industry. "I was naive about it but became less and less so as the years went by. It was about the rubbish that they spoon-feed the public, and still do," says Andy. "Everything you eat is waste/But swallowing is easy when it has no taste," he spat. "Oozing like napalm from the speakers and grilles of your radio/And into the mouths of babes." But, admitting his own part in the play, "Please don't listen to me/I've already been poisoned by this industry."

Dave held the track together with chopping guitars while Andy, his blood raised, managed a passable sax performance. Poor Phil Thornally mixed the track under strict orders to keep everything louder than everything else. And then, right at the end of the album, convinced he had just committed professional suicide, Andy said "bye-bye." "I honestly thought this could be the last thing anyone heard of us on record," he says. "Somebody should have said 'hello' on the next one then," answered Colin.

IN THE SIDINGS . . .

"Frost Circus (Homo Safari #5)"

(Andy Partridge) (B side only, not on album)

Between the first and second *Mummer* sessions, Howard Gray engineered a session at The Manor, with just Dave and Andy present. "Frost Circus" was one of the results, built pass by pass on the Prophet synth. "It was put in the 'Homo Safari' bag, although it wasn't really part of the 'Homo Safari' series," says Andy. "It was just a little instrumental idea but it ended up used as a teenage makeup ad in Japan and on various TV programs." One of these was a documentary about the Coney Island amusement park. Another piece in the same film was by Harold Budd, who was so taken by Andy's music that he resolved to work with him in the future.

"Jump" (Also known as "Jump, Jump, Love and Swimming Pools")

(Andy Partridge) (B side only, not on album)

The first track recorded in any album session is probably a weaker one. "Jump" was so weak that it was rerecorded later in the album sessions, but it still didn't make the album. "Maybe it was just a weak song and the recording process was its last gasp," says Andy. "But I know a lot of people like it. I think we were all of the opinion that it died in our arms. It's almost as close as we get to easy listening." "I think what Steve thought, and maybe we did, too, was that this was a song from an earlier generation. Like something from the fifties," says Colin, though any suggestions that Steve sabotaged the track in production are probably greatly exaggerated.

For a recording on death row, it actually sounds quite a happy one. There's a touch of "59th Street Bridge Song (Feelin' Groovy)" in the guitar figure that's admitted by Andy in the outro scat. But there are also hints of African and Latin fills which make the whole thing quite confusing. "The lyric of the song is me telling myself to loosen up and try things out, take your life in your hands and jump," says Andy. "It's a self-hypnosis thing. And when I don't take that advice, I tell myself off with a song like 'Seagulls Screaming Kiss Her, Kiss Her.' "

"Toys" (Also known as "Oh Dear, What Can the Matter Be?")

(Andy Partridge) (B Side only, not on album)

Andy's passion for toys is legendary. He is a familiar figure at model soldier exhibitions and even designs his own range. He built many games and toys for his children, but has a fascination for the tackiest of mass-produced monstrosities. "Toys" used this interest as a vehicle for exposing our worst traits. "It's how we put all our screwed-up weirdness into toys and how that reflects back on us. Ragdoll gets beaten up by Action Man [the British equivalent of G.I. Joe], who speaks with a commanding voice, but sexually is not all there." The song is antiprejudice, but has just the kind of lyrics to inflame the politically correct, yet ignorant. He admits that the Dolly Concentration Camp idea was a tad tacky.

A rejected verse for "Toys" from Andy's notebook. (CREDIT: ANDY PARTRIDGE)

"Toys" was built around some bluesy G-flat chords that interested Andy, but even he knew it was destined for the B bag. So it sat idle for some time, before being reinstated as a B side on *The Big Express* sessions, mixed by Glenn Tommey at Crescent Studios, complete with the sounds of real mechanical toys.

"GOLD"

(Andy Partridge) (B side only, not on album)

Miles Copeland, manager and family member of the Police, was aware that XTC wouldn't be touring again, but he still tried to poach them from Ian Reid. In a clandestine meeting at The Curry Garden in Swindon, he offered the band a deal, and they declined. Andy arrived feeling quite uplifted. He had just written a song called "Gold," telling himself to appreciate what he had. That even his old red brick town could look gold in the right light. "I walked to the restaurant and it was one of those evenings where the sun was really orangey and all the buildings looked really gold. I thought, Coo! How weirdly prophetic! It was written on a turned-down electric guitar and I think you can tell that," says Andy. "It's as if George Formby had been given an electric guitar—a bit of Formbycation." "There's just about every style under the sun in it," says Colin. "It's sort of Dexy's Midnight Talking Heads Stax Specials," says Andy.

Bob Sargeant tied the jumbled styles together by bringing in a trombonist, Vince Sullivan, to give it a signature. "We just stood there and said, 'Make it more carnival, improvise this and harmonize that,' " says Andy. Dave suggested adding to the carnival atmosphere by making a row, as per that on the Tremoloes' "Here Comes My Baby."

"PROCESSION TOWARDS LEARNING LAND" ("HOMO SAFARI #6")

(Andy Partridge) (B side only, not on album)

Another Prophet synth instrumental from Andy and Dave's Manor sessions with Howard Gray, "Procession Towards Learning Land" reminds Andy of Tibet, though heaven knows why. The only other instrument on this was a toy drum bought from the Early Learning Center. Andy instructed Howard to deliberately overload the desk to give it a distorted sound. "The poor man was tearing his ginger hair out," says Andy.

"Desert Island"

(Andy Partridge) (B side only, not on album)

The quiet that descends on a town on a sunny day and a schmaltzy D diminished chord led Andy to think of desert islands from an oblique angle, a depressing one, thinly disguised as a beach bar cabaret tune. "It's a comment on England in the early eighties, one giant, soulless building site. This wasteland of new buildings and motorways and deserted shopping malls, a deserted island," says Andy.

For the first time on record, Andy and Dave played the backing on nylon string guitars, and the loose feel gave a sunny, beach club sound. "The band sounds playful," says Andy. "This is a case of not giving a damn about a song in a relaxed way and it coming out really well." "The playing sounds like we are your crew," says Colin to Andy. "But if you took the crew away from the captain, it would still sound like a song. It might have been better for just being acoustic."

The song was recorded in various bits and pieces, having been shelved partway through the *Mummer* sessions. It was revived at Crescent Studios, during *The Big Express* sessions, with vocals recorded and the whole thing mixed by Glenn Tommey.

"Cut It Out"

(XTC) (B side only, not on album)

Stuck for another B side, Andy analyzed hours of live recordings to find this, the improvised end section of a performance of "Scissor Man." "It was cut out of 'Scissor Man.' Hence the title," says Andy. "It's probably the listener's reaction, as well, when they found they weren't getting a new song. 'Cut it out!' "

8

COAL FACE

1984

The cover of The Big Express *is filled with a photo of a great, rusting locomotive drive wheel. The vinyl sleeve was trimmed into a circle, but the uncut CD cover exposes a tiny secret. At about the five o'clock position, basking in the warmth of the photographic* lamp, is a cricket. A grasshopper, by Jiminy! A small creature on the verge of being crushed by a vast, unstoppable machine. A bright emerald amid the industrial grime of the Great Western Railway Museum. It had gatecrashed the photo session, but it played a metaphorical role for XTC, a jewel in the mud of Swindon, out on the edge of everything that was happening, on the verge of being crushed by the wheels of industry.

Andy Partridge had often bemoaned that their Swindonian origins made them the target of fashion bigots. He had never really liked the comparisons drawn with Talking Heads, not because he denied the shared musical heritage, but because he thought their cool New York origins had as much to do with their success as tepid Swindon had with XTC's lack of it.

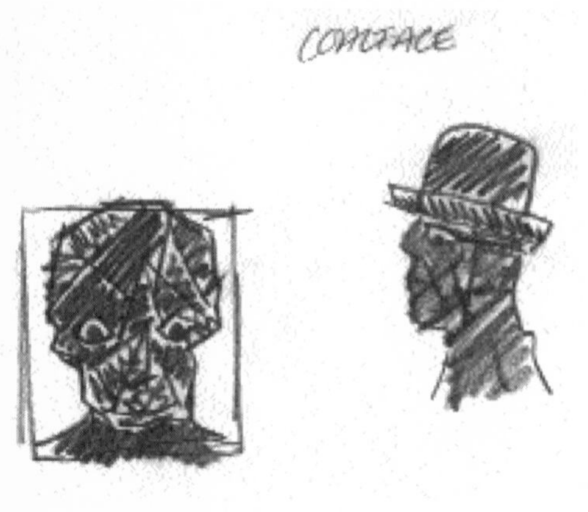

Andy's sketches for the Coal Face *sleeve before the name change to* The Big Express. (CREDIT: ANDY PARTRIDGE)

The Big Express showed a change of mood in the XTC camp. Bitter at the poor response from Virgin, and the lackluster support for *Mummer*, Andy decided to get tough, to stand firm. That meant being proud of his English, and more importantly, his Swindonian origins. He was proud to be from Pig Hill and was willing to celebrate it on a very loud album, a different kind of XTC. Colin and Dave were not prepared for this, but were dragged along by his enthusiasm, unaware that he'd written most of the songs on a guitar with a broken E string! How uncool can you get?

The English city of Bath is only twenty-five minutes from Swindon on the Great Western Railway. But it is a world away in character. Bath was already a resort town when the Romans modernized it 2,000 years ago. It's a wealthy town full of classical, golden stone buildings set in wooded hills. David Lord lived there and produced records in his Crescent Studios. He was also a world away from XTC. He had turned down McCartney's invitation to score strings for "She's Leaving Home" because he didn't think the Beatles made serious music. He was a classical musician and arranger, a traditionalist, a demon on the organ. Andy had worked with him producing *The Naked Shakespeare*, a record by the poetic genius Peter Blegvad. David had engineered, but also contributed his formidable musical knowledge to the album. This made a deep impression on Andy. He hadn't had a musical guru before now. David Lord could hold his own in any musical conversation and piqued Andy's interests in unexplored musical areas.

He had also shown a sense of humor on XTC's thinly disguised "Three Wise Men" Christmas single sessions, which XTC used to test his mettle. This, combined with a production package that gave them unlimited studio time, persuaded Andy, at least, that David Lord should coproduce the next album. So they headed over the hills to Bath for their first exercise in recording excess.

Pete Phipps joined them again, though he had to compete with a Linn Drum, the drum machine of the early eighties. Dave Gregory hated it. It took many hours to program and offered so much choice that days were wasted hunting out the perfect sound. With the tonal colors David Lord's orchestral origins brought to the palette, *The Big Express* dragged out to twenty weeks of recording.

While they worked, armed conflict continued in Mozambique, Iran and Iraq, Lebanon, Guinea, Cameroon, Kashmir, Uganda, and Northern Ireland, shunting the world's arms bill to over $100 billion. In America, Ronnie the Raygun began gunning for a second term win, while most of Central America replaced its presidents. In Russia, Soviet leader Yuri Andropov dropped off to sleep and Konstantin Chernenko took over.

In Bath, a different kind of drama played out. Many of the songs Andy wrote and a couple of Colin's were pure theater, and David Lord emphasized this to the max. The album sessions ran out of spring and soaked up summer. While programming continued for hours, Andy would slip upstairs to toy with an idea for a spoof psychedelic band.

In the end, even Lord ran out of time and moved on to other sessions, leaving the album unfinished, causing much disgruntlement in the XTC camp. They picked up their tapes and trudged off to London, to finish mixing with Phil Thornally in Rak Studios. And as they mulled over the name of the album—*Coal Face? Under the Rusting North Star? Head of Steam? Mindless Sax and Violins?*—they shed the management that had got them to where they were!

THE BIG EXPRESS

TALKING BETWEEN THE LINES

ANDY: *The big express is rolling into town, ladies and gentlemen. Climb aboard for hours of fun. We apologize for any inconvenience caused. The reason is we're really crap and we don't care.*

NEVILLE: *Commercially speaking,* Mummer *was not a high point, was it?*

ANDY: *It puzzled me that* Mummer *wasn't better received than it was.*

COLIN: *It took a dive, really, though I thought it had its high points. But we spent so long remixing and publicizing the thing that there wasn't much time to write the next album.*

ANDY: *Well, Dave found time to play a gig or two with Talisman, the reggae band.*

COLIN: *Did he?*

ANDY: *I know. Can't quite see him wearing dreadlocks. The only locks he's got are on his guitar case.*

NEVILLE: *From reggae to David Lord is quite a leap.*

ANDY: *I'd met David while I was producing Peter Blegvad and was impressed with his pedigree. In the sixties he was seen as one of the angry young composers and he took great pride in having turned down Paul McCartney's request for him to ar-*

range "She's Leaving Home." "Beatles! Pop music!" We tried him out on the "Three Wise Men" sessions and he seemed to understand us.

COLIN: *He wasn't really where I was coming from musically and I didn't enjoy working with him.*

NEVILLE: *It sounds like you didn't have much choice in the matter.*

ANDY: *I liked the fact that he knew where to put a bassoon or a cor Anglais. He was the organist at Canterbury Cathedral and head of music at Bath University. Well in with the "All Gas and Gaiters" brigade. I thought, Maybe we've found our George Martin. Or is it only Millicent Martin?*

COLIN: *But he didn't think about the meaning of the song. I just think he thought about the form. He seemed to think he was playing at the Albert Hall. It was all so grand.*

DAVE: *But the whole thing took so bloody long we didn't get to finish it with him anyway.*

ANDY: *For me,* The Big Express *was a high point. I was feeling pretty dented after* Mummer, *but I was feeling mentally stronger about myself and I think this album contains some of my best songs. Because of the pastoral nature of* Mummer, *everybody thought it was time to put the acoustics aside and crank it up. And with David Lord it created that interesting tension between the orchestral and the metal. Geffen had*

Moulding, Lord, Partridge, Gregory, and Phipps at Crescent Studios. (CREDIT: THE ANDY PARTRIDGE COLLECTION)

been on board since Mummer *and they sent Mrs. Bob Dylan, who worked for them, to check us out. She was like a cross between Hedda Hopper and Joan Rivers, a very nice woman. But she'd psyched herself up for another pastoral album and I think she was a bit shocked.*

COLIN: *It was also the Linn drum record.*

DAVE: *We spent forever programming. I remember a whole afternoon spent trying to find the right hi-hat sound. It was stupid and the album lacks energy because of it!*

ANDY: *I do regret using that thing. It was interesting to work with something that consistent, but it does date the album.*

NEVILLE: *A high-tech piece of kit for an orchestral musician.*

ANDY: *Well, the vibe at Crescent was very old worldly, though they had good gear and knew how to use it. It was really just a couple of old cottages knocked together with even the courtyard walled in as a drum room. One day this old chap turned up, peering through the window, who said he used to live there. He sat with tears in his eyes, saying how he used to eat his porrage by the fire and would sit on frosty mornings doing his homework with his chalk and slate.*

NEVILLE: *So what or why is* The Big Express?

ANDY: *I wanted something about Swindon, and Swindon is famous for its railways. For a long time we were going to call it* Coal Face, *we also thought of* Head of Steam.

COLIN: *That's Gregsy when he's exasperated.*

ANDY: *And* Under the Rusting North Star, *after the old locomotive in the museum, which is where we shot the photos. Tim Bryan, the owner, was running around panicking that we were going to break his trains.*

COLIN: *I was a bit worried when the concept was announced because I thought we might be burying ourselves parochially. We'd been caned for coming from Swindon before and to openly indulge in our history might be seen as being a bit narrow.*

ANDY: *It had always worried me, too. Bands like the Police had this international flavor. One American, one jazzer, and one playing reggae. All flashbulbs at airports. We never got beyond Swindon. Our songs were Swindony, our accents were Swindony, and Swindon will never be cool. We were the anti-Police. But then I realized that what makes a band attractive is its origins.*

COLIN: *I quite like a band that wallows in its own muck.*

ANDY: *So we decided to shoot the cover in the Swindon Railway Museum.*

COLIN: *We had to find ourselves some overalls and I got mine in a secondhand shop on Ferndale Road. Well, I wasn't going to buy a new one for a bloody photo shoot.*

ANDY: *Apparently my jacket is very authentic.*

COLIN: *It was quite a fantasy day out, really.*

ANDY: *Hardly champagne and stockings!*

COLIN: *Yeah, but a trainspotter's fantasy.*

ANDY: *I was picking soot out of my ears for weeks.*

THE BIG EXPRESS

ON THE TRACKS

"WAKE UP"

(Colin Moulding)

Do not adjust your speakers. From jagged Ping-Pong stereo guitars to girls' choir and brain-rattling sub-bass, "Wake Up" ran the audio gamut. David Lord flexed his musical muscles and made a three-chord wonder sound like Haydn's "Creation." But Colin had written "Wake Up" as a small, personal story of daily life—a collage of personal memories culminating in a major personal paranoia. " 'You stayed in bed/You wrote the note' is about me writing notes to skive off work in the early days of my marriage. My missus wouldn't let me go to work for the first few years. We were always at it! 'A morning face' is that face you see every morning, usually a girl on the bus. But the last verse is about this paranoia, this recurring dream I have about being the first on the scene of an accident. If it's the positive version of the dream I resuscitate the victim and save the day. If it's the negative one, I run away."

It was actually a very simple song, too simple in Dave Gregory's estimation. "It was only three chords. The coolest part of the song was the chopping guitars but Colin should have written a better song around that hook. It just went on forever doing nothing. It sounds a good way to start an album but it's not my idea of a musical experience." David Lord saw this simplicity as an opportunity for embellishment. "He took my demo to the Albert Hall and granded it out of all recognition," says Colin. "But he did a good job," says Andy. "He blew it up like one of those hot air balloons in the shape of a palace."

"All You Pretty Girls"

(Andy Partridge)

(Single and album track)

Jimi would have been proud but bewildered. Andy was fiddling around with a Hendrix impersonation on guitar when he came up with the basic two-note blues chords that underlie "All You Pretty Girls." But it came out sounding like a song from Gilbert and Sullivan's "HMS Pinafore."

A playful Partridge slapped a lot of theatrical greasepaint onto several of the songs on the album and this one got the full treatment, including the "ridiculous" theatrical video that went with it. Like

Andy's sketches for singles sleeves for The Big Express.

(CREDIT: ANDY PARTRIDGE)

"Pinafore," its view of naval life was rose-tinted. "I think I always wanted to be a sailor like my dad," says Andy. "An awful lot of the songs in our catalogue are about yachts or the sea and this was the distillation of all my romance about being a sailor." "When Andy first brought this tune up at rehearsals and right up to recording, I didn't know whether we were heading down the hot rails to parody," says Colin. "Certainly a lot of the bass tunes I was playing were the sort of things you'd have heard on 'Popeye.'" The parody continued with the Mellotron choir, recorded from a speaker in the base of a tin bucket. The lyrics set the scene, standing on the deck of a mighty dreadnought, watching the world pulling away. But they concealed sexual images, "rocking in a similar motion." And it revisits the subaquatic dreamland of "Somnambulist." "So am I implying that these dreams are wet ones?" asks Andy of himself. Probably.

"Shake You Donkey Up"
(Andy Partridge)

With Pete Phipps hammering away on a kit made from buckets and trays, a whinnying violin by Stuart Gordon, redneck guitar by Dave Gregory, and a digitally doctored whip crack, XTC kick into Beefheart hillbilly mode. "I always wanted to do something like Beefheart's 'Sure Enough 'n' Yes I Do' from *Safe As Milk*," says Andy. "It's really sassy but with a hayseed edge to it." For all its oddball imagery, "Shake You Donkey Up" is actually a song about Andy realizing his misunderstanding of women. "It's an inconsequential piece of fluff that carries on the 'Down In the Cockpit' theme. I think I was feeling guilty for having unenlightened attitudes about women. The Bible sees women as virgins or whores and I think I saw them as mothers to be bullied or girlfriends who are going to get drunk and attack you. So this song was trying to warn people off this attitude in the song."

"Seagulls Screaming Kiss Her, Kiss Her"

(Andy Partridge)

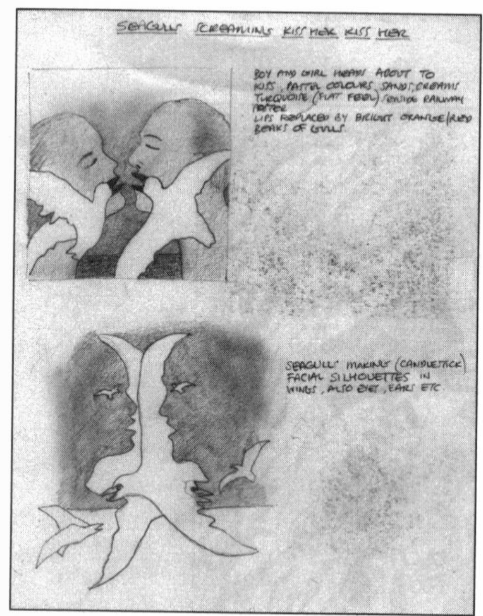

More sleeve sketches from Andy's pencil. (CREDIT: ANDY PARTRIDGE)

Andy Partridge's preoccupation with things sexual never dragged him into the role of rock 'n' roll lothario, far from it. Stubborn loyalty to his chilly marriage held off the inevitable for years. But by this time, Erica Wexler was haunting the back of his mind. She was always writing letters, making Andy's marriage even chillier.

"Seagulls Screaming Kiss Her, Kiss Her" used the theatrical imagery of a desolate English seaside resort in winter to portray his emotional struggle. The visual imagery was so strong that Andy drew sketches of the setting before writing the lyrics. "I was quietly tearing myself apart about her and this song is a slap on the back of the legs saying, 'You fool! You've missed your chance.' She came down to the 'Three Wise Men' sessions and I remember playing her this. I'd just written it and I think she tried to kiss me, but I backed away because I was a married man."

It was the first song written entirely on keyboard, with two fingers on one hand, one on the other. It was free of the editorial conventions that restrict Andy on guitar and had little respect for the conventions of harmony. "It was a little Mellotron tune he'd had for a long time," says Dave. "When we were making *English Settlement*, it was the only thing he could play, but by *The Big Express* he came up with this."

The Davids, Lord and Gregory, were up in arms about the

discords in the song. "I had to stamp my foot because the discordant rub was the essence of the song," says Andy. But David Lord did get to add the delicious euphonium, played by Steve Saunders during overdubs at Odyssey Studios.

"This World Over"

(Andy Partridge)

"The leader with the famous face" had spent a couple of years scaring the pants off the world by now. Reagan's gung-ho attitude toward the Soviets did not impress those elsewhere in the world who hadn't voted for him. His gunslinger speeches rekindled all of Andy's cold war paranoias.

The music rose out of Andy playing the chord shapes for "Complicated Game" with the guitar retuned to E. "I just thought, Jesus! These chords sound fantastic, and suddenly this sad song came out about what a terrible shame it would be if we did unleash nuclear war. My first child was on the way and I just thought that, if I survived, how terrible it would be to have to tell her what life used to be like; that there was once a place called London and it was a fantastic place but it's not there anymore. I did actually break down and cry a couple of times while I was writing the song." Not a single drum on the record is real, as Andy liked the insistence of the Linn drum computer, though he and Colin regret this now. Dave regretted it then, as well, because it took so long to program.

The song was played live on television at a time when Andy was making a futile attempt to grow a chinstrap beard. Only half of it had grown and he wouldn't shave it off, so this beautiful, mournful song was performed with the other half of the beard painted on by the makeup department!

"The Everyday Story of Smalltown"
(Andy Partridge)

Ladies and gentlemeeenn! Introducing the inimitable XTC, imitating Alice Cooper, playing "Autumn Almanac." The musical references are there, and admitted, but "The Everyday Story of Smalltown" is one of Andy Partridge's finer moments. Theatrical to the hilt, "Smalltown" is set on the Penhill Estate, on a sunny Sunday, as the comb and paper band march round The Valley—Penhill's little hell. The teeth-clenching rhymes, "Snoring under blankets, woken by the clank/It's just the milkman's dawn round," are pure Hollywood musical but the image is utterly Swindon. "This is all autobiographical," says Andy. "I'd be woken up every morning by the milkman lifting his foot off the accelerator. It woke me up one morning and I thought, That's got to go into a bloody song." Other elements of Andy's life slip in: the poplars down Whitworth Road, though Colin points out that they are lime trees; his grandfather's description of the black snake of bicycles heading into the railworks; his mother's annual new Terylene nightgown. "It's just a lot of bits and pieces," he says. "It's like saying, 'Who on earth would spoil this little town with all its little foibles?' "

The fun of it overspilled into the recording, which was due to employ some brass samples borrowed from local boys, Tears for Fears, who are credited for their kindness. But the comb and paper arrangement just sounded perfect for this celebration of ordinariness.

"I Bought Myself a Liarbird"
(Andy Partridge)

Due to a legal arrangement with their former management, XTC is unable to discuss the lyrical content of this song!

"Reign of Blows (Vote No to Violence)"

(Andy Partridge)

Andy's hatred of violence is, in a way, contrary to his fascination with battle games. Prior to starting the new album, he was handpainting cards of every uniform worn in the wars of the Spanish succession. His shelves are filled with toy soldiers. But he detests violence and cannot watch violent movies without feeling sick. He hammered that home with "Reign of Blows." "Reign of blows has washed away the corpse of Abel/Cain is now the king in every Babel" was one of his finest lyrical moments. The song was arranged as violently as possible—distorted voices and harmonica (Andy loves playing harmonica through a guitar amp), clashing Keith Richards-ish guitar slammed on open E tuning, cacophonous drums, and a rising multitracked violin squeal by Stuart Gordon that still sets Andy's teeth on edge. Of course, that doesn't mean it works. "I think the song was spoiled in the mix," says Colin. "Everything ended up as loud as everything else. Too many instruments with too much ambience just ends up messy." "I may be to blame," says Andy. "Telling Phil Thornally to make it sound more violent, louder, heavier—what could the poor fellow do?"

Yet more sleeve ideas from Andy. (CREDIT: ANDY PARTRIDGE)

"You're the Wish You Are I Had"

(Andy Partridge)

Two influences that were starting to show in Andy's songwriting by now were the Beatles and Erica Wexler. "You're the Wish You Are I Had" incorporated a hint of each—a touch of "Getting Better" here, a smidgin of unrequited love there. But like the convoluted title, the song is a typically XTC upside-down cake arrangement. The snare plays the hi-hat part, the bass plays a countermelody, the guitar solo twists and bends like Adrian Belew in a blender, and the piano chunkalunks like a pub pianola. All this wraps around the story of a dream girl. "I suppose it's Erica again," says Andy. "It was like making this perfect Eve in a dream and controlling that image with my imagination—making her eat an apple or drink a cup of tea." So this is what Andy's wild imagination could make a girl do!

"I Remember the Sun"

(Colin Moulding)

Chrissy Orral was a bit of a bully 'round Penhill. He was the big kid. He was in the Army Training Corps. He ruled the Penhill Dumps. The Dumps were muddy escarpments at the edge of the estate. There, little Colin and his mates would dig the Great Trench of Penhill for Orral, who was convinced the Nazis were returning and that Swindon needed defending. Years on, two sunny chords and that memory kindled this light, jazzy piece. "That piece of wasteland was immensely evocative in my imagination," says Colin. "My mum hated me getting wet, so I remember the sun because I was only allowed out when it was sunny. The sun was king."

The song sat around for a while during the sessions, the cool grand piano being added at Odyssey Studios much later. "My demo was more rocky because we didn't really know what flavor to give it and when it's like that, we always end up in the jazzy area," says Colin. "It's the place you go when you're searching," says Andy, whose guitar scribbles all over the introduction. "There's certain points of the song where we all get to do our own thing," says Colin. "It's pretty free-form in places." But the song flows in a languid and regular way that stands out on the album, partly because Colin's contributions were thinly spread and partly because Andy was writing loud songs.

"Train Running Low On Slow Coal"
(Andy Partridge)

"I first came up with the idea of this when we were mixing *Mummer* in AIR Studios," says Andy.

"I know. You used to go into that little booth," says Colin.

"That wanking booth," says Andy.

"I think it was a vocal booth, Andy," says Colin.

"Oh! Well, who shall I apologize to?" says Andy.

A happier Partridge on The Big Express. (CREDIT: JO MCKNIGHT)

Boys will be boys, how ever old they are. Which is really the theme of the song. Andy had realized, sitting in the booth, strumming his instrument, that twenty-nine seemed rather old to be a pop musician. "I was worried that I was running out of inspiration, like a train out of coal, dragging two empty carriages, Colin and Dave, downhill." Of course he was wrong, but the pressure to make hits was strong, and Virgin was handing out the orders to him. "I'm a thirty-year-old puppy doing what I'm told," runs the lyric.

The monstrous sound of the record is based around slowed-down Linn drum sounds and the cyclical G riff on open E tuning he had discovered in that vocal booth. He had always seen the song as metallic and deafening, but Colin and Dave thought otherwise. "There were too many machine drums going at once," says Dave. "I wanted to do it like the acoustic version we played on Channel Four's 'Play At Home' show, which we filmed in Swindon's Town Gardens." "The way I saw it was like a Richie Havens or a Joni Mitchell 'Big Yellow Taxi' thing," says Colin. "But the moment I found the train chords, I knew I wanted it heavy," says Andy, whose full head of steam would railroad any argument.

IN THE SIDINGS . . .

"RED BRICK DREAM"

(Andy Partridge) (B side only)

As a child, Andy would walk down Rodbourne Road, holding his grandmother's hand, and wondering at the horrific din that emanated from behind the grim, stone walls of the Great Western Railworks. His grandfather, like three-quarters of the population, worked "inside," as it was called. "It sounded like Dante's *Inferno,*" says Colin. But once the works closed, Swindon seemed to slip quietly into a coma. "Most of the workers came over from Wales," says local historian Colin. "They seemed to have this noble core to themselves. There was this unpretentiousness about them," says Andy, who immortalized them in a poem which recalled the men and the things they made, from buttons and chains to the mighty King- and Queen-Class locos and the old North Star which now sat rusting in the rail sheds. When he was approached to write a song for a documentary about Swindon, he set the poem to music as "Red Brick Dream." "I wanted to write something that didn't just criticize the dump," he said. The film showed him playing the song in the cellar of Crescent, but the song didn't make the album. It was a simple and touching arrangement mixed by Phil Thornally at Rak Studios, who added the metallic clanking of a detuned dinner plate.

"WASHAWAY"

(Colin Moulding) (B side only)

The kids on the Penhill Estate would often slip out of school at lunchtime. The noise of the playground would echo 'round the council estate. While the noise continued, the truants were safe, but the moment the noise died away, at exactly half past one, panic set in. "This is looking at people going about their business but not being where I should be—not being in school," says Colin. "People would look at you like you were a little criminal if you weren't in school." The frivolous little tune was Colin's first piano-written song, though Dave Gregory plays the cheerful Cockney sing-along/"Lady Madonna" ivory-tinkling. Originally called "Half Past One," it is a collage of images from Colin's childhood: Mr. Softee the ice-cream man, Mother boiling cabbage on Sunday lunchtime, condensation dripping down the windows of cheap council housing, and hours spent waiting in the launderette for the washing to dry. "A lot of the lyrics are leftovers from 'Wake Up,'" says Colin. "It sounds like Norman Wisdom chasing a runaway ice-cream van," says Andy. "Print that and you're fired!" says Colin. So fire me!

Andy and Dave in rebearsal. (CREDIT: JO MCKNIGHT)

"Blue Overall"
(Andy Partridge) (B side only)

Andy prefers to pay tribute, rather than steal, and "Blue Overall" drew on Led Zeppelin's bombastic bastardization of the blues. "I like *Physical Graffiti* a lot, which was probably the high point of a band who just played brilliantly together. They just had a funk and a groove that was unbeatable," he says. But he gave the fun job on the record to Dave Gregory, who bottlenecks his guitar to orgasm.

The "overall" pun was a twist on the troubled workingman's clothes and the original title, "Overall I'm Blue," which was a more direct description of the miserable nature of the song. "I get these really depressed moods, possibly now more than ever. I just take the phone off the hook and lie on the couch all day. And I wanted to put those feelings down in a song," says Andy. "It's the equivalent of Winston Churchill's 'black dog' moods," says Colin. "That's Churchill's, not Zep's," adds Andy. "Though I hear he did a great rendition of it."

The lyric alludes to those who criticize white boys for singing the blues and the rip-off sharks who infest music's murky waters. But it was sung so manically as to be almost impenetrable, a deliberate attempt to empty his soul into the song, as per Lennon's "Yer Blues." This he further emphasized by ramming Pete Phipps's monstrous drums, the bass, and vocals to the fore, sinking the guitars in an echoic mire. "It surprised me that Andy wanted to be that indulgent with it," says Colin. "It ended up being a showcase for Dave, which is fine. But he complained, 'That's a rotten mix, my guitar isn't up loud enough.'" "I know," says Andy. "But I didn't want him to do that. I had to get this big thumping headache."

9

DAY PASSES

1986

Dave Gregory tucked enthusiastically into his home-cooked dinner. As an insulin-dependent diabetic, every meal was to Dave like an oasis at the end of a desert march. As Dave's blood sugar levels depleted, he would start to tense up until that vital first mouthful. It was little wonder he was a keen cook. Little wonder Andy and Colin knew only to ask him for favors just after dinner.

But such diplomacy was far from their minds, now. This was the spring of 1986, they were in the wilds of upstate New York, and they were starving. They felt more sympathy for Colonel Gadhaffi than they did for Dave. As he savored the fruits of his culinary labors, their prepacked pizzas sat menacingly before them, less Italian than Martian: "Stick that fork in me and your innards are mine, buddy!" Miles from any restaurant, unable to cook, too proud to ask Dave, they ate pizza upon pizza and spent every dark, Catskills night regretting it.

Woodpeckers start work early. Very early! Every morning! By the time the band trudged up the track to the studio, Andy and Colin had been awake in their beds for hours, finding ways to relieve their frustration! Thousands of miles from Andy's new baby, Holly, and Colin's new home, Dolphin Cottage, they were miserable.

Dave wasn't. Each day was another day in musical heaven, working with a man, nay a genius, with a forehead so high it could only contain the world's biggest brain. It was an education. For Andy, it was purgatory. The only forehead he'd ever seen like it was on "The Munsters" and the man wearing it now seemed determined to trample him into the Woodstock mud. He was being outmaneuvered musically and technically. For the first time since Mutt Lange, Andy was being "produced."

The choice of Todd Rundgren to produce *Skylarking* was born partly out of desperation. *The Big Express* had bombed and with U.S. label, Geffen, baying for a hit, it seemed worth trying an American producer. Of those Jeremy Lascelles listed, they recognized only Todd. Dave Gregory was ecstatic at the idea. The others knew little of him, but Dave's enthusiasm carried them along. Anyway, Todd was willing to do the whole thing on an all-in, flights-beds-tapes-musicians deal.

Colin had been much more productive during the previous year, inspired by his new home at the foot of the Marlborough Downs, an area inhabited since pre-Roman times and still very much in touch with the land. Andy had been writing hard as well, and would visit Dave each week with ideas for string arrangements for him to develop. Armed now with four-track Portastudios, they created more complex demos and sent them to Todd with confidence.

Before they knew it, Todd had listened to them, rejected some, and strung the rest into a loose concept album that expressed all life through a single day. He even came up with a name, *Day Passes*, with a punning sleeve photo concept of a couple of tickets. Nobody had ever treated Andy's songs with such editorial ruthlessness, but he was not in a strong bargaining position with Virgin and meekly accepted his fate.

Few people could outstrip Todd Rundgren musically, but he had a weird way of working. Disciplined to a fault, and determined to be the boss, he told XTC what order the songs would appear on the album and recorded them in that order. He even had them play through the tracks to "book" the amount of tape that would be used, marking start and finish points, and offering little room for improvisation. Just two reels for the whole album. The budget and schedule would be as lean as he was.

Todd's home and studio were outside Woodstock, the world's most rock 'n' roll village. Utopia Studios was a wooden building on his country estate, filled with an idiosyncratic inventory of recording equipment and instruments. He lived in a luxury house but guest accommodation was down the hill, through the woods, in an old and basic, clapboard Colonial house. It was cleaned each week with an evil-smelling polish, the only perfume to challenge the stench of poisoned rodents, who had crawled under the floorboards to fade and fester.

Feeling his power usurped, Andy's relationship with Todd festered rapidly, too. Andy had never played second fiddle to anyone, but Todd wasn't going to let him undermine the producer's authority. Andy respected Todd's musical ability but hated his attitude and sarcasm. Feeling hemmed in, he started taking it out on

Colin and Dave. By the time Todd took them to the Tubes' Sound Hole Studios in San Francisco, Colin was on the point of cracking. Todd had expected him to play the bass parts without drums, a bizarre way to record a rhythm section by any standards. After remonstrations from Colin, he agreed to complete the bass recordings with the Tubes' drummer, Prairie Prince, in Frisco. But there, with Andy and Todd arguing over the minutiae of Colin's playing, Colin stormed out and disappeared for a day. Todd persuaded him to return but, to this day, he hasn't withdrawn his resignation from the band.

On returning to Woodstock, things got worse. Todd didn't want them to attend the mixes, and the band didn't want to spend any more time with him. As soon as the recording was over, they hightailed it back to Blighty, leaving Rundgren with a huge wish list of mixing ideas in a handmade book. But for all their distress, Todd respected those wishes on the whole, and turned out the most individual XTC album to date. Many tears had been shed but the results were incredible. This was a concept album that held together as no XTC album before or since.

A few changes were made. The *Day Passes* concept was scrapped in favor of *Skylarking*, after the skylarks in England's summer skies and the minor naval misdemeanor of playing tag in a ship's rigging. Andy's initial sleeve concept, a male and female pubic area entwined with flowers, was rejected by every record shop in London's Oxford Street.

Todd's musical concept changed, as well. Three of the rejected demos, plus the demo of "Let's Make a Den," which had failed to survive the Rundgren/Partridge wars, were taken to Crescent by Andy and remixed by Glenn Tommey for B sides. And Jeremy Lascelles insisted on reinstating "Another Satellite," which Todd thought didn't belong on the album. With the additional track, Andy took the chance to suggest the removal of the one song on the album that irritated him. Andy was unhappy with "Dear God" and had it relegated to a B side. He thought the song was clumsy in its message and didn't want to draw attention to it. When the album was released later in 1985, "Dear God" was the B side to Colin's single "Grass." But American DJs discovered it and within days, "Dear God" was attracting heavy airplay, rave reviews, and death threats. The Bible Belt was incensed. The colleges adored it. Geffen recalled the album and re-pressed it with "Dear God" included. Despite all Andy's efforts to the contrary, XTC had become a cult hit in America.

SKYLARKING

TALKING BETWEEN THE LINES

NEVILLE: *I assume that it wasn't your decision to work in America?*

ANDY: *It was at Virgin's behest that we chose an American because "an American producer will find something American in your sound that will be attractive to Americans and therefore sell to America and America is a bigger market so go and be sold to Americans!" Jeremy Lascelles gave us a list and we hadn't heard of any of them except Todd. Dave said "Oh my God! I'd love to work with Todd." It was a big fan thing, so we thought, What harm can it do? So I sent him the demos on cassette and he called back and said, "I've edited these demos together and I've got a running order and I've chopped out the stuff I don't like, and I think we'll start on song one and keep going."*

NEVILLE: *You must have been well pleased!*

ANDY: *I felt obliged by Virgin not to argue, to shut up and be told what to do.*

NEVILLE: *Pigs might fly!*

ANDY: *I agreed with Todd that the songs he had chosen in the order he'd done them all rolled into one. It was very well done.*

COLIN: *I was surprised he was doing everything that early in the process. I thought, Well, here's a chap who knows what he's doing. We hadn't really had a real producer up until that point who actually pro-*

duced the whole album, lock, stock, and barrel.

NEVILLE: *So you liked him?*

ANDY: *He was so bloody sarcastic. Which is rare with Americans. He's got it down to an extremely cruel art. He'd ask how you were going to do the vocals and you would stand in front of the mic and do one run through to clear your throat and he'd say, "That was crap. I'll come down and I'll record me singing it and you can have me in your headphones to sing along to." I just thought it was so insulting. On "Let's Make a Den" he picked so many holes in it that I lost all confidence and we dropped it. About two-thirds through the vocal performance I said, "Look, if you don't make this a more pleasing experience, I'm going to catch the next plane home!"*

COLIN: *It was just that the way he wanted to do it was different from yours.*

ANDY: *It was argued to death! He was so patronizing.*

NEVILLE: *But of course, you showed him due respect?*

ANDY: *We thought he looked like Herman Munster and every morning when we saw him coming to the studio, we'd play The Munsters' theme. He never worked out why.*

NEVILLE: *So do you have anything good to say?*

COLIN: *He didn't give you any encouragement. I like some feedback and I took it to heart a little bit. The way he did things was weird. We spent the first week just "booking" tape space. We planned out the album and strummed the songs so we could place the songs on tape.*

ANDY: *Side one was on one reel and side two on another. There were no edits. When we said, "How are we going to get from 'Summer's Cauldron' to 'Grass'?," he said, "Well, you just put your hand on your instruments and stop the strings ringing and then we punch in the start of 'Grass.' I just got the impression he didn't want to spoil his nice reels of tape.*

COLIN: *When we got to Woodstock we spent three or four weeks not getting into the album, putting down bits of percussion and messing with the Fairlight computer. There was a lot of candy floss going on but there were no bones, no foundations.*

ANDY: *I remember you having this confab with Todd saying, "Where do you want me to put the bass because there aren't any drums." And he said, "Well, you just put your bass where you want to and we'll get Prairie Prince to put his foot where you place your bass guitar." It was so ass about face. The bass is the deep glue that holds the drums to the other instruments.*

COLIN: *I think Todd took the point and so we set sail for San Francisco to cut the drums down on these bits of tape space. I was happy working with Prairie Prince.*

ANDY: *Prairie Prince! He's a dead ringer for Robert Mitchum. When we were playing I'd keep looking at the drummer and thinking, Wow! Robert Mitchum's drumming in our band.*

(At the mention of Prairie Prince, and on hearing the album again, Andy and Colin begin to hatch a plan to hijack Prairie and bring him to Blighty for the new album.)

COLIN: *I knew Andy was unhappy with the situation and felt he was taking it out on me. Todd wasn't giving me any feedback and I was feeling rather isolated. We were recording the bass for "Earn Enough for Us." I thought I'd done something worthy and I just felt what I'd put down on tape was being sifted through by Andy and Todd, compounded by the fact that we'd had a rough few weeks and so I . . . well, I overreacted.*

ANDY: *You said, "You can stick the bass up your ass. I'm off!" And that was it. We never saw him again that day.*

COLIN: *I headed in the direction of what I thought was our apartment, following the smell of the fish market.*

ANDY: *It was like Ringo in that scene from* A Hard Day's Night. *I could just see him walking by the river with some kid following him to the sound of an orchestral version of "This Boy."*

COLIN: *I was very tearful. I think Dave rang and said, "What's wrong?" and I lost my rag and said, "I'm leaving the band. I've had enough." So Todd came to see me and said, "Think about what you're doing and give it a few days." It was left in horrible limbo for weeks but it did get better. We got more communicative.*

NEVILLE: *Still, there was always the peace of the Woodstock countryside.*

ANDY: *I was woken at four every morning by that bastard woodpecker!*

COLIN: *Woodpecker? That was me wanking!*

ANDY: *With his wood pecker! So I'd throw something out at it but then I'd be lying awake with nothing but an archaic copy of* Hustler *for company.*

NEVILLE: *You sad bastard.*

ANDY: *Well, what else are you supposed to do with nothing but woodpeckers and raccoons for company. I was thinking about paying the woodpecker commission to knock out another hole for me, a little closer to the bedroom window.*

COLIN: *It was one of those colorful, clapboard, eighteenth-century New England places. Nice but very primitive.*

ANDY: *Very Clampett! I objected to the smell of rotting rodents.*

COLIN: *And that strange American polish.*

ANDY: *You'd stagger down the hill after a hard day grappling with your songs and you couldn't even breathe for the overpowering stench of rotting rodent and floor polish. That smell has burned a chemical hole in my brain and I can still smell it now.*

DAVE: *I'd stayed in worse. It was part of Todd's estate and it was quite comfortable. I don't know what they were complaining about. I just remember the gas oven had no thermostat.*

COLIN: *Of course, it was self-catering, as well. And you know what that means.*

ANDY: *It means we lose weight.*

COLIN: *I prefer full board myself.*

ANDY: *Full board is what those pizzas tasted like.*

COLIN: *Andy and I lived pretty frugally because our culinary skills were very limited. So we lived off these frozen pizzas from the store fifteen miles away.*

ANDY: *But Dave was all right. He could cook himself up a storm, rattling those pots and pans and preparing himself a beautiful little banquet.*

COLIN: *It was, "*Mmm, *that looks rather nice, Dave."*

ANDY: *"Wouldn't you like to try a piece of my pizza, Dave, if you could just give me a morsel of your meat and potatoes?" We'd just have to forage for ourselves and there's Dave looking like a chef with big piles of grub. "Mmm. This whole roast ox is divine! Don't you wish you could cook?" "Yes, Dave."*

DAVE: *They were eating the worst shit imaginable. If we'd had a pact where we pooled resources I would have cooked. But they didn't ask me to cook and I didn't offer. It's that simple.*

NEVILLE: *San Francisco must have been better.*

DAVE: *We stayed at the Crystal Tower block of flats. It was quite comfortable, half a mile from Fisherman's Wharf, and I'd go for a walk by the sea every morning. I managed to save enough money to buy my first Les Paul '53 Gold Top. That changed my whole style. For years I'd been fiddling around with amps and pedals and at last I had the guitar of my dreams.*

ANDY: *We were in the Tubes' studio, the Sound Hole, with the emphasis on "hole." It was a converted factory with a makeshift studio in it and all the Tubes' weird props. There was this funny little tape op called Kim Foscato and she lived in a little box up a ladder on the wall of the studio. She would climb in there and go to bed.*

COLIN: *I thought the setup was rather bohemian for my taste. It was a bit grimy.*

ANDY: *You did wonder whether everything was going to work the next day. It was funny because we did two-thirds of the album in a glorified log cabin in the hills of upstate New York and the other third in an empty factory in San Francisco. So how the hell does it sound so English?*

COLIN: *It's my favorite album so far. I just wish that we could find a way to make an album that good without having to go through so much misery.*

ANDY: *I suppose it's one of mine, too.*

NEVILLE: *So why call it* Skylarking?

ANDY: *My dad always used to say it to me, "Come on, now. Cut out your skylarking and get off to school."*

COLIN: *It was definitely a word from the last century.*

ANDY: *I think he brought it back from his days in the navy. It just meant stop messing about. But it also has that summery connotation. It's definitely the sound of an English summer, skylarks singing over the fields.*
NEVILLE: *You must have something good to say about Todd?*
DAVE: *I still like the sound of* Skylarking. *I liked the fact that we had some input from a genius musician, which more than compensated for the standard of the recording. I was quite happy to be directed by Todd instead of Andy.*
ANDY: *He did do great things musically. The arrangements were brilliant and I don't know how he came up with them. Virtually over a couple of hours one night he could come up with a string arrangement and this was a man who couldn't play keyboards with more than two fingers. He'd just work them out one note at a time. "Sacrificial Bonfire" he more or less did overnight, which was shocking. The bloke is ludicrously smart when it comes to certain things.*
DAVE: *He'd made a hell of a lot more records than us. It was like eating and drinking for him. We have to prepare for months to make a record. I was just thrilled to have Todd producing my record. What a treat! He saved our career and gave us a hit record.*
ANDY: *I liked the fact that the album used sound effects in a musical context. It gave it a filmic atmosphere.*
COLIN: *I've got nothing but admiration for Todd's skills as a producer.*
ANDY: *You can put me down for that, as well . . . with hindsight. But at the same time he did have this really destructive thing with people.*

Promotional shot for "Skylarking."

(CREDIT: BY PERMISSION OF VIRGIN RECORDS.)

Colin: *He was never like that with me because I wasn't a threat to his domain, whereas I think he thought Andy was a threat to his authority. Our philosophy was that the songwriter makes the final decision. He was from the old school and in his book, if you pay him to be producer, then he has to see it through his way.*

Andy: *That was his way with production. He just broke you down so you'd do what he wanted. Perhaps I fought too hard. One bunker—two fuhrers.*

SKYLARKING

ON THE TRACKS

"Summer's Cauldron"

(Andy Partridge)

Andy's poetic side has yet to be exploited and is possibly the theme for another book. He can kill and caress with his wordplay and books of discarded poetic genius fill his study shelves. One hot afternoon in Swindon (hot, at least, by Swindon standards), he sat on his decrepit wicker garden chair and wrote a fluid, semi-abstract poem about all things hot and summery, "Summer's Cauldron." With its rolling phrases "mats of flower lava," "boiling butter," "fruit of sweating golden Inca," it reminded him of Dylan Thomas. "Not that I'm saying I'm a Dylan Thomas. More of a Terry Thomas, really," he says. He hadn't intended it to be a song, but he loved its pagan naughtiness and the rhythmic feel, so during one of his visits to Dave's little house on Stanier Street, he hammered out a musical idea with him.

Todd saw it as the album's opening track and wanted to build a collage of summer sounds around it. He bought piles of sound effects records to sample into his Fairlight computer and assembled them with Andy—crickets, bees buzzing across the stereo image, distant dogs barking, and a pulsing rhythmic quality. "I suggested that it should be rhythmic," says Andy. "But it sounds more American than English. We don't have that intensity of crickets and doesn't that dog have an American accent?" It was the first thing they recorded on the album and Todd decided to run it straight into "Grass," rounding off with the same insect chorus. But for all his passion for technology, he still insisted that, at the point where "Summer's Cauldron" finished, they should just damp their strings, and then record "Grass" from that point on, an extremely unconventional way of recording. One slip on the record button could have lost part of the previous track.

"Grass"

(Colin Moulding) (Single and album track)

Colin hadn't experimented much with open tuning, but on one day he was fiddling around with the chord shapes of Thunderclap Newman's "Something In the Air" on an open E tuning and the rich chords of "Grass" popped out. They reminded him of teenage days round Coate Water, a parkland area outside Swindon, immortalized by the eighteenth-century poet Richard Jeffries, who lived there. For hundreds of years, it was a place to mess around, get drunk, and experiment with sex. Colin had continued the tradition. "A lot of people think the song's about marijuana, but it isn't," says Colin. "It's just about Coate Water."

Even at demo stage, Colin could hear the violin/guitar blend, an idea picked up from John Lennon's "How Do You Sleep." But Todd expanded it to include a Tipple (a tiny guitar) and suggested the Fairlight pizzicato strings which Dave played hurriedly and was never given time to correct. He also brought in Mingo Lewis to play congas, though the role almost went to a hanger-on at the Sound Hole called Carey Colbert. "He kept grabbing me and saying, 'Colin, you must let me play on your song. I have the touch!' It went on for days and in the end Todd said, 'Okay, we'll give him a go.' But he just went to pieces. I felt really sorry for him."

Colin's vocals almost went to pieces, as well. "Todd said, 'Don't sing so deep. You sound like a bit of a molester.' So I just did the Bowie thing and added an octave above it."

"Grass" became the first single from the album, with a video that brought Colin close to his first screen kiss. Andy lusted over the actress but Colin wasn't so sure. "I'd rather have kissed you, Partsy," he says. Supposed to be a sunny video, but shot on a wet English day, it was filmed in a tent on the grass under bright lights, but despite the promotional push, the single became subservient to its B side, "Dear God."

"The Meeting Place"

(Colin Moulding) (Single and album track)

When they were in their late teens, Carol Moulding worked at Swindon's borough press and Colin would meet her for lunch. Years on, experimenting with open tuning, a childlike riff came from Colin's guitar that reminded him of those days and inspired "The Meeting Place." "I think it was a bit like the Stones' 'Waiting for a Factory Girl' but because the riff was more like 'Postman Pat,' we were just figures on a Toytown landscape viewed from above. It was me meeting her at the gates for a sandwich in The Beehive pub, embroidered with the suggestion of a lunchtime quickie." Around the same time, Andy would lunch with his grandfather, George Reeves (typical of Andy to have a relative with the same name as the first Superman!). When the works hooter echoed out over Swindon, George would head back to the railworks as others had for a century, and his grandson sauntered back to college. When the works closed down and that hooter sounded for the last time, a documentary was made and Dave kept a recording of the haunting wail. It was that final gasp of Swindon's soul which Todd blended with industrial sound effects and coconut shell horse hooves, to create

Utopia Sound Studios, Woodstock.

(CREDIT: COLIN MOULDING)

the Victorian atmosphere of "The Meeting Place." It was more historical than Colin had imagined but he was happy that it was true to the simple sentiment of the song—a girl standing by the factory gates meeting her man.

"That's Really Super, Supergirl"
(Andy Partridge)

Oscar Wilde said the English and the Americans were two nations separated by a common language. Although Todd could be outrageously sarcastic, British irony rarely goes over in America and didn't for many people in this case. "That's Really Super, Supergirl" should be spoken in snide tones because this was a song about a woman, nobody in particular, who thinks the world of herself and treats her man badly. Mentions of superheroes abounded in the lyrics, including Kryptonite and Superman's Fortress of Solitude. "Where he went for a bit of privacy, and probably a superwank, from the look of the place," says Andy, tastefully.

When he wrote it, Andy was worried about the loungy-sounding chords becoming a bit smooth and suggested toughening it up with a Tamla–type snare beat. Todd had just such a sound on the multitracks of Utopia's Beatle-spoof album *Deface the Music*, and he sampled it into the Fairlight. This left Prairie with the nightmare of playing all the drums without hitting the snare. Todd also had an amazing selection of instruments, including Eric Clapton's old psychedelic Gibson SG guitar, which he lent to Dave to play the solo. It was a dream come true for Dave and he spent hours rehearsing the solo to make the most of his place in the guitar's lineage. "I'd go into his little room, smelling of aftershave and guitar wax and dead mice, and he'd be rehearsing this solo over and over again. I can still see him playing it," says Andy.

"Ballet for a Rainy Day"
(Andy Partridge)

Swapping sun for rain (of which Swindon has plenty), Andy continued in Dylan Thomas mode with "Ballet for a Rainy Day"; a rolling collage of fruity colors and images of a town in the rain—bright raincoats, wet, shiny fruit on street market stalls, collapsed hairstyles like misshapen pineapples. "The one thing I remember about the rain as a child was my mother cursing that her new hairdo was going to get ruined," says Andy. "My mother was the same. Rain equals ruined hairdo and the countryside just means mud and untidiness," says Colin. Blended with the Peter Pan imagery of a different, rooftop world, in admitted homage to the Blue Nile's influential "Walk Across the Rooftops," "Ballet" forms a rather cheerful look at a miserable day, in contrast to the subsequent track.

Todd was convinced that Andy's desire for lyrical fluidity had created "Miracle Play" in error, and got into a heated discussion with Andy about it. "He argued for about two hours that I should have said 'Passion Play' but I wanted the alliteration of 'melting miracle play.' " Andy was correct. The Miracle Plays were medieval biblical performances to educate the English peasantry.

"1000 Umbrellas"
(Andy Partridge)

Todd's flow from "Ballet for a Rainy Day" to "1000 Umbrellas" was almost seamless. For weeks, Dave had been working on a string arrangement for Andy, to create a heavy sense of damp misery, and the multitracked quartet in San Francisco gave a good rendition of it. "There was very little time to do the strings for the album, so they had one run through and then recorded it," says Andy. "Their balls were on the line but they turned in a pretty fine performace."

The miserable little song, about being dumped on by a woman, was the second such theme on the album. It would probably require a chat with Andy's analyst to find out why. But the lyric struck a chord with Dave. "He took me on one side and said, 'I know what you mean by that lyric, "How can you smile and forecast weather's getting better, if you've never let a girl rain all over you," ' " says Andy. "And I thought, How very enigmatic of you, Gregsy."

Whatever the reason, Dave turned out an exquisite arrangement that stands out amid Todd's more syrupy, off-the-cuff arrangements. It found him a lot of work in the years after and it saved the song from rejection. "Todd had only heard the demo with acoustic guitars and he had put 'Dear God' in that slot on the album," says Dave. "The string arrangement, which took for ages, with Andy's help persuaded him to record it."

"Season Cycle"
(Andy Partridge)

Todd Rundgren sank into his deepest Tony Bennett club style and crooned "about the baby and the umbilical." He taunted Andy for weeks over the line, which he thought was ridiculous. It was just that sort of thing that would wind Andy into a knot. He is painfully frank and is hardly innocent of the occasional snide comment, but he hates hurtful humor and has been sensitive about being the butt of it since schooldays.

"Season Cycle" was, and is, one of Andy's favorite songs, inspired by walking his dog, Charlie Parker, on The Lawns near his home. It had nothing radical about it. It was just a well-structured, good all-rounder. "I felt that, maybe, I had finally laid the ghost of Ray Davies 'fore me and written a song that could stand up against, say, 'Shangri-La' or even, dare I suggest, 'Autumn Almanac,' " says Andy. "And the funny thing was, it took this cartoon style of Beach Boys singing to do that." Dave had only introduced Andy to the eccentric brilliance of the Beach Boys album *Smiley Smile* in recent months and it was already playing a big part in his music. The backing vocals for the album are even credited to The

Beech Avenue Boys, a hybrid of the kings of surf music and one of the ugliest streets in Swindon.

The content of the song was simple enough, more or less summed up in the title. It was a positive song, but it caused some upset with Dave, who objected to the occasional atonal rub Andy had written. "Luckily Todd backed me up for once and Dave backed down but it was the same argument I had with 'Seagulls Screaming,'" says Andy. "Dave runs his ship by the book," says Colin. "We don't. But real musicians can get too pernickety."

"Earn Enough for Us"
(Andy Partridge)

Found "in the same dole office as 'Love On a Farmboy's Wages,'" "Earn Enough for Us" was an autobiographical memoir of the days when Andy had a "real" job. The humiliating and hurtful boss was the Middle Mr. Tunley, of Tunley's paint shop in Swindon, where Andy sold artists materials and mixed paint. "He was a tiny, whingeing little man who sucked in his snot when he spoke," says Andy. "I'd work there for a pittance and this bloke used to come in and humiliate me for no reason," he says, demonstrating the chink in the Partridge armor through which Todd loved sticking the needle. "He'd come into the shop and go, 'Snort! snort! Look at ya, you fuckin' useless little cunt, snort! snort! You got a fuckin' girl's haircut, ya little cunt, snort!'"

Prairie Prince and Todd Rundgren in the Sound Hole Studio. (CREDIT: COLIN MOULDING)

Andy's home was still in a state of disarray, as well, "with a roof held together with holes" and the arrival of little Holly had emphasized the paternal, homebuilding instinct in him. It was a simple message for a simple song, which was bordering on the mundane until Todd squeezed the opening riff out of Dave. "He said, 'Come on, Dave. You can think up one of those melodies every kid in his bedroom wants to learn to play,' " says Andy. And he was right. The finished song was so catchy, people still think it was a single, which it wasn't. But it was the straw which broke the camel's back for Colin, who suggested Andy use his rectum as a bass guitar case and stormed out during a futile argument over bass parts. "All it means to me is that bloody song where we had that bloody argument," says Colin. "But it's the only real argument we've had in twenty years, so it says a lot for the marriage, really."

"Big Day"

(Colin Moulding)

Retirement from touring had at least allowed Colin to enjoy bringing up his children. Lee, his son, was heading toward his teens and Colin was considering the fatherly duties that lay ahead when he wrote the paternal pep talk, "Big Day." "My son wasn't marriageable at the time but this was aimed at the time when he would be," says Colin. "I'd been messing around with the chords of Labi Siffre's 'It Must Be Love' and with a little moving around, it became this sort of fanfare to a big event, a ticker tape parade for a big day." Colin wrote "Big Day" for *The Big Express* but wasn't confident about the song, and hid it until the Dukes of Stratosphear sessions. "But the guys said keep it for the next XTC album. I was a bit surprised because I thought it was a bit of a B side."

Andy even saw it as a single and drew up a very cynical sleeve idea with a man in his wedding suit with a bag over his head awaiting marriage and/or execution.

"Another Satellite"

(Andy Partridge)

Whether Andy wanted it or not, Erica Wexler had become a part of his life since he had met and fallen for her in the early eighties.

She had turned up at the *Three Wise Men* sessions and added backing vocals. Whenever XTC was in America she would be there. "America equals Erica," he says. She also wrote numerous letters to Andy, gumming up the atmosphere between himself and Marianne. He tried to pass her off as the mad fan who would probably pull the trigger, though not believing it for a second. Dave had dubbed her "Whacky Wex." Andy wanted to avoid the truth. When they met, he would be painfully polite and would avoid kissing her. On one occasion, he chickened out of a date with her in New York. She was so furious, she threw her XTC memorabilia collection from her apartment window. "Our records were Frisbeeing all over New York," he says.

Confused and frustrated, he wrote "Another Satellite" to try to tell Erica to leave him alone with his family. It was a brilliant song woven around a guitar chord sampled onto a $100 children's Yamaha synth, but today he regrets releasing it, because it hurt Erica deeply.

Todd didn't want it either because it didn't fit the concept of *Skylarking*, but Jeremy Lascelles loved it and insisted on its inclusion. Dennis Fano, the guitar maker, loved it so much he named his guitar range "Satellite," despite the fact that there is only the sample of a guitar on the track. "The story had a happy ending," says Andy, "because Erica and I finally got to express the emotional bond that was always there. I regret writing it because things turned out so marvelously with the person it's all about."

"Mermaid Smiled"

(Andy Partridge) (Not included on later U.S. releases)

Children prize the strangest things. Andy's childhood treasure was a book about the sea, in which he peered through cutout illustrations of sea caves and portholes at plastic fish swimming in a sachet of real water in the back cover of the book. "You'd shake the book and the fish would move around in the water. I was fascinated by it," he says. "For a while I'd wanted to write a song

Dave, Andy, and Todd in a rare moment of harmony. (CREDIT: COLIN MOULDING)

called 'Book Full of Sea' about this book, it was a big symbol of my childhood naivete." So mermaids, a slippery myth believed only by the naive, became a natural theme for a song about the way childlike naivete slips through our fingers.

Andy believes the song is an "underrated gem" in his repertoire. Once Mingo Lewis added his extraordinary bongos, Andy saw its bizarre D 6th tuning as somehow Indian, but Todd checked his attempts to sing flattened quarter tones. Colin saw it more as a Bobby Darren number with its muted trumpets and Prairie's big band swing style. But for all its qualities, it was sacrificed to make way for "Dear God" on the Geffen version of the album.

"The Man Who Sailed Around His Soul"
(Andy Partridge)

"The Man Who Sailed Around His Soul," completely out of character, found the Three Swedebashers from Pig Hill and a Woodstock hippie creating the first example of beatnik, existentialist spy music. Andy's original demo was completely different: "An accidental cross between Leonard Cohen and Can, played on nylon string guitar with a seven/four rhythm." But he already liked the idea of it having a Vegas cabaret/Bond music feel and Todd knew just how to create it. "He said, 'Let's do a John Barry thing' and, literally overnight, came up with this arrangement with brass and flutes. It's bang on. Cod spy music."

It was very smooth. To add a touch of extra "hipness," Todd auditioned the band for finger clicks, with Dave and Andy failing miserably and Colin cutting the mustard with ease. "Well, you know what they say about finger clicks—big click, big . . . !" he boasts. Andy even laid on a velvet, cabaret vocal croon—the walrus gets a tux! But the silky and tongue-in-cheek nature of the arrangement concealed a blunt yet poetic lyric that would stand scrutiny in any beatnik basement. "It just says you're born, you live, and you die. Why look for the meaning of life when all there is is death and decay," says the ever-optimistic Andy.

With the mass of arrangement, Andy didn't get to play any instruments, comfortable, at last, that to write and sing the song was sufficient. It was also one of the few Partridge songs he thinks has been covered well. Hats off to Ruben Blades.

"Dying"
(Colin Moulding)

Colin's father, Charlie Moulding, died suddenly of a heart attack in 1983, and the natural assumption was that "Dying" was about him. But it wasn't. Colin had bought Dolphin Cottage, a semi-detached house in the Wiltshire countryside. The adjoining cottage was a ramshackle tangle of weeds owned by an old man called Bertie. "We didn't see him for the first six months and thought he might be dead. But people in the village said that he'd recently lost his wife and had become very quiet and sad," says Colin. With time on his hands, Colin befriended the old man and would sit with him, drinking tea and discussing the past. "He used to get these attacks and be very short of breath," he says. "But he loved to talk about the old ways."

Bertie didn't die in the house, though he did a while later, in a rest home. But the sadness around him, and the way children abuse old people inspired what Colin, and others, believe to be one of his most beautiful songs.

In the studio, the song became a little filmic vignette. The sampled sound of a clock ticked out the rhythm, reminiscent of thousands of railway workers' retirement clocks on mantelpieces around Swindon. Colin also wanted something like a bass clarinet and Todd said he had a similar sound on the ancient Chamberlain keyboard down below the studio. But he didn't think it worked. Dave "Handyman" Gregory saved the day, evicting the mice and shovels full of their droppings, and breathing life into the old instrument to create the melancholic clarinet solo to the sad, unfinished-sounding song.

"Sacrificial Bonfire"

(Colin Moulding)

Dolphin Cottage was situated at the foot of the Marlborough Downs, the site of many Celtic settlements, and close to many ancient monuments. Colin was quite a keen local historian and, on finding a pagan-sounding riff on the acoustic guitar, decided to create a scene from some Iron Age ritual. "There was a touch of 'The Sorcerer's Apprentice' and a bit of Arthur Brown's 'Fire' in it, I suppose. But I wasn't moralizing. It was just that this was an evil piece of music and good would triumph over it."

Colin's initial demo repeated the basic arrangement throughout, and he would have been happy to keep it that way, but Todd saw bigger things for the last song on the album. He wrote a dramatic, reverb-laden string part for the climax. "It had to be recorded very quickly, so it was full of mistakes, but I liked it," says Andy. "It was a bit too Vivaldi for me," says Colin. "But it had to go somewhere, I suppose."

The string players and Dave played almost everything on the song leaving Andy and Colin with little to do. But Todd wanted something akin to tapping sticks marking out the rhythm. Experiments with twigs didn't work, so Todd brought piles of cheap, leftover, Chinese Fourth of July rockets into the studio and Colin and Andy tapped bundles of them instead. Even the cellophane firework wrapping came in handy for the fire effect in the middle of the song and Colin is credited with playing bonfire. "It was a good ending to the album, fading deep into the night," says Andy. "It just leaves you in blackness with the slightest hint that dawn is coming."

"Dear God"

(Andy Partridge) (Single B side and album track)

"Todd said, 'I don't want you guys around when she's singing,' " says Colin. " 'No disrespect meant, but she's quite temperamental when she's singing and I'd rather you guys went in to town or something.' " And with that, XTC was excluded from the session that helped break them in America. Jasmine Veillette was the eight-year-old daughter of a friend of Todd's. She would occasionally get up with her parents' country band and sing, and she was the nearest thing Todd knew to the boy singer Andy envisioned singing the introduction to "Dear God." In the video, her words were lip-synched by a boy.

Andy didn't mind too much. He didn't want the song on the album and anything that might help it become a B side suited him.

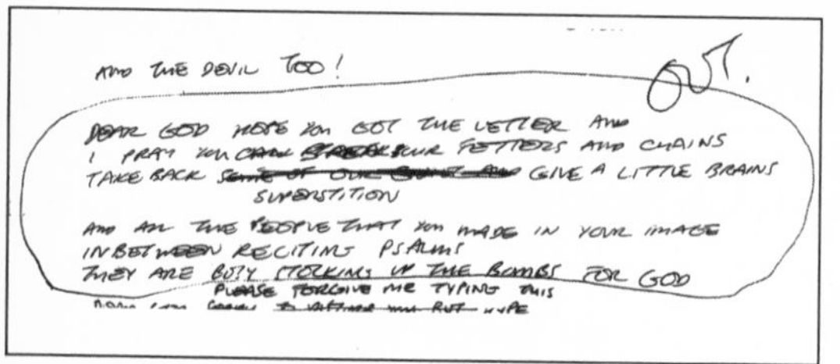
AND THE DEVIL TOO!
OUT.
DEAR GOD HOPE YOU GOT THE LETTER AND
I PRAY YOU ... YOUR FETTERS AND CHAINS
TAKE BACK ... GIVE A LITTLE BRAINS
SUPERSTITION
AND ALL THE PEOPLE THAT YOU MADE IN YOUR IMAGE
INBETWEEN RECITING PSALMS
THEY ARE BUSY STOCKING UP THE BOMBS FOR GOD
PLEASE FORGIVE ME TYPING THIS

A rejected verse from "Dear God" from Andy's notebook.

(CREDIT: ANDY PARTRIDGE)

In fact, Jasmine did a pretty good job, and the whole song came out well, but Andy still disliked his lyrics. "It is such a big subject and I'd been wrestling with it for years, but how can you cover it in three-and-a-half minutes?" he asks. "I felt kind of tricky about it; not because I'd upset anyone, that wasn't it. If anyone gets upset by this song then they deserve to be upset by this song. If they're that anal about their religion that you can't have a different opinion without them wanting to firebomb your house then that's their problem. But I didn't want it on because I didn't think I'd done it well enough. I thought it had failed tremendously and I asked to have it nipped off the album."

The song was inspired by the *Dear God* books of children's letters to God, which Andy had seen as sick exploitation of children. He had recently concluded that there was no God and therefore the idea of a child's to-God letter questioning God's very existence might be a poignant irony. He'd been trying to write it for a long time, but the song didn't come together until one day, while Andy was playing around with an old favorite, Paul McCartney's "Rocky Raccoon."

As a fifteen-year-old art college student, Andy had earned the name Rocky for playing his one-song repertoire while the teacher was out of class. "Because I was the youngest, they'd physically lift me onto the desk, give me my guitar, and say, 'Play "Rocky Raccoon" or you're not getting down.' I'd play it over and over until the teacher came back."

In 1985, jokingly fiddling around with the song's hillbilly picking and slipping in the odd minor chord, he discovered a vehicle for his song about God. A few sessions with Dave in Stanier Street added the string arrangement. "I said, 'Think of "Summertime" with that slightly wicked edge' and we came up with a piece of mock-Gershwin," says Andy.

Try as he might, the song became less and less of a B side. Even when it was released on the back of "Grass," the DJs in America picked it up. "It did us a lot of good, although it upset as many people as it pleased," he says. This is an understatement. A radio station in Florida was threatened with firebombing for playing the track. Andy was deluged with hate mail from "Christians," and a student in an American college held the principal and his assistant hostage at knife point, demanding the song be played over the school PA. He was led away by a SWAT team and, thankfully, no one was hurt. But the huge public pressure forced Geffen to re-press the album, removing "Mermaid Smiled" and inserting "Dear God." The song single-handedly reestablished XTC in America.

IN THE SIDINGS . . .

"EXTROVERT"

(Andy Partridge) (B side, not on album)

Andy would often use songs to give himself a pep talk, but with the recording of "Extrovert," the song's instruction to rid himself of shyness involved some alcoholic encouragement. It was one of the first songs written for the album but was the last recorded and is the only recording on release of Andy singing drunk. "I was feeling pretty bad about the project and I wanted to celebrate the end of the sessions. I thought, This is only a B side, so fuck it! and got quite drunk." He had previously promised himself not to do this, as the first take of "Living Through Another Cuba" (on a pint of vodka) had been a disaster, but luckily, "Extrovert" could be sung in a state of inebriation without mishap. "Never mind where his head was when he sang it, I don't know where it was when he wrote it," says Colin. "It sticks out like a sore thumb in this collection." He was right that it probably belonged on *The Big Express*, but it was safe out of reach of *Skylarking* as a B side.

Three days after recording it they got on the plane and raced for the safety of Swindon. Todd agreed to add some sampled brass after they left, but when they got the final version Dave was astonished: "Bloody hell! He's got the chords wrong!" Dave was right, but by then, who cared?

"TERRORISM"

(Andy Partridge) (B side, not on album)

Terrorism had been a factor in people's lives outside the United States since the early seventies, but it was the birth of Holly Partridge that fueled Andy's paranoia about bombings. "I thought, Great! I'm going to be shopping with Holly and a bomb will go off in a waste bin and that will be it." But he didn't want the song to preach to anyone in particular and aimed it at all people and all religions. It had a slightly Eastern air to it, thanks to its "Paint It Black" insistence, but Todd thought it inappropriate for the album, so the demo version was mixed at Crescent by Andy and Glenn Tommey and it became a B side.

"THE TROUBLES"

(Andy Partridge) (B side, not on album)

Carrying the terrorism theme a stage further, Andy wanted to say something about Northern Ireland, a difficult subject for anyone to write about, especially an apolitical Englishman like Andy. "I knew nothing of what was happening there, only the bombs in pubs and shops here. We weren't taught the origins of the crisis or that it had a religious basis. It just seemed so ludicrously senseless." Aware of his own ignorance, Andy chose not to take sides, but to approach the subject as a lullaby (with a Bo Diddley rhythm!), comforting a child with the idea that "the troubles" will all be over soon. Again, thanks to Todd's strict *Skylarking* criteria, only the demo version appeared, remixed by Andy and Glenn Tommey on a B side, though at one point, there was some talk of the Chieftains recording it for the tribute album, *Testimonial Dinner*.

"LET'S MAKE A DEN"

(Andy Partridge) (B side, not on album)

Todd saw "Let's Make a Den" as a candidate for *Skylarking*. He liked the theme of children playing mum and dad, continuing the game into adulthood. "I was fascinated by the idea that you play all these games and then do it in real life. First it's a den and then it's a real house," says Andy. "I had finally got my own home and didn't like the idea of losing it because England might get caught up in a war caused by Ronald Reagan's 'Star Wars' saber rattling."

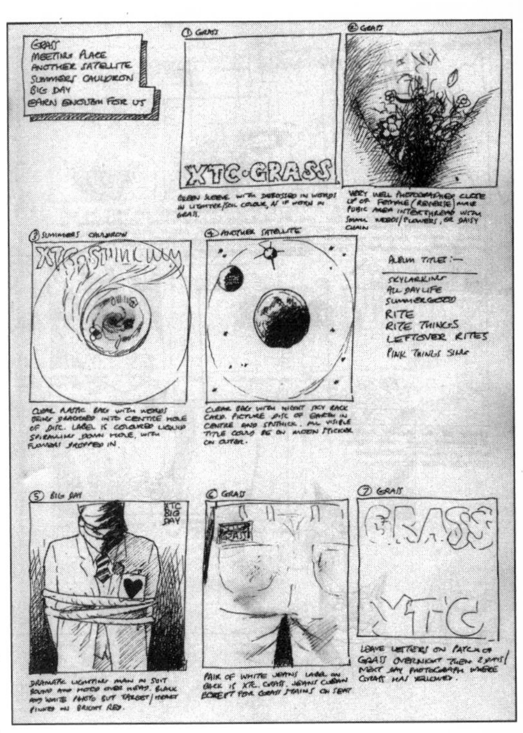

Andy's ideas for Skylarking *singles sleeves.* (CREDIT: ANDY PARTRIDGE)

The childlike approach to the theme fit Todd's all-life-in-a-day album concept. But he wanted changes. "Lots of it was in seven/four but he wanted it in eight/four, which sounded too rested and complete to me," says Andy. "I wanted this keenness and childish joy which you get from the seven/four meter. I also wanted the rhythm track to have banging Coke cans and stuff, the things that kids would do." But Todd wanted none of it. He didn't like Andy's vocals either, and complained so much that Andy threatened to walk out of the sessions. In the end, Andy preferred not to record it rather than butcher it and so only the demo appeared, as a B side, remixed at Crescent with Glenn Tommey.

"Find the Fox"

(Colin Moulding) (B side, not on album)

Colin had never witnessed a traditional English foxhunt firsthand and probably wouldn't want to but the galloping nature of the guitar rhythm he was playing with seemed to demand an equestrian theme. "I had the idea of doing a mysterious nursery rhyme-type of song, along the lines of Syd Barrett's 'Scarecrow.' But I had this unusual measure of triplets playing over fours, right across the rhythm," he says. "So I thought that, in my mind's eye, I could put over a picture of what a foxhunt might be like." It was a song that Colin was very happy with, but Todd didn't see it fitting into his concept for the album, so it remained in demo form, to be remixed by Andy and Glenn Tommey during some downtime at Crescent Studios.

10

COLONELS, KINGS, DUKES, AND JESTICLES

This is supposed to be a book that discloses hidden facts, but exposing the reality of XTC's schizoid other self is like opening a vintage wine—once open, that's it, exposed to the atmosphere, its secrets divulged and decaying in moments. It would be much more fun to say that the

The Dukes of Stratosphear: E.I.E.I. Owen, Sir John Johns, the Red Curtain, and Lord Cornelius Plum.

(CREDIT: BY PERMISSION OF VIRGIN RECORDS.)

Three Wise Men were Middle Eastern kings, cashing in on 2,000 years of fame by making a Christmas record. It would be preferable to disclose the Colonel as some errant guardsman who wanted to be a pop star and was subsequently drummed out of the regiment. It would be great to describe the Dukes of Stratosphear as four rich and chinless products of Eton and Cambridge, the sons of royal equerries (barring E.I.E.I. Owen, the illegitimate issue of some well-connected gentleman farmer), holed up in the Welsh hills with their guru. It would, perhaps, be better not to describe Johnny Japes and His Jesticles at all! But the truth will out.

All these projects, these personae, were just alter-egos for an XTC that needed a little injection of levity—a bit of a laugh!

THE COLONEL (1980)

The Colonel was a little light relief for Colin, who was more than a little irritated at not having made a bigger contribution to *Black Sea*. "We hadn't had a lot of time to write *Black Sea* and Virgin wanted a quick follow-up to 'Nigel.' I felt pressured but Andy was champing at the bit to redress the balance and prove that he could write a chart hit, too. I was peeved at being hurried and I wanted to do something fun with a different band and girl backing singers."

Virgin was happy to support this. Colin had laid the golden egg on the previous album, perhaps he would lay another. But the Colonel proved to be less golden goose than turkey. The team was good. Mick Glossop produced and engineered, being available, amiable, and affordable. A team of musicians was plucked from Mick's and Barry Andrews's phone books. Only Terry Chambers joined from XTC, lured by a few free beers. Andy and Dave weren't invited because Colin thought they wouldn't like the track and would harass him; "I'd have been laughed out of the hall," he says. The name was a continuation of the "Generals and Majors" theme. "I thought it led people gently to who was doing this mysterious track but nobody got it, and nobody wanted to know, so bollocks to them!"

"TOO MANY COOKS IN THE KITCHEN"

(Single only, released by the Colonel)

Whether there was a link between the title and Colin's feelings about the band or not, he is not saying. The Colonel more or less wrote the lyrics in the studio and, as is often the case with Colin Moulding songs, the melody led to the phrase and the phrase inspired the lyrics. "It was a very unXTC sound, more like the sort of thing Jonathan King would have done in the seventies under a name like 'the Piglets.'" In fact, if it had been released then it might have been a hit. "But it wasn't and it didn't and that was that."

"I Need Protection"

(B side of single, released by the Colonel)

This is just a blur to the Colonel now. "I can't remember what the lyrics were about," he says helpfully. "But it was a song rejected from the *Black Sea* rehearsals. There's probably a little bit of 'Supertuff' in there." Which is curious, because Colin didn't like Barry Andrews's "Supertuff" at all. But there is certainly something of the thug in the song, as, no doubt, there is in us all.

THE THREE WISE MEN (1983)

This festive folly was Andy's idea, though, of course, he stole the names. Although he had wanted to write a Christmas song, it was supposed to be sung by the Virgin Records staff. "There seemed to be a lot of people there called Mary and I thought it might be nice to release a record by the Virgin Marys. Virgin is not known for shying away from controversy, but the Marys weren't interested, possibly for reasons of common decency." So XTC recorded it with David Lord engineering.

"Thanks for Christmas"

(Kaspar/Melchior/Balthazar) (Released as a single by the Three Wise Men)

Disclosing that this was written by Andy is like telling a child that Santa doesn't exist, especially as the three-way credit would imply the only ever joint-writing effort by the band, but he wrote it and, after the refusal by the Marys of Virgin, XTC decided to record it. "Maybe they thought it was blasphemous or something," says Andy, innocently. "So I said, 'Well, *we'll* put it out then.'" It was recorded at Crescent Studios and Andy, at least, is not embarrassed by it. "But we didn't want people's first exposure to the band to be a tinselly Christmas thing so we did it under the name the Three Wise Men." Just as well, really!

"Countdown to Christmas"

(Kaspar/Melchior/Balthazar)

(B side to "Thanks for Christmas," released by the Three Wise Men)

This might have been an opportunity to try out David Lord, the Linn drum, and Crescent Studios, but festive Anglo-funk in the ABC/Scritti Politti mold is not something XTC should do too often. They did it here, and that should be enough. The most interesting thing about the track is one of the backing vocalists, a certain Erica Wexler.

THE DUKES OF STRATOSPHEAR

25 O'CLOCK (1984)

Long before Sir John Johns, the Red Curtain, Lord Cornelius Plum, and E.I.E.I. Owen came into being, the name the Dukes of Stratosphear was on Andy's lips. In 1975, when the name the Helium Kidz was considered too "glam," they needed something snappy, something memorable, something NOW! One idea was XTC and the other, for reasons known only to Andy, was the Dukes of Stratosphear. Had the band not chosen XTC, this book might never have been written. For the moment, thank goodness, the Dukes were shelved.

In 1978, the idea of a psychedelic spoof record was mooted by Andy to Dave. Dave was a friend then, rather than a colleague, but with a legendary propensity for pastiche—he could mimic any band you could choose. But this idea was also shelved, probably

"Curtains" Moulding (left) with the Helium Kidz, Andy Partridge, Terry Chambers (in false beard), and Dave Cartner. (CREDIT: MARTIN CHURCH)

on the same shelf as the Dukes, because in 1984 the two concepts were brought together, thanks to Andy and John Leckie being sacked from a Mary Margaret O'Hara production.

Left with time on his hands, Andy squeezed five grand out of Virgin's coffers and booked Chapel Lane Studios in the appropriately silly-sounding village of Hampton Bishop. The Christian couple who ran it were unaware of the irreligious goings-on that were occurring under their roof and supplied hearty meals to the five funsters. Dave's brother, Ian (otherwise known as Eewee), was invited to play drums as he wasn't famous and would not draw attention to the band's true identity. Everybody assumed suitable names: Andy became Sir John Johns, apparently upper-class British but actually an homage to Jon Jonzz, the Martian manhunter of DC comics. Colin became the Red Curtain, after his teenage nickname, Curtains (because his hair was as long at the front as it was at the back and you couldn't see his face) and because Andy and Dave thought he was a bit left-wing (which he denies emphatically: "The things they'll say for good copy!"). Dave became Lord Cornelius Plum, a name lifted from an American book about psychedelia and altered to sound more British. His brother, Eewee, made the short hop to E.I.E.I. Owen. Not to be outdone, John Leckie used his Indian spiritual name, Anand Nagara, with the professional prefix of Swami. The rules of engagement were simple: all tracks were to sound like something from 1967/68 with suitable psychedelic credentials and nothing was allowed more than two takes. Six tracks were completed in the two weeks and Andy created a suitably acid-trippy *Disraeli Gears*-influenced cover from bits of copyright-free images of Charles Atlas and Gammidges ads, photocopied and pasted together on his kitchen table.

They were, of course, deluding themselves if they thought they could remain incognito but the humor of the project, coincidentally released on April Fool's Day, was better received than the previous two XTC albums and, until years later, the minialbum sold more copies than *The Big Express*!

25 O'CLOCK

TALKING BETWEEN THE LINES

ON MARY MARGARET O'HARA

ANDY: *I was asked to produce Mary, who is, I believe, a couple of spoons short of a full set of cutlery. I went down to Rockfield Studios and was sacked before they'd recorded a note. Her manager took me for a short walk up the lane and said, "Mary doesn't think your vibes are right."*

NEVILLE: *So John Leckie got sacked because your vibes weren't right?*

ANDY: *He said, "She doesn't want him either because he belongs to a cult that supports free love and she's a Catholic." So I called him up and said, "What are you doing for the next two weeks?" and he said,*

"Nothing. You just sacked me." So I said, "Would you like to do the Dukes of Stratospbear?" I think he did it for nothing.

ON PREPAREDNESS

COLIN: *I was caught on the hop again. Andy tends to do this. He'll write all these songs for a concept and then say, "We're going into the studio next week. Have you got anything?" The rotter!*

DAVE: *It's true, he does that sort of thing.*

ON THE MERITS OF PSYCHEDELIA

ANDY: *I loved British psychedelic music from '67/'68. In the school youth club we'd all listen to "See Emily Play" and "Arnold Layne" and "My White Bicycle" and think, When I grow up I want to be in a band like that.*

DAVE: *Psychedelia to me was all about making the silliest noise you could with a guitar.*

ANDY: *It was different for Americans. It was more hard drugs and avoiding Vietnam. For England it was garden parties and Edward Lear and school uniforms on boating lakes which turn to jelly. The Dukes*

The Dukes in all their "glory."

(CREDIT: THE DESIGN CLINIC. BY PERMISSION OF VIRGIN RECORDS.)

were the ghosts of every band in 1967 smashed into one.

NEVILLE: *Ah, you mean a load of bollocks?*

DAVE: *When Andy first suggested the idea to me in 1978, I was driving a van for a living, so I said, "Okay. I'll put a new battery in my fuzz pedal," but in the age of punk I couldn't think of anything more stupid to try and do. Then we heard Nick Nicely's "Hilly Fields 1892" and thought we'd better get on and do it.*

COLIN: *It wasn't really where I was coming from.*

DAVE: *That's because Colin was a bit younger than us and hadn't been through that. He knew all the hits but the only psychedelic thing he really knew was* Sgt. Pepper.

COLIN: *And* Their Satanic Majesties Request *but most of the stuff Andy and Dave were into was guitar hero stuff, not melodic enough for me.*

ON SWAMI ANAND NAGARA

DAVE: *We couldn't have done it without John Leckie. The fact that we got it down in the time we did was down to his skill. He knew exactly what we wanted and how to get it.*

ANDY: *He has this reputation for being up to anything unusual you might want to try.*

ON CHAPEL LANE STUDIOS

ANDY: *It was a Christian studio. Very nice people.*

DAVE: *We were very respectful to them whenever they came in but as soon as their backs were turned we were moaning about the accommodation, which was freezing.*

COLIN: *She made nice cakes and preserves, though.*

25 O'CLOCK

ON THE TRACKS

"25 O'CLOCK"

(Sir John Johns)

Refer back to the Electric Prunes, if you dare, and you will find their entire career compressed and repackaged in this rabid fuzz guitar and reverb-drenched monstrosity. "It's a mixture of them and the subpsychedelic sixth-form British bands—all doom-laden nonsense poetry and doomier chords," says Sir John Johns. He strongly refutes claims that the clocks were purloined from Pink Floyd. "*Dark Side of the Moon* was years behind. It was already passé on *Yellow Submarine*." (Reference material: the Chambers Brothers' "Time Has Come Today," early tracks by the Welsh band Man, the Electric Prunes' "I Had Too Much to Dream Last Night," and Tomorrow's "My White Bicycle.")

"BIKE RIDE TO THE MOON"

(Sir John Johns)

If anyone deserves to be the King of Psychedelia, it is Syd Barrett, latterly of Pink Floyd and now in residence with his mother in Cambridge. "Bike Ride to the Moon" is, as Sir John insists, "complete and utter Cambridge." "It's just daft," is the considered opinion of Lord Cornelius Plum. The Red Curtain's buzzing bass is actually more of the Move's school than Floyd's but in every other way this is pure Syd. (Reference material: Pink Floyd's "Bike" and the Move's "I Can Hear the Grass Grow.")

"My Love Explodes"
(Sir John Johns)

When R&B bands like the Yardbirds headed into psychedelia they usually set off in the direction of India, though more often than not, they got no further than picking up a bit of electric sitar and a tabla—about as far as XTC got with "Beating of Hearts." "My Love Explodes" nodded in that direction, with a touch of "Electric Prunes' 'Get Me to the World On Time' feedback, and Theramins meet Bo Diddley," says Sir John, as if that meant anything. But its lyrical content was more basic than spiritual. It's about an orgasm, so the vociferous complaint at the end is understandable. It was recorded by Swami Leckie during a trip to New York, and is a genuine radio listener's tirade about a broadcast performance of "Go Fuck Yourself with Your Atom Bomb" by Tuli Kupferberg of the Fugs (who can be heard saying these words in reverse of the run-out groove; the only use of the "F" word on an XTC record). It is not, contrary to popular belief, Woody Allen. (Reference material: the Yardbirds' "Over, Under, Sideways, Down.")

"What In the World??"
(The Red Curtain)

Caught short by the Dukes project, Colin had only one offering suitable for *25 O'Clock*, but Lord Cornelius Plum called it "a great song." "What In the World??" initially sounded like a 1961 B side to "Telstar" meets Zager and Evans' "2525." But with "Only a Northern Songish" tape effects, it became a passable candidate for the Dukes. "I think our grandparents would be shocked by the things our kids discuss with us and I just thought, Where is it all leading to?," says the Red Curtain. *Deep!* (Other reference material: the Beatles' "All Too Much," Manfred Mann's "Semi Detached Suburban Mister James.")

"Your Gold Dress"

(Sir John Johns)

The vast majority of original psychedelic hits were based around one, second-rate, I-just-bought-a-guitar-and-I'm-gonna-be-a-star riff. Sitting in Crescent Studios while *The Big Express* was mixed downstairs, Sir John Johns developed "Your Gold Dress" around such a riff. "It's sub-Troggs for Christ's sake! I was thinking about things like the Smoke's "My Friend Jack Eats Sugarlumps," says Sir John, demonstrating his encyclopedic knowledge and dubious taste. Sadly, he blew it by making the song too good. "The Nicky Hopkins's style piano was probably one of the high points of the record," says the Red Curtain, who recognized the florid Stones' flavor of Lord Cornelius's playing, if nothing else on the album. (Other reference material: Nicky Hopkins playing on the Rolling Stones' "She's a Rainbow," the Beatles' "Strawberry Fields.")

"The Mole from the Ministry"

(Sir John Johns)

In the late sixties, somebody sent a key to BBC Radio One, saying there was a package in a locker at Paddington Station. The package contained a record called "We Are the Moles" by a mystery band called, coincidentally, the Moles. The correspondent said the artists were very famous and DJs, especially Alan Freeman, decided it had to be the Beatles, with Ringo singing. In fact, the whole thing was a spoof by Simon Dupree and the Big Sound, but it caused a stir for a while. Inspired by this, one crisp Herefordshire morning Sir John tinkled on the piano and wrote the best song on *25 O'Clock*, "The Mole from the Ministry," a deep and meaningless exploration of that favorite sixties, cold war subject, spies and double agents, or "moles." "When Andy played us the songs for the Dukes, I thought they were just stupid," says Plum of Sir John. "But afterward, I realized that some of them, especially 'Mole,' were really good songs." Which is what happens when a brilliant songwriter tries to make a Beatles psychedelic pastiche. Sounds of "I Am the Walrus" and "A Day In the Life" blend with backward seagulls and the repeated word *loam* is *mole* in reverse (in case you needed assistance). Endless effects and noises were spun in, including the odd hint of XTC (a snippet of "Life Is Good In the Greenhouse" played on Zippy Zither, for instance), fun for all the family to work out on cold nights.

Andy's unused cartoon for "The Mole from the Ministry."

(CREDIT: ANDY PARTRIDGE)

A promotional film, exploiting every psychedelic visual effect, was filmed in the gardens of Nailsea Court, near Clevedon in Somerset, which stank of cat urine. It remains one of XTC's few credible video productions. (Reference material: Any Beatles, and the sayings of Benjamin Franklin.)

PSONIC PSUNSPOTS (1987)

The little dinghy pitched on the broad Fowey River as they clung to the Mellotron and amplifiers. The Dukes were heading downstream and everything they owned was in this unstable little boat

Sir John Johns and E.I.E.I. Owen drift downstream from Sawmills Studios.

(CREDIT: COLIN MOULDING)

with its spluttering outboard motor. They heaved a sigh of relief as they turned under the little bridge into the creek and drew up beside the old pink sawmill, Cornwall's quirkiest and most remote recording studio. Blocks and tackles hauled the equipment onto the jetty and the Dukes and their guru prepared for three weeks of recording and going native.

Colin had a pretty good idea that they hadn't seen the last of the Dukes of Stratosphear and had quietly stored away a few songs, just in case. So, when Virgin suggested they do a full album, he brought a little more to the table than before. He was also determined to include a few tributes to bands that he recognized.

With £11,000, three weeks in Sawmills Studios, and genuine record company interest, Dave knew that it wouldn't be as much fun as last time but it would still be a relief after the stress of *Skylarking*. What was clear was that this album would have a more united feeling, linking the songs with sound effects and nonsense phrases, as per Lear or Carroll. It had been hoped that these would be read by the English character actor Derek Guyler, but as his agent wanted most of the album budget, they used the studio manager's daughter, Lily Fraser, who made a superb Alice.

The Red Curtain and various grades of accommodation at Sawmills Studios.

(CREDIT: DAVE GREGORY)

Virgin's excitement over *25 O'Clock* meant that more resources were to be poured into promoting *Psonic Psunspots* and a double A-side single was released with a video of one side. Not surprisingly, the side with the video was the one that earned the least airplay but the album did well and both 25 *O'Clock* and *Psonic Psunspots* were released together on the new compact disc, under the name *Chips from the Chocolate Fireball*. Fortunately, the CD was not issued in the same finish as the psychedelic splatter-colored vinyl album, which came out looking more like a chip from a chocolate cow!

PSONIC PSUNSPOTS

TALKING BETWEEN THE LINES

ON MONEY

ANDY: *We got 5,000 [pounds] for the first one and did it for three and gave back the change, which was stupid. We got eleven for the next and spent nine but kept the change. I've felt guilty about it ever since, even though it was our money.*

ON SEQUELS

ANDY: *I usually hate sequels but we'd had so much fun not being ourselves, so I'd been secretly storing up songs for the eventuality.*

COLIN: *I thought that if I had any songs this time, I would try to make them sound like the bands that I liked.*

DAVE: *It wasn't as much fun. We spent three weeks on it and it shows. It's a bit more serious.*

ON SAWMILLS STUDIOS

DAVE: *Very rural. Like a holiday camp, living in shacks in the woods.*

COLIN: *You could only get there at high tide. A great place to bring up kids but very cold at that time of year.*

DAVE: *We had fun bringing all this stuff in on the boat. We were dicing with death there.*

Andy: *The only way in was by boat or by walking down the railway tracks. Once I was in, I couldn't be bothered to walk to the village or get in the boat, so most evenings I just watched the "Nearest and Dearest" video again and again.*

PSONIC PSUNSPOTS

ON THE TRACKS

"Vanishing Girl"

(The Red Curtain) (Single and album track)

The Hollies were perhaps a bit too poppish to fit the Dukes' bill but, as Sir John Johns points out, "King Midas In Reverse" was one of Graham Nash's finest psychedelic moments. "Vanishing Girl" was undoubtedly Hollies in origin, but from probably a year or two before psychedelia hit Britain, exposing the Red Curtain's shaky credentials in the kaftan and acid department. "All I had was this very smooth-sounding melody," says the rouge-draped one. "So we amped it up and got the tempo going and Hollies'd it up." 'Twas fortunate that Lord Cornelius was a fan of Tony Hicks's guitar playing, otherwise this might not have gained acceptance. But it provided a single, which found favor with the West Coast radio jocks. (Other reference material: the Hollies' "On a Carousel" or "King Midas In Reverse.")

"Have You Seen Jackie?"

(Sir John Johns)

"Arnold Layne" is the archetype of all psychedelic records and "Have You Seen Jackie?" is in tribute. Endless songs about English eccentrics followed Syd Barrett's masterpiece, including numerous cross-dressing themes, so it seemed appropriate that the Dukes should do the same. Though how appropriate it was to let young Lily Fraser narrate the tale of Jackie's gender dilemma is a matter for the child psychologists. The Red Curtain believes that it was originally titled "Have You Seen Sydney?," though this was probably too close to the great space cadet for comfort. (Other reference material: Anything by Keith West and Steve Howe's band Tomorrow.)

"LITTLE LIGHTHOUSE"
(Sir John Johns)

Holly Partridge was only a few months old when Andy penned this song about her for *Skylarking*. Todd Rundgren's production was rather too industrial and, according to the Red Curtain, "It didn't fit his scheme." So the song was passed on to Sir John Johns for redecoration in paisley print. Suddenly, the song about a little angel's marble-colored, rubber-textured skin and the way her eyes lit up made much more sense. Well, if it didn't, who cares, because psychedelia is about more than mere words, isn't it, maann?

Lily Fraser as Alice and Sir John Johns as the Mad Hatter.

(CREDIT: COLIN MOULDING)

The arrangement borrowed more from West Coast American acts like Steve Miller and Love than was the Dukes' norm. Sir John is not quite sure whether they stole the foghorns from Steve Miller's *Sailor* album, but then those were hazy days and who would expect him to remember anything? (Other reference material: Anything by the Electric Prunes, early Grateful Dead, the Blues Magoos, Quicksilver Messenger Service, and the entire contents of CBS Records sampler *Rock Machine Turns You On*.)

"You're a Good Man Albert Brown (Curse You Red Barrel)"

(Sir John Johns) (Single and album track)

Andy Partridge wouldn't have penned a song like this. He could only have written such a blatant biographical tale of his grand-pater, Albert Partridge, and the wartime nurse he married, Elsie Brown, under an assumed name, such as Sir John Johns.

British psychedelic bands, expecially those of R&B roots, all seemed to record at least one druggy knees-up pub song—"Lazy Sunday" for the Small Faces, "Lazing On a Sunday Afternoon" for the Kinks. "Albert Brown" was the Dukes' attempt at the genre and "Curse You Red Barrel" enhanced the sixties/pub/war story conjunction. "Watney's Red Barrel was the beer that shot down the sixties," says Sir John, and the Royal Guardsmen's confusing tribute to Snoopy and his First World War exploits ("Snoopy vs. the Red Baron") included the immortal line "Curse you, Red Baron!" The combined phrase summed up the sentiment of the song in a sixties framework.

"Collideascope"

(Sir John Johns)

"Andy is the Mike Yarwood of pop," says the Red Curtain, in a dubious compliment, comparing Partsy to Yarwood, the reformed alcoholic British impersonator. Certainly, Sir John Johns does a passable Lennon and the ascending E-minor chords and the brutal surrealism of the lyrics to "Collideascope" are utterly Lennonesque. But "Collideascope" is so much more. "It is one of the best things he ever wrote," says Lord Cornelius Plum, still missing the point that "Collideascope" is a tribute to their sojourn in the Sawmills—the wood-sawing solo, for instance, an idea previously employed by the Turtles on "Sound Asleep"; "Bloody Nora!," and "Any changes here will be made over my dog's body," the odd quotes of Jimmy Jewel and Hilda Baker from the Dukes' favorite video, "Nearest and Dearest"; and the crashing "snare" sound of a drum case full of tambourines being dropped. It's a trip, and a rather ugly one at that. (Other reference material: possibly the Move's "Blackberry Way.")

"You're My Drug"
(Sir John Johns)

It is just possible that this is the track that inspired Andy to ask Dave's participation in a psychedelic EP, because "You're My Drug" was too Byrdsish to be an XTC track when it was written in 1978. "It's a bit 'Eight Miles High' to me," says the Red Curtain. "More on their druggy side. I preferred the melodic stuff." "It's a straight lift of the Byrds," Sir John concurs. "That and every band that tried to be them, like the Animals' 'Monterey.' " It is also a rather cool and mellifluous track, a love song, perfect sunny afternoon, festival fodder.

"Shiny Cage"
(The Red Curtain)

Demo recordings of "Shiny Cage" were made for *The Big Express* but, according to Colin Moulding, "It was too like something else." Well, "something else" is what every good psychedelic song needs and once the Red Curtain got hold of it, "Shiny Cage" became an amalgam of everything in the Beatles' *Revolver*, especially "I'm Only Sleeping." "It's so stupidly like the original you think, Oh dear!" says the Curtain. "But it's okay because it's just a big laugh."

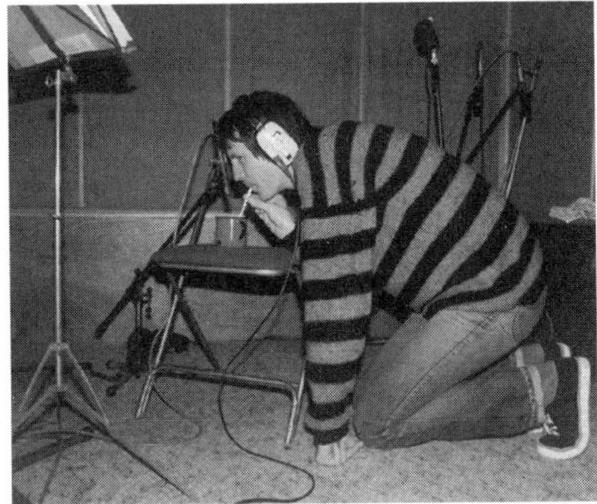

Lord Cornelius Plum in virtuoso bubble-blowing mode for "Brainiac's Daughter." (CREDIT: COLIN MOULDING)

"Brainiac's Daughter"
(Sir John Johns)

Sir John casts the first stone and makes a splash for "Brainiac's Daughter." (CREDIT: COLIN MOULDING)

From Lennon to McCartney, Sir John's versatility knows no bounds. "Brainiac's Daughter" married Macca with DC comics' evil master Brainiac. The result was a bubbly little number akin to "Martha My Dear," "Penny Lane," "Maxwell's Silver Hammer," and "Good Day Sunshine," all fat-fingers piano and nodding heads. The lyrics concerned a "whacky chick [probably Erica] with lots of Superman comic ideas, like the 'Bottle City of Kandor,' where Superman's powers were neutralized," says Sir John. The sound effects were equally childish. "Instead of a cymbal at the start, Leckie ran a microphone out of the window and we threw a bloody big rock in the creek," says Sir John, like an excited infant. It was also his first ocarina solo, which has undoubtedly transformed his musical career ever since.

"The Affiliated"
(The Red Curtain)

Dave and Andy thought Colin hadn't quite got the point of the Dukes and Colin probably agrees. They suggested that "The Affiliated" was more an XTC track but after giving it a "Day In the Life" doom-laden flavor, it was shoehorned into Dukes style. "The middle section was more Jack Jones 'Wives and Lovers' stuff, really, but that is sixties, isn't it?" says the Red Curtain, clutching at straws. "More like Unit Four Plus Two after a snort of Drano," says Sir John encouragingly. The song was actually about a man escaping those famous workingmen's clubs that Colin was dragged to as a child, though it's doubtful that the Red Curtain would frequent such blue-collar establishments. The announcer at the beginning is genuinely taken from the BBC report to tell the British people that Adolf Hitler was dead. Sir John wanted the whole message included, but Dave said to take it off.

"PALE AND PRECIOUS"
(Sir John Johns)

"This is the best record the Beach Boys never made," says Lord Cornelius Plum. "It's better than any other attempt to copy them, even the Ivy League's records." Strong praise indeed from a lifelong Beach Boys fan, the man who converted Andy Partridge, and so Sir John Johns, to the joys of "Smiley Smile" and "Surf's Up." Without a doubt, the musical side of "Pale and Precious" is a masterpiece, hidden from many who would have loved it had it not been given the Dukes treatment—the Fraser girls whispering at the start, the "Up she rises" ending vocal, and Sir John drumming because E.I. was too drunk. "I was kicking myself that we put this song on this record," says Andy. "Dave said, 'You're an idiot. This is really good and should be on an XTC album.' But the only reason it came into existence was I was trying to write a fake Beach Boys song." And that he did.

Swami Anand Nagara demonstrates a relaxing yoga position to Sir John Johns.

(CREDIT: COLIN MOULDING)

JOHNNY JAPES AND HIS JESTICLES (1987)

It feels a tad uncomfortable, having got this far into the book, to start talking in the first person, but at this point I make my ignominious entrance to the tale. While the Dukes were hiding in the Cornish wilds, I was recording the comic actor/songwriter/pop "superstar" John Otway and his erstwhile partner, Wild Willy Barrett, in London. Andy Partridge had introduced me to Viz Comic, a glorious slapback against the politically correct brigade run by a group of unemployed "lads" in northern England. Otway and I were instantly hooked to characters such as Terry Fuckwit, Johnny Fartpants, and the Bottom Inspectors and he suggested that we make a record about one of the characters, Scooter Dolphin Boy. But as he had been badly injured and jailed for causing unnecessary suffering to his late dolphin, we decided to choose the more popular Buster Gonad and His Unfeasibly Large Testicles. A quick call to enlist Dave Gregory, master of the four-track reel-to-reel machine, resulted in Andy volunteering and, ultimately, railroading the project to produce "Bags of Fun with Buster," recorded during one day in Drive Studios, Swindon, and released by John Brown Publishing on the specially created Fulchester Records. Many fans have asked why Andy and Dave should have made such a banal record. I can only say that it was probably the truest example of the depths to which their humor can sink—and we had a great laugh doing it.

"Bags of Fun with Buster"

(Neville Farmer, Andy Partridge, and Dave Gregory) (Released as a single by Johnny Japes and His Jesticles featuring John Otway)

There is little to say. This is no more than the everyday story of a superhero, a boy whose testicles were struck by a meteorite as a baby. They swelled to enormous size and he believes they have special powers, which of course, they don't. I wanted a ska beat to this and started the song off but Andy soon took over. He and Dave played the majority of instruments while I added special vocal effects and Otway "sang" lead and played the excrutiating sax solo. Only on release as a seven-inch vinyl single, and not many copies being sold, it is now a collector's item.

"The Scrotal Scratch Mix" on the B side is probably the better comedy track, involving some typically British toilet humor from Otway and myself and the awesome crotch scratching of Dave Gregory, who was the only one wearing the type of corduroy trousers that make a loud scratch!

TERRY AND THE LOVE MEN (1995)

The shelved contender for the title of *Black Sea* was revived, long after Terry Chambers's departure, for a special version of Colin Moulding's "The Good Things," recorded incognito (just about) for David Yazbek's *Testimonial Dinner* XTC tribute album, or *Testicular Dinner* as Andy insists on calling it. "We thought it would be really tacky to appear on our own tribute record and that's why we did it. It was recorded in Drive Studios in Swindon," says Andy. There is now a pub band playing the West Country of England with the name Terry and the Love Men, but don't get excited, they just borrowed the name.

11

SONGS OF SIXPENCE

1988

The sun burned down on Sunset Strip as usual. From their vantage point in Summa Studios on the junction with La Cienega, XTC was leching over the high-class whores who shopped for their leathers across the street. The studio control room was a mess. The usual track sheets were stuck around the walls, one song per sheet with a list of the instruments in the arrangement. And there were too many people in there—the band, percussionist Pat, producer Paul, engineer Ed, tape jockey Joe, Mark Isham, Mike Keneally, me, others. There was excess everything. "Excess," the name marketing men would have given to Los Angeles had the Spanish not got there first.

Riding high on the success of *Skylarking*, XTC leapt into the next album with a bright, loud, smiling attitude and a fat budget. Virgin wanted to continue the American success with another American producer—a pop producer. Paul Fox had impressed Jeremy Lascelles with his remixes of Boy George and Yes. XTC was simply overwhelmed that any producer would fly to Swindon to see them. They accepted him without such second thoughts as, Wouldn't it be better to work with an experienced album producer? Or, Can we afford him *and* his engineer, Ed Thacker?

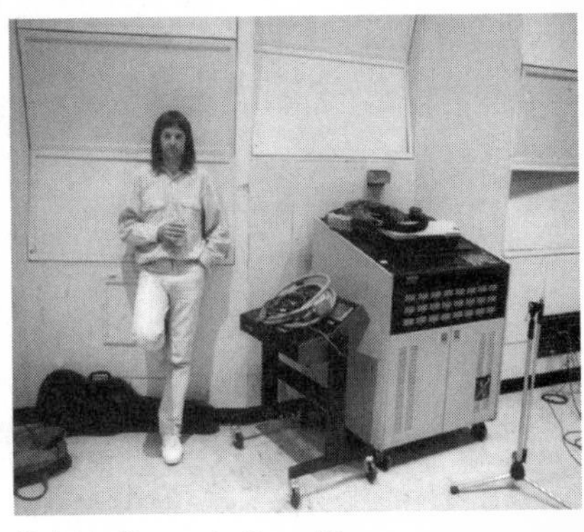

Cool Mr. Gregory in Ocean Way. (CREDIT: PAUL FOX)

Songs of Sixpence, as Andy named the album, would be another Made In America recording, but this time there would be no woodpeckers and copies of *Hustler* for company. The entire Swindon posse would come along: kids (four), wives (two), guitar collections (one plus Andy's and Colin's oddments). They set up camp in the Valley, in the pleasant-sounding Oakwood Apartments, all mod cons, pool, security, etcetera.

As the XTC bandwagon rolled into town, they got there to find that everybody wanted to jump on board. The "session" drummer, Pat Mastellotto, lately of Mr. Mister, was so happy to be working with them, he would always beat them to the studio. His wife, Connie, even had THXTC as her license plate after her favorite sci-fi movie and her favorite band. For the first time in years, XTC felt wanted.

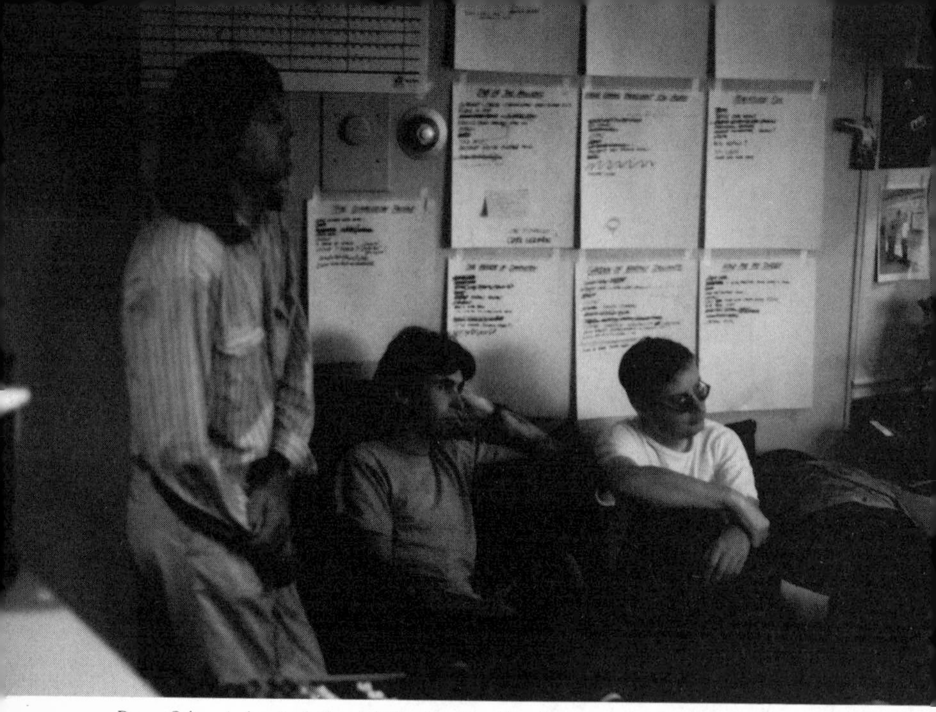

Dave, Colin, Andy, Paul Fox, Ed Thacker, Pat Mastellotto, and Joe Fiorello mixing it in Summa Music. (CREDIT: NEVILLE FARMER)

In the first month, Paul put them through a grueling rehearsal schedule at Leeds Studio in the San Fernando Valley. Then it was into Ocean Way's famous Studio One, home of the Beach Boys and many, many more. Three weeks of drumming, strumming, and plucking and it was on to Summa Music, a less imposing studio but beautifully equipped. Summa belonged to Paul Fox's manager, Rick Stevens, a man with gleaming white shorts to match his gleaming white teeth.

But L.A. is a fickle place. The apartments were not what they seemed. The band shared their accommodation with thousands of tiny nonpaying guests, and the pool with some rather unsavory heavy metal characters with odd chemical habits. Stuck in California with nothing to do, the families retreated to Swindon after a couple of months, leaving Andy and Colin to transfer into one apartment where they could share their homesickness.

As the sessions dragged on and on . . . and on, Andy became

more and more stressed. At home, armies of lawyers and accountants were gathering to fight a battle between XTC and their ex-manager. Long before it would come to court, the legal and accounting bills were amounting to far more than they could hope to win. Andy started hitting the bottle and crying himself to sleep. Dave was worried about it, too. But he was also having a hard time with his diabetes, making him fractious. He wasn't getting much joy in the making of the album either. Paul's inexperience gave Andy more control than usual and Paul would always defer to the composer in arguments over songs. Dave didn't write, so Dave invariably lost. Even Andy felt guilty about it.

Colin was nervy. He'd be laid-back in a nuclear assault, but after taking such a prominent role writing *Skylarking*, he was unhappy with his latest offerings. Virgin was unhappy, too. Five months of recording ran up a bill topping half a million dollars and Jeremy Lascelles threatened to halt proceedings. As the album credit says, "Simon and Jeremy—Hands off that plug." Only humble begging from Andy saved the day, plus his agreement to cut costs by coming

Colin and Pat in Ocean Way. (CREDIT: ANDY PARTRIDGE)

home, leaving the mixing to Paul, Ed, and Dave. Andy was happy with that arrangement anyway. He could see his career going down the pan if he didn't get home to sort out the mess. He was confident that *Oranges and Lemons*, as the album was to become, was the most commercial and excellent record to date. He was correct in the former and, arguably, in the latter judgment, as well. *Oranges and Lemons* was as lush and lurid as its cover and made sure that radio stations across the country wanted to play it. Andy conceded to a live radio tour, playing acoustically on American stations and live on *Letterman*. They even recorded an MTV unplugged session before MTV called such things "unplugged." It was an expensive gamble, but *Oranges and Lemons* paid off.

ORANGES AND LEMONS

TALKING BETWEEN THE LINES

ANDY: *After* Skylarking, *we decided we wanted to do something bold and commercial.*

COLIN: *We were optimistic that we were going to do good things with this album, on the back of* Skylarking. *We wanted to capitalize on what we'd done.*

ANDY: *I think it was Jeremy Lascelles or Simon Draper who said, "There's this young chap called Paul Fox doing remixes in L.A. He's just done one for Boy George which is fantastic." Which it was.*

COLIN: *He so wanted to do the project and obviously enthusiasm counts for a lot.*

ANDY: *The fact he was willing to come to Swindon was a big swayer. Being an American, he didn't have the English hang-ups. Short of removing his trousers and daubing his genitals with Marmite I think he would do anything to please. It was a very snap decision. Because Paul was new at this game, he really wanted to get it right with us, and he came with an excellent engineer called Ed Thacker. It was kind of an expensive dynamic duo.*

NEVILLE: *So it was off to L.A.*

COLIN: *It was a bit of an uproot.*

ANDY: *Because we were there for so long.*

COLIN: *Five months.*

DAVE: *Longer for me. But it was nice to spend six months in the sun and watch the West Coast go by.*

ANDY: *I took the wife and kids and Colin took the wife and kids and Dave took his guitar collection.*

COLIN: *Those are his kids.*

ANDY: *The Oakwood Apartments looked superficially okay but because so many people had gone through, they'd become flea-ridden.*

DAVE: *I had a hornet's nest on my balcony.*

COLIN: *What was disturbing was we'd been out there for three-and-a-half weeks and we hadn't recorded a note. Paul was a stickler for detail in rehearsals and we were in Leeds rehearsal room for a month. This band never rehearses, or hardly ever, and I just remember feeling so tired every day.*

DAVE: *Pat Mastellotto made all the difference.*

ANDY: *Paul recommended Pat and he was a great drummer, a big fan of the band, and again ready to please. Oddly enough, you could have shut your eyes [and] thought he was Terry on a good day.*

DAVE: *Pat was a real godsend. He was always in the studio before us, working out what he was going to do. The difference between U.S. and U.K. musicians is the work ethic. Americans are obsessive about doing the job and not failing.*

NEVILLE: *Did Paul get any say in the track listing?*

COLIN: *We sorted them out at Leeds because I remember he didn't want to do "Cynical Days" and I had to really fight for that.*

DAVE: *I had a real downer on "Merely a Man," but Paul wanted to do it so we did it as a favor to him. It ended up as one of my favorite songs.*

COLIN: *So we started recording at Ocean Way down on Sunset, mainly for the big room to get the drum sound. It had that delicious feel about it that you were there to make a record.*

ANDY: *A lot of the good things that came out of L.A. came out of that room and you hoped that maybe that would rub off on you.*

DAVE: *Ocean Way was brilliant. A fantastic studio.*

ANDY: *I remember we had a lot of cheap porn mags going around and I made this huge sort of German officer's peaked cap and stuck these pussies all over it. If anyone was being difficult they had to put on the Colonel Cunt Hat and wear the Thumb of Decision. It was like a way of humiliating them.*

COLIN: *I think it was made for you.*

ANDY: *Strange. It fitted perfectly.*

COLIN: *Once we'd recorded all the live drums at Ocean Way, we moved into Summa.*

ANDY: *It belonged to Paul's manager, Rick Stevens.*

COLIN: *All alfalfa sprouts and tennis and the Bacharach lifestyle.*

ANDY: *We had an awful lot of hangers-on coming into the studio. A girl called Logan lived on the hill behind the studio and painted* XTC KISS KISS KISS *on her window. In the end she would visit with her dog.*

Tarquin Gotch, our new manager, said, "There's this young actor called River Phoenix who's a big fan and he'd like to come down." I didn't know him from Adam until one day I saw this disgusting-looking, smelly kid in the lounge who I thought came in off the street. After about five minutes, he introduced himself as River Phoenix. I thought, Bloody hell! If he's a successful actor, at least he could have his shirt ironed. He'd come 'round and hang out and rant for hours and hours. He was a total and utter anal fan.

COLIN: *He was very pleasant. He got me some work. He lived next door to T-Bone Burnett in Hollywood who was looking for somebody to play bass on his wife's album, and River said, "Have you heard of XTC's Colin Moulding?" And I got a call.*

ANDY: *River asked me would I speak to a friend of his who was also a big fan and I said, "Okay." There was this very nervous voice at the end of the phone going, "Oh wow! Shit, man! Shit! Wow!" That's all he could say. He said he was in rehearsal with his band and that his name was Keanu Reeves. Members of Zappa's band would be hanging 'round, as well, notably Mike Keneally, who was very pleasant and ludicrously musical and Scott Thunes who was very musical but was the sort of person you could get into a big argument with and I did.*

NEVILLE: *The families must have enjoyed themselves.*

COLIN: *If you're not actually working in Los Angeles, it's a bore.*

ANDY: *They went home after a while. There was too much weird stuff going on. They'd spend days 'round the pool and there'd be all these weird characters hanging out there, wannabe bands.*

COLIN: *Drugs played a big part in the scene. People there seemed to think if you didn't do drugs, you weren't a real band. So the girls buggered off home after a couple of months.*

ANDY: *After the girls went, I started drinking heavily and I don't think I ate too well.*

COLIN: *When I'm in the studio I like the domestic duties to be taken care of. I don't like to come home and have to make dinner and, really, we had to fend for ourselves.*

DAVE: *A lot of problems stem from my health and I forget that when it starts going wrong I get in a really bad frame of mind and that affects everybody.*

ANDY: *One of my overriding memories is sitting in the lounge area of Summa waiting for them to sort out another take and watching videos of old black-and-white English movies. We were so homesick we couldn't get enough Englishness.*

Erica came over to these sessions because my wife had gone home. She made it really difficult for me and I decided I was going to tell her once and for all to leave me alone because I was a married man. It really hurt me to do this. Because all female companionship went home we suddenly felt very lonely. And we started to fret about the problems because at the time we were going through the run up to the court case with our ex-manager. We'd also spent an awful lot of money making Oranges and Lemons, *and by three quarters of the way through, Jeremy Lascelles said, "You've spent a quarter of a million pounds and I'm pulling the plug." I had to beg him not to. "Please don't do it. This is the best thing we've done to date and if you pull it, what are you going to end up with?" Things got very weird. I'd started drinking whisky, which I never drink, and I'd stay up until about three or four in the morning, standing there with my head against the TV screen, crying about the court case.*

COLIN: *I think it was Tarquin who came to our rescue really. He convinced us that the case was a fruitless endeavor.*

DAVE: *Tarquin told us what was wrong and said, "Get rid of the lawyers, you silly fuckers." After that it all became clear.*

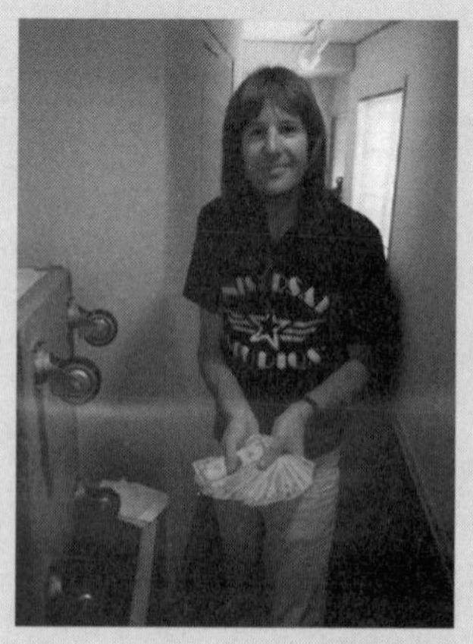

Dave in a rare sighting with per diems.

(CREDIT: COLIN MOULDING)

ANDY: *By the time we'd got everything recorded, I felt really good about Paul and Ed overseeing the finishing off of the album so we could go back to England to see to this court case.*

DAVE: *I was left there with Paul and Ed to mix the album, but Paul had been doing Andy's bidding the whole time and when he left, Paul was a bit flummoxed about what he would want. I really had to fight him over a few issues.*

ANDY: *Because Paul kept adding more and more options, there were a lot of decisions put off and put off until the mix. You'd record maybe three different hi-hat patterns for a song and say, "Let's pick it in the mix." But it never got picked in the mix. We'd have all three. But I think Paul did very well and he was one of the few producers I would work with in the future because of his conscientious midwifery, getting the thing born. I remember being in tears in the manager's office about the court case and the poor bloke got so involved in it he was crying as well. He was emotionally involved in the whole record in a deep way.*

DAVE: *Paul was a nice guy and although he was very inexperienced, he made a good album.*

COLIN: *He was very good at coaxing the best out of you. Making you feel as though you were doing a good job, and I think it was some of my best playing on that record. I think that's mainly due to him guiding me down a certain route. It's something that's overlooked with a lot of producers.*

ANDY: *I wanted to call the album* Songs of Sixpence. *I like nursery rhymes. But because the album was coming out so shiny and fluorescent and so sleek and fast, the title* Oranges and Lemons *seemed about right. In L.A., they are the colors you see everywhere. This bold color comes off the music and it fitted the criteria of a nursery rhyme title.*

I was talking to Gregsy and said wouldn't it be nice to do a really pop art sleeve and he said he'd always liked the sleeve to the Who's A Quick One. *I liked the idea of a pop sleeve for a pop album. The lettering for the sleeve came from the cover of Andy Williams's* Love, Andy *album which I found in a secondhand Graphis annual from 1968. And I'd always loved a radio station poster Milton Glaser had done with all these people playing bendy instruments with these sunset rays behind them, so I got the Design Clinic to redraw that, but as if Heinz Eidelmann, who designed* Yellow Submarine, *had drawn it.*

COLIN: *Sheila Rock, who took the photographs, realized what an—well, I wouldn't say ugly bunch. But let's say we were in need of a little attention. Unkempt.*

ANDY: *The Unkempt Brothers.*

COLIN: *She actually got her makeup artist to do a good job on us. Do you remember spending a long time in makeup doing our hair?*

ANDY: *I don't actually because there's not a lot you could do with mine. It was so busy falling out. I know Gregsy really likes this session. He's really the face of '68 on the back cover there. Unfortunately, it's 1568.*

COLIN: *I always thought you had your fingers in your ears.*

ANDY: *No, I'm just sitting there having a think about that knife and fork in my hat. It was a set of Victorian cutlery that somebody had left on a London Underground train. I've still got them to this day.*

COLIN: *Personally, I didn't feel happy about my contribution to the songwriting, with the exception of "Cynical Days." Also, a lot of the sentiments of the songs on the album are overviews. I like sort of simpler, more personal sentiments.*

ANDY: *"Chalkhills" was very direct and so was "Cynical Days," but I know what Colin's saying. Things like "The Loving" were just a grand statement.*

COLIN: *It was less English, I suppose.*

ANDY: *But it didn't seem to do us any harm. In fact, I think it did us nothing but good.*

DAVE: *They were great songs but probably too many songs, to be frank. There are not too many that I didn't enjoy. It was overproduced and I would have preferred two less months and five less songs, but that wouldn't have been XTC, would it?*

ORANGES AND LEMONS

ON THE TRACKS

"GARDEN OF EARTHLY DELIGHTS"
(Andy Partridge)

The birth of Harry Partridge required a fanfare, a welcome to planet Earth and all its delights. The title "Garden of Earthly Delights" had been sitting around waiting for a song for a few years, and now seemed as good a time as any to write it. It was an extravagant song with an air of Persian mystery, tales of the Arabian nights, and references to great observers of the world's small wonders—one-eared Van Gogh and Chekhov (the playwright, not the *Star Trek* character!). Paul Fox made sure that it sounded big, bold, exciting, and new. "I wanted it to sound like a Persian rug," says Andy. "And Paul did a great job." But there was precision under the clatter—a programmed drum pattern as well as Pat drumming and Colin's bass parts sampled and repeated.

Andy's early four-man drawing for Oranges and Lemons.

(CREDIT: ANDY PARTRIDGE)

The sample of a real Arab market was a whirlwind opening to the album. But the fuzzy guitar and vocal line is more like the opening of Frank Zappa's "We're Only In It for the Money" as it builds to Gregsy's extraordinary high-speed harmonized guitar battle with Paul's fuzzy synth. The ending, which sounded like the whole whirling circus disappearing into the dust, was actually a trial run-through recorded at Ocean Way, live, without overdubs. It was a raucous launch for Harry and the album.

"Mayor of Simpleton"

(Andy Partridge) (Single and album track)

The switch from "Garden" to "Simpleton" came as a welcome relief. It was a perfect, sweet, innocent single of a song and became a West Coast radio hit. But it was also one of those impersonal songs that Colin scorned. It was simply the imaginary love poem claiming that the author's ill-educated mind didn't reduce his capacity to love. "Lyrically it's a little remote," admits Andy. "I'm not a backward person. I'm fairly smart. I learned nothing at school but I'm proud of being in touch with my intuition."

The song was almost ditched in its early incarnation as a slow reggae sea chantey, but the riff changed it. Dave played the Byrds-ish twelve-string while Colin had to crank up his bright-sounding Wal bass to separate the notes on the rapid bass line. "Andy came up with the bell-sounding 'collegiate' bass line but it was so fast it would blur if it sounded too bassy," he says. Colin invented the rest of the bass line itself, which is one of the finest and fastest on any XTC track. But if the playing was complex, the song was not. "I was rather embarrassed by its simplicity," says Andy.

The single was a minor hit across America and the video earned heavy rotation, causing many fans to question the inclusion of "Terry the Fish" and "Barry the Car." "They were added by Tarquin Gotch in the edit after we'd gone," says Andy. "It was a bizarre example of his humor and I have no idea what it means."

"KING FOR A DAY"
(Colin Moulding) (Single and album track)

"King for a Day" was the second single on the album and was performed on David Letterman's show. Built around an incredibly awkward guitar riff with normal tuning but two open strings, the song was a cynical view of the world, atypical of Colin's lyrical style. "It's not one of my best songs," he says. "The lyrical content took second place and it's not a centered-enough subject to write about." But the musical side fired up Dave. "I think Dave was sexed up because we were straying into Steely Dan territory," says Andy. "He even brought in a cassette where he'd programmed how he thought the chords should be." "I had to rap his knuckles because it was getting too loungy," says Colin.

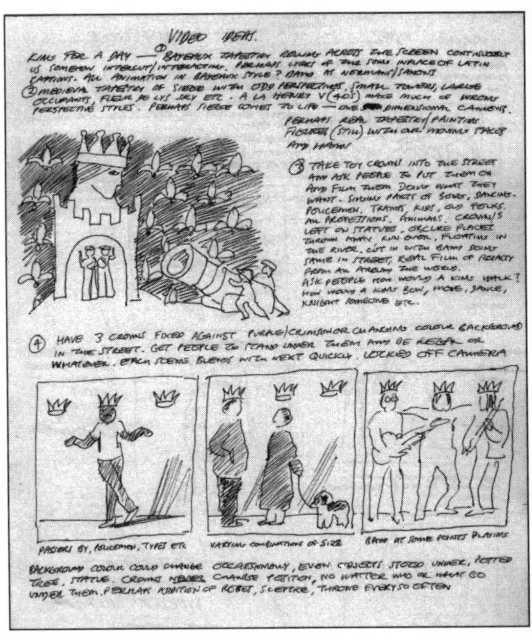

Andy's rejected video ideas for "King for a Day." (CREDIT: ANDY PARTRIDGE)

The bittersweet song found a mixed reception. Paul's production led it toward a Tears for Fears sound and one critic called it "Everybody Wants to Rule the World for a Day." But the worst came when the record company had the song remixed. "I was really embarrassed that this happened. They pulled it apart," says Andy. "The worst thing was they put it out under our banner," says Colin. "And they charged us for it," adds Andy.

"Here Comes President Kill Again"

(Andy Partridge)

For the second time, Alan Sillitoe's *Travels In Nihilon* influenced one of Andy's songs. President Nill, the nonexistent president of Nihilon, was a randomly selected photo, as likely to be a gorilla as a man. President Kill was inspired by him. "Democracy is just a pacifier," says Andy. "Presidents are supposed to be voted in but they don't really make the decisions. This is about our powerlessness over governments' ability to kill." "They're all Blue Meanies, really," adds Colin, appropriately bringing up the Beatles. "The middle section is the whole *White Album* compressed into a few bars," jokes Andy. The live-sounding arrangment was also an introduction to the brilliant trumpet of composer Mark Isham, who played throughout the album.

"The Loving"

(Andy Partridge) (Single and album track)

The opening crowd scene of "The Loving" made use of the many hangers-on, including myself, who cluttered up the control room at Summa Music. It was a song of musical excess with a simplistic message of love and peace. "It was too wordy for its own good," says Andy. "Was 'The Loving' a group, a product, or no more than an ad man's vision?" "It was a strange blend of early Tamla and stadium rock," says Colin. "Preposterous as it seems, it came out of the Supremes' song 'The Happening' and the chords of the Honeybus' 'Can't Let Maggie Go,' " admits Andy. "But it became Diana Ross on one knee at Wembley Stadium playing a screaming Les Paul." Ms. Ross's guitar parts are played here by David Gregory. "It was the nearest we ever got to sounding like Mott the Hoople," says Andy.

"Poor Skeleton Steps Out"
(Andy Partridge)

Trust Andy to find the oblique view on things. At a time when equality and human rights were an issue for the whole world, Andy decided to take the side of the poor skeletons inside us which have to put up with the brain and flesh's misdemeanors without any say in the matter. "They're the same quality of skeletons whether they belong to a truck driver or the Queen Mother," he says. "Lyrically it hit the nail upon the head."

"Musically a sort of thank-you to Captain Beefheart," he says of the clumsy, bone-clattering arrangement. But the clumsiness was carefully orchestrated, from the varisped digital cymbal sample (the legendary vacuum cleaner noise) at the start to the loose-strung opening guitar and the paper-threaded banjo guitar sound. As with "King for a Day," Colin played two basses, Wal and Epiphone and Paul Fox's singer/songwriter wife, Franne Golde, Jean McLean, and I added rear vox. Pat's drumsticks dropping onto the Ocean Way studio floor gave the song that moment of studio vérité.

"One of the Millions"
(Colin Moulding)

Colin is not one to impose his will, which is just as well in XTC. He would rather accede to Andy's wishes and leave him with the responsibility for the band. It has helped him survive, but "One of the Millions" was a personal rebuke to himself for always taking the soft option. "I think I'm giving myself a bit of a ticking off for not speaking out," he says. "I hate making a scene but there are times when you have to stand up for yourself." The idea was inspired by the bass riff, which sounded to Colin like a rocking boat. Dave augmented it with the bell-like guitar riff and Andy, for want of anything to do with the song, came up with the synthesized clarinet trill. "I felt like a spare prick at a wedding until I came up with that," he says of this rare example of Andy on keyboards.

Paul Fox squeezed the maximum out of everyone for this. Pat's drum part and tambourine were all played at the same time and Colin's vocal is one of his finest. It ended sounding less XTC than Jethro Tull, according to Colin. "Jeremy Lascelles thought it sounded like Tull and I suppose it is. I've always had a thing about them."

"Scarecrow People"

(Andy Partridge)

Andy's voice has always been a worry to him. He was several albums down before he recognized his true singing style or even admitted he could sing. "Scarecrow People" was not an easy song to sing and took two days to complete. But "Scarecrow People" remains one of his favorite songs. Andy had long had a fixation about L. Frank Baum's *Wizard of Oz*, but around this time he had become quite paranoid that he, Colin, and Dave were growing uncannily like the Cowardly Lion, the Scarecrow, and the Tin Man, respectively. But this is not a song about Colin. "It came from stumbling over a strange chord shape that sounded like the land, the American Midwest dustbowl," he says. "The idea is that junk culture people are actually dead. That junk culture makes junk people." The hillbilly nature of the sound was enhanced by a bluesy lick that was actually lifted from the bass line of Prince's "Sign O' the Times,"

Gregsy scoring in the Oakwood Apartments. (CREDIT: ANDY PARTRIDGE)

believe it or not! "I don't usually nick stuff but I wanted to do something of a similar feel," says Andy, though there was little common ground between this and Prince. The clatter was enhanced by Pat's ultratight drum heads and the scattered scrap percussion (laid out on a trestle table in Ocean Way and played at random), topped off with an exquisite guitar solo by Signor Gregory.

"Merely a Man"

(Andy Partridge)

Both Dave and Andy had doubts about this song. "I just thought it was a bit too blatant," says Andy, who nicknamed it "I'm Merely a Ham." Dave hated it, but Paul Fox insisted that it had single potential. "He had some strange ideas about singles," says Colin. In the end, after a grueling rehearsal schedule, it became one of Dave's favorites. Andy wrote it almost out of spite. Jeremy Lascelles had rejected much of the album at demo stage. "He suggested doing something like ZZ Top, the bastard! So I thought, We'll show him." They did. "It was a song for Dave," says Colin. "It was as if Paul wanted us to wear leather armbands and long hair. But where does that trumpet fit in?" The mock-baroque trumpet solo was a Gregory masterpiece, scored by him and played by Mark Isham, whose double-tracking was so perfect it had to be triple-tracked to hear the difference. The rest of the music was hard-nosed rock 'n' roll played to unrock rhythms and lyrics. "It's about government and religion and nerdy men like me," says Andy, nerdily. He had always wanted to use Jimmy Swaggart's name in a song and did so in the line "Gadhaffy Duck propelled from Jimmy Swaggart's tommy gun."

"Cynical Days"
(Colin Moulding)

Unlike the previous track, Paul Fox hadn't shortlisted "Cynical Days" for the album, but Colin fought for what he believed was his only really good contribution to the album. "It was too downbeat for Paul," says Colin. "I wasn't feeling cynical when I wrote it. I think it had more to do with the melancholy nature of the chords. Sometimes you play something and these sentiments descend on you."

The overall sound of the track was, as Colin puts it, quite "loungy" with Mark Isham's muted trumpet and Parthenon Huxley of P. Hux on tambourine, though Andy's "Twin Peaks" tremolo guitar part broke the mold. But much as Colin might love the song, it was an unlikely subject for one of life's most laid-back individuals.

"Across This Antheap"
(Andy Partridge)

Todd Rundgren rejected the swampy-sounding demo of "Across This Antheap" for *Skylarking*. Paul Fox thought it was a single for *Oranges and Lemons*. The song was written around open E tuning, as an observation of the trivialities of life and man, seen as ants. The insectlike hissing of the programmed earlier parts progressed into a monstrous arrangement with Pat having to record his drum kit in mono to make room on tape for the epic orchestral finale. Paul had wanted something slick and had continued the muted trumpet of "Cynical Days," but his plan for a bigger brass ending fell foul of budgetary restraints and he had to settle for a synthesized orchestra. Colin found it a confusing song for a bassist. "It had a bluesy verse and this 'Alfie'/'Long and Winding Road' chorus." But the Beatles reference gave him another idea. "Dave was working on strings for the end, when I suggested the sort of climbing chord section I'd heard on 'The Long and Winding Road,' " says Colin. "That end piece gets me really choked up," says Andy. "Keep taking the tablets," says Colin.

"Hold Me My Daddy"

(Andy Partridge)

Johnny Partridge got on pretty well with his son but Andy was a rebellious brat who played guitar and truant with equal fluency. The usual conflicts would arise, with young Andrew challenging his father's authority. "I had a few sticky moments with Dad as a teenager. But you can't hit your dad, whatever gets said. I was constantly seeking approval but never got it." By now a father himself, he had started to recognize his father's reactions in himself and wanted to write a song about it. "People are not supposed to write about their relationships with their fathers. But this was a song hoping to break through that." "Hold Me My Daddy" wasn't a direct open letter to his father, though he must have heard it, which worried Andy at the time. So he tried to make it lighter in feel, adding the African highlife guitar ending at demo stage. At Summa it was added to with overlapping riffs and songwriter Andy Goldmark on bass vocals. It became slicker but it really didn't work. "It sounds like the Equals playing highlife," laughs Colin. "I wanted a joyous ending so what better style to do it, but I realize now that we just can't play highlife," says Andy.

"Pink Thing"

(Andy Partridge)

Andy claimed later that he hated people writing songs about their children, but this is probably the most ignominious example imaginable. To end any controversy about this song, "Pink Thing" is about the birth of Harry Partridge *and* about Andy's penis. "Harry was called Pink Thing when he was born but I love my dick and I'm not afraid to tell people. So it's about both," says Andy defiantly.

"Pink Thing" proved XTC's ability to flip with the most flippant. "There has always been finger-pointing about us taking ourselves too seriously. But 'Pink Thing' is one of my faves," says Colin. "Light and frivolous, almost like a Martini advert." It was, however, a serious musical undertaking to get that Club Tropicana feel, especially Dave's glorious version of Joe Pass's guitar solo from "Relaxing At Camarillo."

"Miniature Sun"

(Andy Partridge)

It is perhaps ironic that this was written on the same little sampler synth as "Another Satellite," which dealt a heavy lyrical blow to Erica, the supposed other satellite. This time the song pointed at Andy as the sun around which everything revolved, changing mid-song from the positive force of life to the powerful cause of death and destruction as he discovers he's been cuckolded. It was prophetic, as some years on he would find himself in that position with his marriage.

Musically it grew into something much more complex than "Another Satellite." "Dave wanted it as a sort of jazz combo thing," says Andy. "But I thought that would be too cheesy." Nevertheless, Dave ended up playing all the guitars and keyboards with Colin on bass, Pat on drums, Paul on piano, and Mark Isham on electric midi trumpet. "Mark really rose to the challenge on this," says Andy, who played nothing, but sang the lead and added some vocal percussive sounds.

"Chalkhills and Children"

(Andy Partridge)

The "God Only Knows" majesty of the song hides the true meaning behind "Chalkhills and Children." Written chord by chord on a keyboard in his garden shed, Andy drew on the influences of

Terry Riley's music and Carla Bley's "Escalator Over the Hill" to weave a song questioning his career in light of his fatherhood.

"This is remarkably honest for me. I usually wear a mask in my writing, but this is me. Do I really want to be here? How can I be a rock god when I'm changing the baby? The whole song is questioning being in show business." "At our age, it's very unrespectable being in a band," agrees Colin. "The long-dead dreams are the teen ideals that got me into this," says Andy. "But perhaps I flew too near to the sun and my wings melted." "It's better than a real job though," says Colin. "My mum and dad don't think so," says Andy. "And I still get tradesmen coming to the door and saying, 'Still in the band? Got any bookings?' "

The lyrics formed a melancholy, dreamlike poem. The music, too, influenced by Andy's late interest in the Beach Boys, has a hypnotic quality. "I don't mind it being Beach Boysish if they don't," says Andy. "This is one of the best things I've ever written." "It's a landmark track," says Dave. "And if we're to be remembered for anything, it is this song."

IN THE SIDINGS . . .

"My Paint Heroes"

(Andy Partridge) (B side only, not on album)

As an art student, Andy's key influences were Miro, Dali, and Rousseau. Today, he hates Dali but in 1988, this home demo was a tribute to them, with a verse for each. The demo was recorded with a beat box in Andy's attic.

"Skeletons"

(Colin Moulding) (B side only, not on album)

In opposition to Andy's "Poor Skeleton Steps Out," Colin's home demo of "Skeletons" suggested that skeletons don't set you free. But it wasn't a favorite. "It doesn't connect. It was a half-hearted attempt to tell my kids to watch what they do but I'm not very good at demos." "Dave and I find that charming," says Andy.

"Ella Guru"

(Don van Vliet) (B side and album track for Captain Beefheart tribute album)

After weeks of study, and weeks of programming the drums, Andy mananged to copy Captain Beefheart's classic "Ella Guru" for a tribute album. "It was the first time I'd tried to unravel someone else's record, inspired by Dave's precise microsurgery experiments as 'Arch Marble and the Hallmarks,' " says Andy.

Colin helped Andy make it in Drive Studios, though he was no big Beefheart fan, and it came out so well, they decided to use it as a single B side, as well. "The bastard was working it all out. I didn't see any point in trying to do a different interpretation because the original was so amazing. When we met Mike Keneally of Zappa's band in L.A., he told us that it sounded like a quantized version of the original," says Andy proudly.

"Living In a Haunted Heart"

(Andy Partridge) (B side only, not on album)

Andy proudly played this vaguely Elizabethan dance to all visitors when he wrote it, including myself. But it received a lukewarm reception from the band and remained a demo. "It was written in my attic studio," he says. The attic collapsed shortly after while he was sitting on the toilet below. "It was a strangely prophetic song, really, predicting that I was going to get dumped by my wife, which I was five years later."

"The World Is Full of Angry Young Men"

(Colin Moulding) (B side only, not on album)

Originally recorded during the *Mummer* sessions but unused until now, "Angry Young Men" was a pretty straightforward song. "It's basically about the way you lash out at everything when you are young," says Colin, who seems unlikely to have lashed out at anything ever. Pete Phipps's drumming was kept from the original recording, but after *Oranges and Lemons*, XTC went into Townhouse's three studios and rerecorded the piano, guitar, and vocals.

"The Good Things"

(Colin Moulding) (B side only, not on album, also released by XTC as Terry and the Love Men on David Yazbek's XTC tribute album)

"If you can imagine a father reading from a book called *The Good Things In Life* to his children at bedtime, that just about sums it up," says Colin. "But my kids were old enough to stick one on me by this stage." The four-track demo was a contender for the album which ended up in the B bag. "I would have done it for the album," says Andy. "But the demo is very charming." They did record it in the end, under the assumed name and proposed title for *Black Sea*, Terry and the Love Men.

"Happy Families"

(Andy Partridge) (Released on the sound track of She's Having a Baby*)*

There is an old card game called Happy Families, in which players have to collect cards representing the members of four-person family units. It's a children's game, common in Britain but hardly relevant in today's divorce-addled society. Way back in the days of *Mummer*, Andy brought forth a little wordplay song about dysfunctional families based around altered names of the characters in the game—"Miss Carriage," "Master Charge," etc. But the song didn't seem to be working in the studio, so it was shelved until

Tarquin Gotch introduced XTC to filmmaker John Hughes in the late eighties. Hughes asked for the song for his film *She's Having a Baby* and the band recorded it at The Manor with engineer Glenn Tommey and mixing engineer Tom Lord Alge. "The track was ruined by my insistence on machine drums," says Andy, though you could barely hear it in the film, anyway.

Soon after, Andy was producing the Japanese artist Saeko Suzuki, who asked if he had a song to offer to the project. Once again, "Happy Families" was taken down off the shelf, though this time it was translated into Japanese.

12

THE LAST BALLOON
1991

Tarquin Gotch had a cunning plan. He had been offered a small fortune to get XTC on tour in America and it seemed like the only way he or the band were likely to make money. But Andy wasn't having it. He had retired from the road and never wanted to know its tor-

ture again. Cajoling him with luxury hotels, private jets, guaranteed rest days, large and capable crews, *cash!*, all failed to have any effect. The only way was to trick him into it.

Tarquin's plan required a little collusion with the rest of the band. The idea was to pique Andy's vanity, to play on his insecurity, to tease him into playing. So they agreed to tell Andy that they had asked Thomas Dolby to front them on tour.

It was a lie. They hadn't even asked Thomas, although his earlier application to replace Barry Andrews made the story more plausible. At first, Andy fell for the ruse and, wounded by this undermining of his power, suggested that he might come on for a couple of numbers at each gig. Tarquin jumped too soon. "You can play every number if you want!" he exclaimed. Andy realized he'd been duped and the plot collapsed. Instead they spent money touring America's radio stations, playing live but unplugged into hundreds of thousands of eager home bootlegger hi-fis. Andy wasn't so much bitter as irritated that Tarquin had tried to trick him. Tarquin was exasperated that he couldn't make any money out of managing the band. They parted on friendly terms. Andy started writing another album and Tarquin went off to work on the music of *Home Alone*.

As the eighties ended and the Berlin Wall came down, XTC settled back into Swindon, sheltered from their American success and getting on with their respective sidelines of producer/cowriter, producer/arranger/session guitarist, and homemaker. Colin did play one gig, with a Swindon fit-up band called David Marx and the Refugees, featuring a certain Barry Andrews on keys. Dave even played reunion gigs with Alehouse and Dean Gabber and His Gabberdines but he spent more profitable time producing Cud and playing for Marc Almond, Johnny Hates Jazz, and some interesting Italian sessions with Francesco Messina. Andy retired, puzzled from producing The Mission U.K. and managed more successful productions with Peter Blegvad. He produced Stephen Duffy's band, the Lilac Time, in Chipping Norton Studios and Rockfield Studios, two old studios that were new to him. He even compered a pilot children's TV quiz show, "Matchmakers," though it didn't make it to broadcast. By 1991 a new album had also been written and Andy had dubbed it *The Last Balloon*.

Short of a manager but determined to go it alone, XTC poured through their phone books and record collections for a new producer. *Oranges and Lemons* had convinced them that they preferred to record in England. Colin's wife, Carol, hated Colin being absent for months on end and he didn't much like it either. Andy also had two young kids and he didn't want to miss their childhood as Colin had missed much of Lee's and Joanne's.

Their first choice of producer, Tears for Fears hit-maker Chris Hughes, was incredibly keen but it didn't work out. So they tried Steve Lillywhite who suggested re-creating his partnership with Hugh Padgham. It looked like fun and the superstar producer Hugh Padgham was willing to compromise his usual fees. So a studio was booked and rehearsals began.

Ian Gregory suggested Dave Mattacks of Fairport Convention as drummer. He had worked with everyone on the planet and, despite his diminutive stature, could out-thump any drummer on the block. Ian had read an interview with Mattacks saying that the band he wanted to work with was XTC. So he was met with, taken to, and booked for a few weeks before his tour with Jethro Tull. Rehearsals started in a church hall in Gorse Hill, Swindon, but Steve Lillywhite didn't turn up as agreed. Before they knew it he'd pulled out to sort out his marriage with Kirsty McColl. Without the old team, Hugh backed out, as well. Suddenly, XTC was a band with a studio, a rehearsed set of songs, and no producer. In case anyone should ask, neither Dave nor Colin wanted Andy to produce.

Dave Mattacks suggested Gus Dudgeon, the veteran producer of Elton John's greatest work, David Bowie's single of "Space Oddity," the Bluesbreakers during Clapton's days, and the Bonzo Dog Doodah Band. Dave loved the idea and Andy was taken by the idea of the Bonzos' producer. So they asked him down to Swindon. Andy claims that his instincts have helped XTC survive a number of disasters. So why he decided to ignore them now, heaven knows. He knew from the moment Gus stepped out of the blue personalized Aston Martin, in his squeaking trousers, loud shirt, and deafening cologne, that Gus was wrong for the job. But as he told me later, "He was so wrong he had to be right." Andy was wrong.

Gus Dudgeon is a wonderful English eccentric; an entertainer, wit, and raconteur. His productions have sold in hundreds of millions and he has forgotten more about engineering than most engineers will ever know. But he works his way and Andy works his. Gus has a fatherly, almost schoolmasterly nature about him. Andy was a lousy scholar and now, at thirty-eight, he was even more resistant to lessons. Ironically, they had booked Chipping Norton Studio, itself a converted school, in the honey stone Cotswold market town of the same name. Barry Hammond, the house engineer, would be the engineer on XTC's album. Best of all, Colin didn't have to cook.

The sessions started well enough. Gus worked like a dog to get the best performances out of everyone, farted like a trooper, and had an endless supply of celebrity anecdotes. Barry was a great engineer. But Andy and Gus soon started to needle each other. Gus had read that Andy was awkward and made sure he wouldn't have any truck with uppity artists. Andy felt a sense of déjà vu, of Toddism creeping into the sessions. He started feeling that his ideas were being discarded and when Gus suggested that, rather than struggle with "Rook," they should dump the song, things started turning ugly.

The merry banter continued. Gus still keeps DATs of Andy's in-studio wit, worthy of bootlegging. But professionally, battle lines had been drawn. When Gus told Andy he didn't want him present at the mixing sessions in Rockfield Studios, Andy snapped. Colin and Dave agreed to stay away, hoping that they would have another *Skylarking* on their hands, but Andy wasn't happy and insisted on turning up.

The mixing sessions were very uncomfortable. Barry was willing to listen to Andy's ideas but Gus was determined to get the album done the way he felt he had been employed to do it. Andy hated the first three mixes and Virgin wasn't that happy either. For the first time in XTC's career and possibly the first in Gus's, the producer was ousted.

XTC was up the creek without a paddle. Jeremy Lascelles came to the rescue with the suggestion of Genesis mix man Nick Davis. Andy hated the music but liked the mixes and said "Yes" without even talking to the man. He was lucky. XTC liked Nick and liked the way he worked. He liked the music and although Gus was very unhappy with the results, the band and the label were happy.

The Last Balloon was supplanted by the name *Nonsuch*, the arrogant name of Henry the Eighth's fabled and lost palace. A village was flattened to build Nonsuch Palace. Egos were flattened to build *Nonsuch* the album.

NONSUCH

TALKING BETWEEN THE LINES

ANDY: *We really went 'round the houses with producers. In the early days we were hanging around with Chris Hughes. We were courting him for ages and then he went for a meeting with Virgin and that was the last we heard of it. So we went to see Steve Lillywhite and he suggested getting Hugh Padgham involved and getting the old team back together. Hugh said he'd cut his fee in half to get the job done. We had the rehearsal space and the drummer booked between tours with Jethro Tull so we had to start at that date. We rehearsed this in your front room basically.*

COLIN: *Well, we struck out the chords in my front room but we rehearsed it in Gorse Hill in the church hall in three weeks there.*

ANDY: *Oh yeah, you're right. It was taken over by this little chap who wanted to start a rehearsal stu-*

dio but I don't think it lasted that long.

COLIN: *No, I think he's lorry driving now.*

ANDY: *He's probably making a lot of money.*

COLIN: *He also had a printing business in there and all this ink wafted around.*

ANDY: *You couldn't sing for being asphyxiated with printing ink. And Steve Lillywhite didn't turn up once. Then a few days before we were due in the studios, we got a message from Virgin saying Steve Lillywhite has gone on holiday to the Caribbean with his missus.*

COLIN: *I think they were trying to patch things up.*

ANDY: *I said, "Well, at least we've got Hugh Padgham." And then a few hours later we got a fax saying Hugh doesn't want to do it anymore. So we were stuck totally high and dry. It was a case of whoever comes through the door next is producing the album.*

NEVILLE: *And who should come through the door but Gus Dudgeon.*

ANDY: *As soon as he got out of his big car, I knew he was wrong, but by that time it was difficult to go back.*

COLIN: *Gus dressed very loudly, didn't he?*

ANDY: *He should come with a volume control on his chest.*

COLIN: *I remember we had to meet him at this pub near our place and he pulled up in this huge car with GUS 92 on his number plate. There was this huge bloody thing parked up our lane and he got out all in black and white, looking like some villain from* Batman. *I was looking at him from the pub and thinking, Will I ever be able to hold my head up in the village again?*

ANDY: *Don't let him in this pub. They'll kick him to death if he comes in like that.*

COLIN: *He created quite a stir.*

ANDY: *And he gave off this headmasterly vibe.*

COLIN: *But he wasn't all bad.*

DAVE: *Gus is a man who, as an avid record collector, I'd seen on more records as engineer and producer than almost anybody. The Bluesbreakers with Eric Clapton is a milestone for any guitar player and I thought, This man has a history and is keen and available.*

ANDY: *He was superficially fun in the studios.*

DAVE: *He was a bit eccentric but he had a sense of humor and was a fund of interesting stories. I just wanted to pick his brains. I like him very much.*

COLIN: *I think that he was a good nurturer and he spent hours comping vocals and performances to make the thing sound complete. He put in long hours doing that.*

ANDY: *He did put a lot of donkey work in but ultimately he wasn't the right producer for us. He might be all right for some bands but we weren't prepared to jump through hoops. I know a lot of the problem was he'd read an interview saying I didn't get on with Todd Rundgren and thought, That Partridge must be a difficult cunt. I'll sort him out from day one. And I don't think I'm a difficult cunt. I'm just a know-what-I-want sort of cunt. He told me that he'd read that I was difficult to deal with so he was going to make sure that I did as I was told.*

DAVE: *The* Nonsuch *sessions were reasonably fluid apart from a couple of hiccups where Andy and Gus fell out. It was only when they went down to Rockfield to mix that it went wrong.*

ANDY: *Gus and I had been getting on bearably well. And then toward the end of the sessions, Gus took me on one side and rattling his gold jewelry at me, he said, "I'm afraid you won't be coming to the mixing. I don't want you there and I want to get on with things without you."*

DAVE: *He said, "You can come down when I've done the first mixes and listen and stay for the recalls," but Andy wouldn't leave his babies alone.*

ANDY: *I said, "Gus please! These are our songs. We really would like to be at the birth of our baby." But he refused. This was about a month before the end of the sessions and the relationship became very strained because of it. Eventually, we just weren't getting on.*

DAVE: *It wasn't really fair on Andy because, inflexible as he is, without his input, our records would be a lot duller.*

COLIN: *I was told to stay away* so *I stayed away because it had worked with Todd Rundgren and I didn't see why it couldn't work again.*

ANDY: *But surely you want to be around when they're your mixes. You want to have an opinion, don't you?*

COLIN: *It's handy to have an opinion once the mixes are completed but I think it's essential to have just one mind on the job.*

ANDY: *Oh yeah, well, that worked out well with Nick Davis. But what happened with Gus is the ingredients were raw. They weren't cooked. We'd shopped for all these ingredients and Barry Hammond at Chipping Norton is a great shopper. He can buy beautiful fresh ingredients for you and we had them all chopped up and ready to go, but the trouble was Gus couldn't cook this stuff and it just sounded like a bunch of raw ingredients.*

Barry Hammond at Chipping Norton.

(CREDIT: PRAIRIE PRINCE)

NEVILLE: *These days that might be considered healthy.*

ANDY: *We'd booked Rockfield Studios in Monmouth and I said, "Look Gus, I'm coming. I'm sorry, but I'm going to appear." I remember taking the train down there feeling very trepidatious. It was utterly pissing down with rain and I arrived totally drenched. Gus and Barry just sat there staring at me for five minutes not saying anything. They just didn't want me there.*

COLIN: *He did three mixes.*

ANDY: *And he sent them to Virgin and we went down there to listen and the atmosphere was just horrible. I never want to be in a situation like that again.*

COLIN: *I think "Peter Pumpkin" was the best of the three.*

ANDY: *Somebody at Virgin said, "These mixes give off icy blasts," and they did.*

DAVE: *Andy came storming back to Swindon and called Simon Draper and said, "Sack the producer." Personally, I heard the mixes and was not impressed. It was an unfortunate situation.*

ANDY: *I came back from Rockfield*

and thought, Well, what the fuck are we going to do now?

DAVE: *Nick Davis had just finished a Genesis album and was free, so he came down to Rockfield and mixed it in two-and-a-half weeks.*

ANDY: *I don't like Genesis but the things he'd recorded with them sounded great. And there wasn't time to worry about his personality or anything it was just, "Hi, I'm Andy, you must be Nick, and I'll meet you at Rockfield tomorrow." He came along and saved the day.*

COLIN: *He was a very good mixer and we had a good system going. When we were doing my songs, I virtually left him to it to mix them and we'd get to a stage where we were ready virtually to put it to tape and I'd come back and say, "I don't like this or that," and he'd make those changes and then you'd take it.*

ANDY: *He was willing to please. Nick Davis was great. He'd say, "Disappear for a couple of hours and I'll get this straight and you can give me your input." So you'd put in your input and disappear for another couple of hours. He was willing to please and that was a great feeling.*

I guess Gus and I weren't destined to get on, but despite all that, I think we ended up with a pretty fine record. The ingredients were well shopped by Barry and were beautifully mixed by Nick Davis.

DAVE: *I listen now and maybe it's a bit safe. At the time I was really excited but I still think it's a great record. I really rate it. Now that I'm in my forties that's the way my head's going. I still love the noisy stuff but that album had a touch of class about it.*

ANDY: *I'll tell you what I wanted for the sleeve for this album. But it never came to pass. You buy those records of musicals like* South Pacific *and you open up the book and you get those real Eastman color matte photographs from the film.*

COLIN: *When are we going to do one of those, I'm waiting.*

ANDY: *What I wanted was the sleeve of a fake musical from the late fifties called* The Last Balloon *which has that connotation of Jules Verne's* Around the World In Eighty Days. *You'd open up the book and there'd be these big color pictures with the band in stovepipe hats and frock coats in ludicrous colors like lilac or turquoise.*

COLIN: *Mary Poppins–type things.*

ANDY: *And we'd all be in the basket of a balloon just leaving and there'd be all these equally ludicrously clad civilians waving hankies and we'd be singing over the basket of the balloon. And then we'd fake other scenes from the musical. But it looked crap on a little CD sleeve.*

COLIN: *I've always wanted to do something like that. Of course, calling it* The Last Balloon, *you're inviting comment that it might be the last record.*

ANDY: *Yes. So, I read about this marvelous palace instigated by Henry the Eighth. They leveled a village to build this thing. But I loved the name Nonsuch Palace, meaning there is no such thing that is better than this. I thought wouldn't it be great, this is a great tongue-in-cheek, pompous title, like calling yourself the king of everything.*

COLIN: *The bestest!*

ANDY: *There was a little illustration of the palace front in this book which was perfect for the cover. Then I saw a lot of miniatures of people and I liked the way that they framed them at this time and always wrote "Aetatis Suae," meaning "at this time" they were however old. I thought it would be a nice thing to do in photographs, as well. It sort of fell together like that. The word* Nonsuch *was this big conceit really. I like the idea of this ridiculous Christmas cake of a palace because the album was like that.*

NONSUCH

ON THE TRACKS

"THE BALLAD OF PETER PUMPKINHEAD"

(Andy Partridge) (Single and album track)

Andy had produced some of the previous two Peter Blegvad albums before falling out over money matters and Peter believes that "The Ballad of Peter Pumpkinhead" is lifted from his own "King Strut." But it developed independently, from an attempt to write a Bob Dylan–style epic. Stuck for a subject he used the rotting remains of his children's Halloween jack-o-lantern, sitting on a post outside the shed studio. "I just started writing about this perfect sort of Jesusy character who just happened to have a pumpkin for a head." The character's rise to fame and subsequent persecution was certainly not unique to "King Strut."

The song was simple enough, and didn't especially inspire Andy, though it was almost as long as a Dylan epic and allowed him to exercise his fetish for amplified harmonica. But it made it through the prealbum debate and into the studio. "He'd done a pretty fleshed-out demo so it was just a matter of making this five-minute song a little more interesting," says Dave. "I just came up with some Harrisonesque guitar and we added some Hammond organ to give it that Al Kooper, *Blonde On Blonde* feel. It might have been a hit if it had been chopped down."

"It certainly wasn't earmarked as a single," says Colin. But a single it became, with a Kennedy-killing video of which Andy is justly dismissive. It wasn't a hit for XTC, but the Crash Test Dummies did pretty well when their almost-direct reading became part of the *Dumb and Dumber* movie sound track. "I was really jealous of them for that," says Andy.

"My Bird Performs"
(Colin Moulding)

It took poor Barry Hammond a whole night to loop a few bars of Dave Mattacks's complicated shuffle to a full four minutes. The band, meanwhile, had a good night's sleep. Barry did not feel good about Colin's feel-good song, "My Bird Performs."

"The song was a metaphor for feeling good about how life's going," says Colin. "I hadn't got fond memories of my thirties and naivete got me through my twenties, but as I came closer to my forties it all started to come clear and this, I suppose, was the start of that awakening in me." The awakening displayed itself in bright brassy fanfares and flourishes by Guy Barker, and a lyric awash with positive metaphors. Dave, a stickler for musical minutiae, pointed out that it sounded like "Jump" in reverse and it was suggested that the bird might be Andy, though Colin denies this. "I did get a bit of stick for the title though," says Colin. "It was all, 'Oh yeah! Your missus is good in bed, is she?' "

"Dear Madam Barnum"

(Andy Partridge)

Gus Dudgeon, man of history, had been recording the Elton John Madison Square Garden gig when John Lennon had reappeared from his "lost weekend." Stuck for a suitable crowd cheer for "Dear Madam Barnum" twenty years on, he edited in the roar as John Lennon walked onto the stage. He also had the best showman voice in Chipping Norton and was recruited to the other side of the desk to announce, "Ladies and gentlemen! Introducing for the very last time." "He speaks fluent ringmaster," says Andy.

"Dear Madam Barnum" was another of Andy's prophetic songs about the future demise of his marriage, though he was unaware of it. He wrote it as a commission for the Australian film *The Crossing* while he was producing Blur in Rak Studios. The commission was for a song which would sound good on a 1965 jukebox. "It was a sort of hybrid of Manfred Mann, the Hollies, and English folk rock, but when I found out the producers weren't going to give me any money for the song I said they couldn't have it." Dave Gregory was a fan of the song and suggested including it on *Nonsuch* and much fun was had in the production. Dave Mattacks got to use another couple of his fifty snare drums—forty-nine after Andy fell through one of them.

"Humble Daisy"
(Andy Partridge)

Since moving to Swindon's Old Town, Andy had walked his dog, Charlie Parker, over The Lawns. They were all that remained of the Goddard family estate, the house having long been ruined. It was Andy's only regular touch with nature and dog-walking pace became the meter of many of Andy's songs. "Season Cycle" was one, for instance. "Since Charlie died, I've lost touch with the seasons," he says sadly.

In late spring, The Lawns would be carpeted with daisies, inspiring the short "nature-defeating-technology" poem that became "Humble Daisy." It was a piece of near-Stratosphearic psychedelia, swamped in the Loving Spoonful and Beach Boys references, aimlessly wandering from one key to another. "It's a piece of dream logic," says Andy. "Every few bars sound like they come from different songs." "It has the same whimsy as 'Ladybird,' " says Colin. "But from the next field over," answers Andy.

"The Smartest Monkeys"
(Colin Moulding)

"This is pomp! yeah! yeah!" Two different fans were so inspired by Colin's despairing song about mankind's stupidity that they each sent Andy home videos for it. But it was the most deliberately pompous arrangement Colin had ever got away with. "It was an excuse for a bit of pomp rock," he says. "Even in the demo, I had Genesis at the back of my mind. It was all sort of Deep Purple, John Lord, Rick Wakeman." "*What!* You were actually thinking about that?!!" exclaims Andy, his punk credibility dissolving before him. The most obvious pomp sections are the Tullish strings and Dave's wah-wah-Wakeman synth solo. "It sounds like someone rubbing a bit of polystyrene against a monkey's ass," explains Colin, poetically.

"The sentiment is pretty self-explanatory," says Colin. "We all think we've come so far but there are people living in boxes in London."

Playing accurately with the echo proved a nightmare for the band and most of Andy's guitar chords were actually dropped in as samples. "I suppose the lesson is never play with your own echo," says Colin, "or you'll go deaf."

"THE DISAPPOINTED"

(Andy Partridge) (Single and album track)

Andy gets "Disappointed" with video shoots.

(CREDIT: MARK THOMAS. BY PERMISSION OF VIRGIN RECORDS.)

During a cowriting project with Terry Hall, Andy suggested "The Disappointed" as an idea for a song but Terry didn't come up with any lyrical ideas, so Andy completed it and created a catchy pop single from a miserable subject. It gave Andy his first Ivor Novello Award nomination, though he was pipped at the post by Clapton's "Tears In Heaven" and Annie Lennox's "Why."

The song's club-of-the-broken-hearted theme may signify some disillusionment about love and marriage but Andy started on a different tack. "It was going to be called 'The Disappeared' after I saw this television documentary about the mothers of the Disappeared [*Los Desaparecidos*], of Argentina," says Andy. "But I thought, This is preposterous. I know nothing about this." Not that it ever stopped Sting.

Some of the original lyric survived, "Their placards are the same with a number and a name," but the arrangement took the song into a jaunty, almost surf-pop flavor. "It sounds like the Four Seasons to me," says Colin. "And the middle section sounds like Fleetwood Mac," says Andy. "I hate the L.A. version of Fleetwood Mac. It's like prechewed food for old people." So that's his invitation to the next presidential inauguration down the pan!

"Holly Up On Poppy"
(Andy Partridge)

Holly Partridge desperately wanted a rocking horse for her fourth Christmas and as soon as she saw it and its red rosette, she named it Poppy. Andy wrote this about her, riding it in her bedroom, around a delicate fairground carousel sound which sounded, to Andy, very like a rocking horse. So those fans who think it is a song of opium can return to reality now.

Andy also had fond memories of a rocking horse and had written a previously unreleased song about one, "Ra Ra for Red Rocking Horse." There had been a huge one at his grade school which he would ride into a dream world, so long as school bully, Harold White, didn't want it first. Today, Harold runs Whites Coaches, a bus company in Swindon and Holly is a young teenager who would rather not have people know about the song and her rocking horse. "I hate people who write about their kids and I tried not to make this too chocolate-box sicky," says Andy. "I think I got away with it but I know some of Holly's teachers are fans and the last thing she needs is to have them playing this to the class." Though it would be nothing compared to Harry's teachers playing "Pink Thing"!

"Crocodile"
(Andy Partridge)

"Wouldn't it be great if we had a crocodile sound, growling as it's stomping toward you," said Andy. "I've got just the thing," said

Dave Mattacks, and produced a sample of a pig grunting! Why Mattacks had a sample of a pig probably should remain a mystery but tuning down the sample made it a little less friendly and it seemed to work.

"Crocodile," a song which combined Andy's love of theatrical staging with Dave's country show band past, was an uncanny prediction. "I didn't see it at the time, but it's as plain as day now. I was about to be unceremoniously dumped by my wife and I predicted my own future in this song." It would be a couple of years before Marianne actually walked out but things were not good, and sitting in his shed, scratching away on Holly's plastic crocodile guiro, he scraped out the rhythm of a jealous, green-eyed beast stomping through his head. In the end, the beast that overtook him was less jealous crocodile than bitter and angry black dog.

The country flavor of the song, blending English folk rockers Lindisfarne and Stealer's Wheel with a little of Gregsy's bluegrass picking, was counter-melodied with the "charming" mock Egyptian playground tune, "All the girls in Spain do a wee wee down the drain/While the boys in France do the same thing in their pants." The scene-by-scene nature of the lyric and the presence of the croc was not unlike a Punch and Judy play. It wouldn't be the first or last time he had written a song as a playlet.

"Rook"

(Andy Partridge)

The rasping cries of rooks are a distinct and dismal feature of the English countryside and a number of XTC records. Andy hadn't written a note for about two months and was beginning to despair when he found the four-chord progression that formed "Rook." "The chords just sounded so dark and I started singing nursery rhyme gibberish to them. I was so delighted and yet genuinely frightened by this thing that I'd found that I cried like a baby. I thought, My God! I'm going to die." That fear of imminent death infused itself into the lyrics, depicting the out-of-body experience of dying, of the soul rising above the world as the death knell tolls. "It scares the shit out of me even now," says Andy. "I wondered if it was going to affect people the way that it affected me, like some secret musical formula. Obviously it didn't, and it would ruin it to try to do it again."

Musically, "Rook" was important in other ways. The orchestral arrangement, string quartet, and brass, led by Dave Gregory on piano and synth, was a portent for what was to come on the next album. " 'Rook' is extraordinary," says Dave. Thank heavens Andy fought his corner with Gus, who wanted to drop the song during the difficult initial stages.

"Omnibus"

(Andy Partridge)

Hidden in the high-speed, twiddling noise before verse two of Pink Floyd's "See Emily Play," there lies a lightweight tune climbing a simple scale. It was this, decelerated, that formed the basis of the verse melody of "Omnibus." It had appeared previously in a turgid, harpsichord form beneath Peter Blegvad's poetry for the *Orpheus* project, a promising collaboration which collapsed with their friendship, but otherwise it remained unused for a long time.

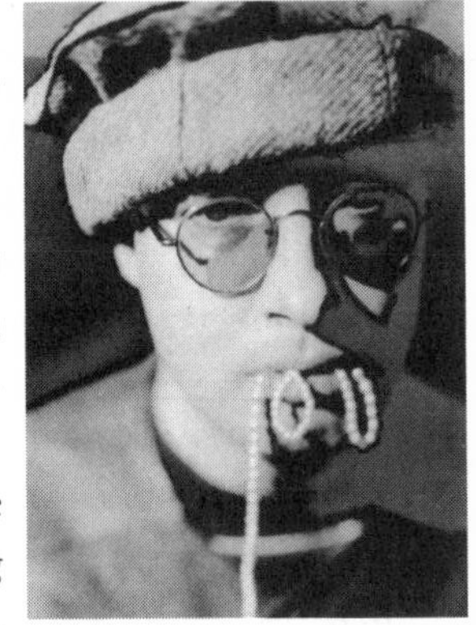

Andy hides the naked truth beneath an Afghan cap. (CREDIT: KEVIN WESTENBERG. BY PERMISSION OF VIRGIN RECORDS.)

"Omnibus" was an open letter to Dave Gregory, in West End musical style, urging him to sample the women of the world. Barring his brief relationship with Aimee Mann shortly after *Nonsuch* was released, Dave was quite the solitary bachelor. He seems happy enough that way but Andy, who cares greatly about Dave, said, "I just wanted him to find the right partner."

"Omnibus" was supposed to sound like a West End musical impression of a bus ride through London in the fifties—all jolting rhythms, clanking and hooting with a scrapyard percussion section and bell-like trumpeting from Guy Barker. It was not the sort of song Andy could compose on guitar. At that speed, it was not the sort of thing he could play on piano either, so it was left up to Dave. Whether or not he realized that he was the subject of the song, he found it incredibly hard to play. "I remember in rehearsals, the poor bloke's hands were in knots," says Andy. In the end, they returned to Andy's programmed keyboards instead.

"That Wave"
(Andy Partridge)

Just once in the sixties, the Partridge family (Swindon branch), made a change from Weymouth and went to Newquay in Devon for their summer holidays. Newquay is noted for its surf and as a child, Andy experienced one of these waves head-on and was knocked unconscious. "It probably contributed to my fear of water," he says. It also contributed to the theme of "That Wave." "It's just a wave of love knocking you senseless," says Andy. It rose from an open tuning so unusual Andy had to note it down in his book for future reference. It became a psychedelic monstrosity. "It was like a grenade going off in a psychedelic boutique and blasting cushions, feather boas, and goldfish out of the doors in slow motion," he says. "It was a blend of the sets from *Barbarella* and a scene from *Electric Ladyland*."

"I didn't know what to do with it when I first heard it," says Colin. "But once I got together with Dave Mattacks, it all fell into place with the two of us going at it like a pair of brontosauri." Dave Gregory knew that his solo at Chipping Norton hadn't cut the mustard and had anticipated Andy's call from the mixing sessions at Rockfield by writing a new one. "It was a fantastic tumbling solo that came scorching at you out of the stratosphere," says Andy, still in awe.

"Then She Appeared"

(Andy Partridge)

"Gus bullied me into doing this because he thought it was a single," he says. "Aha! Dudgeon the Bludgeon," adds Colin. "Guff Dungeon himself," says Andy. The song required some lyrical adjustment to bring it up to XTC scratch, but Gus's choice of this aerated ditty was a sensible one after the energy-sapping weight of "That Wave." "Then She Appeared" sounds like a song to Erica, but Andy says not, indeed the tricolor and Phrygian cap in the lyrics refers to the French equivalent of Britannia or Uncle Sam, whose name, by coincidence, was Marianne.

It was originally recorded by the imaginary bubblegum band the Golden (Partsy in disguise) for a cover-mounted spoof sixties flexidisc on the psychedelic music magazine *Strange Things Are Happening*, but the magazine folded before release. Gus revived the pretty "Then She Appeared" with its nonsense lyrics, adding festive-sounding Gregorian twelve-string guitar and a bizarre "ripping" percussion track. It certainly sounded like a single, but Andy thought it was "inconsequential fluff," and it didn't make the grade.

"War Dance"

(Colin Moulding)

"War Dance" showed a political side of Colin which he rarely exposes in public. "It started life in 1983," he says. "I brought it up for *Mummer* with different music, in reponse to the patriotic fervor drummed up by the Falkland War. Every so often Britain gets this war fever." The Gulf War gave the song new poignancy.

In the studio, Nick Davis completely altered the initial mix, though Colin kept in his shuffling shaker to carry the song. Andy's biggest disappointment was the synthesized clarinet. "I wish we'd done it with a real clarinet," he says. "It's too exposed. It sounds like a singing penis."

"Wrapped In Grey"

(Andy Partridge) (Album track and aborted single)

Somewhere out there are about 5,000 singles of "Wrapped In Grey." "I remember hearing this on the car radio, riding across the Golden Gate Bridge and feeling really proud. The boy from Penhill made good," says Andy. "It was one of our finest moments," says Dave. "It was the great cot death single," says Andy. "They pressed it and then withdrew it. Such a shame. It was the last straw in making me want to leave the Virgin label."

Andy was so proud of this prospective single that he drew a storyboard for a video, based on a Lottie Rheinegger shadow film, but he didn't play anything on the recording. "Lazy sod," says Colin. The song was another step toward the orchestral with a lovely string arrangement by Herr Gregory. Gregsy also played the Bacharach piano and Dave Mattacks and Colin just blended into the rich *Pet Sounds*–influenced mix. "The music is like sitting in the barbershop in 1960 and listening to the 'Light Programme' on the radio," says Andy. It does up until the Badfinger-ish coda, at least. "My dad listened to the coda and said, 'Now you've gone and spoiled it!' " says Andy. "Trust Johnny to slap me down."

"The Ugly Underneath"

(Andy Partridge)

There is a hint of an earlier XTC in "The Ugly Underneath," an angry but simple verse rolling into an ecclesiastical chorus with a snide lyric riding over Dave's electric razor E-bow guitar orchestra—"Like a turd on a velvet cushion," as Andy so delicately puts it. The theme combines Andy's disillusionment with politicians in general and his marriage specifically. "It's lots of things smashed together. You get married and it's all sweetness and light, then you move in together and you start to see the ugly side. It's the same with politicians. During the election it's all honey smiles and sweet talking and then you find you've voted in a rottweiler and the one it's going to bite is you."

The song is very short at well under three minutes and would have been shorter had it not been for Dave's organ-izing at the end. "It's a trifle self-indulgent at the end," says Colin. "The song was quite short so we thought we'd take different elements of the song and do a bit of a J. S. Bach on it." "We wanted a beautiful second half to balance the ugliness of the music and lyric in the first. It's an organ extravaganza to summon up the ghost of John Paul Jones's haircut," says Andy. "The John Holmes Organ Centre would have been proud of it."

"Bungalow"

(Colin Moulding)

Driving to London with Andy and Dave, Colin heard Andy's tape of "Sparky's Magic Piano" and was so taken with the unusual diminished chord change under the voicing of "Sparky" that he decided to work it out. The changes over the single chord, he discovered, gave him the rhythm of the word *bungalow*. That, plus his love of Noël Coward's "Let's Fly Away," and childhood summer holidays in Weymouth, "Swindon-On-Sea," gave him "the best thing Colin's ever written," according Andy. "I wish I'd written it." "His demo was even better," says Dave.

The recording summed up everything about the glorious awfulness of a British seaside holiday. The organ was typical of the clubhouse cabaret organ in British holiday camps. "The clarinet sound was pure Acker Bilk and 'Strangers On the Shore,' " says Colin, though he later discovered that the clarinet riff was more like "Postcard" by the Bonzo Dog Doodah Band, a track Andy used to play to Colin years earlier. "I also hammed up the voice to sound a bit Noël Coward. And then Dave found the Welsh male voice choir sample. When I heard it, I almost went through the ceiling and screamed, 'That's it! Put that in!' " The choir was augmented by the band, singing along in best male voice choir impressions. Even Dave Mattacks's stiff drum pattern evokes the sound of some cheap combo warming up in the camp club. "It's really a little film. A bit of Mike Leigh-On-Sea," says Andy.

"It was the only song I've written on piano apart from 'Washaway,' " says Colin. "It was really my parents' dream to save all their lives and retire to a seaside bungalow. Of course, they never did."

"Books Are Burning"
(Andy Partridge)

The extraordinary reaction to Salman Rushdie's book *The Satanic Verses* shocked Britain. For depicting a love scene with the prophet Mohammed, the former advertising copywriter was placed under a worldwide *fatwah* (religious license to be killed) issued by the Ayatollah Khomeini to the entire Muslim world. Rushdie had to go into hiding as British Muslims were seen burning the book and effigies of him in the streets of London.

To Andy, the sight of burning books was especially frightening. "Heinrich Heine said, 'Whenever books are burned men also, in the end, are burned.' I love books. They are above criticism. They are the wisdom hotline to history. They are our roots and we must never lose that." This passion showed through in the lyric Andy wrote, perhaps overdramatizing a bit by comparing the smell of burnt books with that of burnt human hair. But the words waited for a song until one day when Andy was "dicking around" with the chords of the Beach Boys' "I Get Around." There he found the chord changes that brought out the structure of "Books Are Burning."

The arrangement of the song was simple enough. It was run at the majestic pace of a death march, speeding up for the climactic middle eight. Originally, Andy had planned a "Hey Jude" drawn-out ending, but Gus and Dave suggested the uncharacteristic dueling guitar solos of Messrs P. and G. (possibly the best opportunity to compare Dave's precise and intricate style with Andy's more instinctive playing) before fading with the remains of the "Hey Jude" idea, sung by XTC, Mattacks, Dudgeon, and myself.

"Books Are Burning" was the first song XTC had performed live on BBC TV in many years. Sadly, the performance on *The Late Show* was marred by the BBC's legendary inability to get a decent sound for live bands. "It sounded appalling," says Andy. "We ran through seven times to get their camera angles right but they wouldn't let us sort out the sound. What could you do but go and get drunk?"

IN THE SIDINGS . . .

"Down a Peg"

(Colin Moulding) (B side only, not on album)

As was often the case, B sides would be home demos, more to give something special to the fans than to save money, though doubtless that helped. "Down a Peg" was one of Colin's home demos, and although he laughs at the suggestion that it is aimed at Andy, he says it is not. "It's probably more to do with going home and being brought back down to earth by your kids. Having a family is a great leveler. You can easily let all this pop nonsense go to your head and it's good to be taken down a peg when you get home."

"Gribouillage" and "Somesuch"

The French Virgin label released "Gribouillage," the first five demo recordings for *Nonsuch*, as a limited edition CD for the fans. That, in turn, inspired Andy to propose *Somesuch*, with all the demo tracks for *Nonsuch* in the identical order. Harry Partridge, then about four, was also commissioned to draw the sleeve, but Virgin lost the tapes and they have never been heard of since.

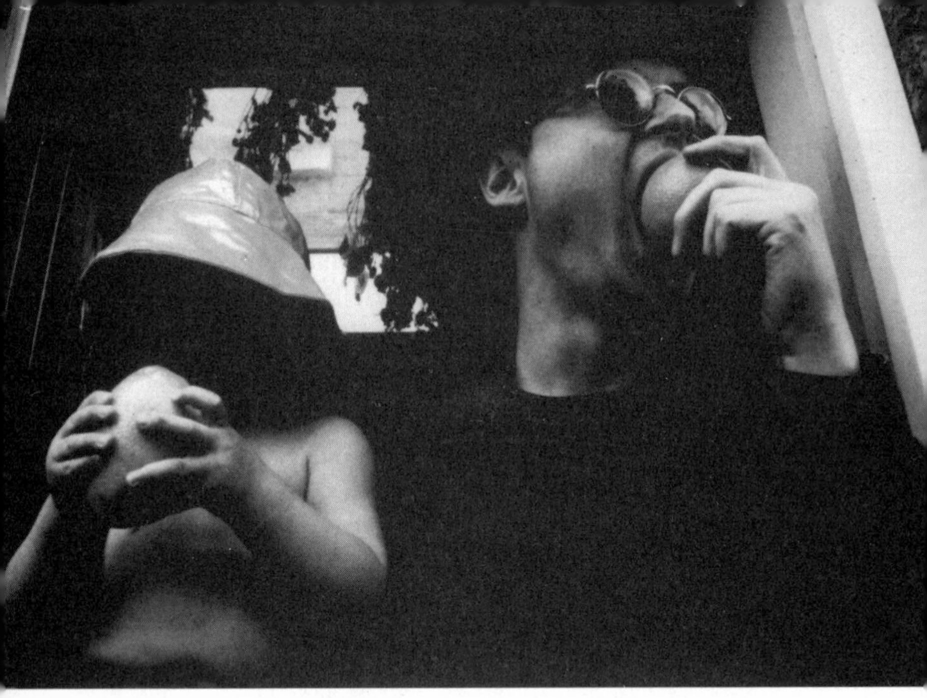

Oranges and lemons, Andy and Harry. (CREDIT: THE ANDY PARTRIDGE COLLECTION.)

"Cherry In Your Tree"

(Andy Partridge) (Released on Out of This World with Carmen San Diego, *children's game show sound track)*

Every song on the ill-fated bubblegum album project was about sex. "Cherry In Your Tree," supposedly by the "famous" sixties band the Captain Cooks, was an obvious example. Yet it was taken, in a slightly softened form, for the second children's album to be released in conjunction with the American game show "Where In the World Is Carmen San Diego?"

David Yazbek, XTC fan and friend, was musical supervisor for the show and called Andy to ask for a track for the album. He offered "Cherry In Your Tree" and it was accepted so long as the line "Making love with you" was altered to "Baking love with you," which actually fitted better with lines like, "Roll it in the flour now/Knead it for an hour now," all harmless, innocent fun on the face of it.

Dave Gregory was away on tour with Aimee Mann and so missed the session. Andy was visiting Erica in New York and as David Yazbek lives there, Colin flew over and David produced the track with They Might Be Giants drummer, Brian Docherty, at Kampo Studios on the Bowery. "It certainly wasn't in the sixties pop style that the Captain Cooks were supposed to do it in," says Andy. "More sort of cheesy contemporary really." So the resultant cheesecake was baked under the name XTC.

13

THE HISTORY OF THE MIDDLE AGES

1998

In the first fifteen years of recording, XTC's royalties had never outstripped their advances. During the boom and bust of the Thatcher years, XTC just stayed bust. The court and accounting costs in the late eighties had cost upwards of $800,000, borrowed from Virgin against future earnings. To secure this loan, they agreed to a deal that no self-respecting music lawyer should have recommended. Most debut acts expect royalties of around 12 percent of retail price, minus around 30 to 40 percent of questionable deductions concocted by record company lawyers. This isn't a great deal, but success should give an artist some negotiating clout to improve future deals.

Despite increasing record sales and international acclaim, XTC's lot had actually worsened. After deductions, they were lucky to earn enough to pay the record producer's royalties. The only income that could keep them alive was publishing earnings for writing the songs and only a small part of that was passed on to Dave. They had sold over three million albums and attracted huge income from radio performance but had seen almost nothing for it. Andy calculated the total turnover on XTC music to be around $50 million. His figures may have been wrong, and much of the real amount didn't end up in Virgin's coffers, but the band was understandably sick of being poor while others profited from their efforts.

Dave on Hammond as Haydn Bendall looks on.

(CREDIT: NEVILLE FARMER)

Nonsuch was not as successful as *Skylarking* or *Oranges and Lemons*, but it sold in the hundreds of thousands. By the early nineties, in contradiction to the John Major economy, XTC finally looked like breaking even, so they decided to ask Virgin for a more equitable deal. Despite being the longest-lasting signing on the label, they had few friends remaining and Virgin wouldn't bend far enough.

In an attempt to maintain positivity, Andy proposed a humorous aside project for the band and Virgin, a bubblegum pop compilation by spoof sixties bands. He and Colin wrote an album's worth of sixties-style sugar pop songs and suggested that Virgin announce that they had purchased the "famous" Zither Records catalogue and would be releasing their "classic hits": "Candy Mine," "All Aboard for Bubble Land," "Visit to the Doctor," "I'm the Kaiser," "It's Snowing Angels," and "Cave Girl" amongst others. The artists would be called Anonymous Bosch, the Four Posters, Herbert Fountain, the Brighton Peers, the Captain Cooks, the Twelve Flavours of Hercules, and suchlike. Virgin were completely baffled by the idea and turned it down flat.

After that, the gloves came off. XTC asked to leave the label but Virgin refused. So they went on strike. Possibly the only act to do so since Michelle Shocked. This naturally endeared them greatly to the label and a pointless five-year stalemate ensued.

In the meantime, Andy Partridge's wife, Marianne, left him for another man and a messy and painful divorce followed. After years of waiting, Erica Wexler finally moved in. Andy also went through a terrifying period of partial and total deafness through ear infections. Colin Moulding's wife, Carol, suffered years of illness that kept Colin at home, making stained glass rather than writing songs. He played for others, though, recording a Sam Phillips album and with the L'Affaire Louis Trio. Dave Gregory bought several guitars and a new but modest house and fell in and out of love with Aimee Mann. Dave and Andy spent their extracontractual activities producing, arranging, playing, and cowriting with the Chills, Mark Owen, Martin Newell, Verve Pipe, Harold Budd, Stephen Duffy, Cathy Dennis, Terry Hall, Aimee Mann, Herbert Groenemeyer, Lloyd Cole, Iva Davis, Nicky Holland, and Chris Difford. Andy even guested, for a rendition of "Collideascope," onstage with Dave and Aimee. He wasn't great and his bowels were "not my best friend that day," but he actually enjoyed it.

While XTC remained silent, the fans communicated with each other on the Internet (two unofficial XTC sites being in the top five visited on the Web) and through Pete Dix's fan club, The

Little Express, and at XTC conventions. David Yazbek coordinated and produced *Testimonial Dinner*, a worthy tribute album of XTC music by numerous signed admirers, including three mysterious blokes from Swindon called Terry and the Love Men. Richard Pedretti-Allen produced the semipro counterpart, "Chalkhills Children," as a tribute from the fans. The BBC released *Drums and Wireless*, a collection of XTC radio sessions. Virgin and Geffen each released compilations, *Fossil Fuel* and *Upsy Daisy Assortment*. The Crash Test Dummies found success with a cover of "The Ballad of Peter Pumpkinhead" in the movie sound track of *Dumb and Dumber* and Robbie Williams rerecorded "Making Plans for Nigel" for an audience that wasn't even born when it was written. XTC demos for the next album were leaked everywhere to an eager bootleg market.

Hopeful of a resolution to the dispute, Andy continued writing enough for an album every two years which Virgin expected to release. The first would have been rich and orchestral, the second hard-nosed and electric. But the songs remained in demo form, adding to the legal problems as submitting the demos to Virgin gave them the publishing rights. But they were useless without being released by XTC and there was no shifting them. Eventually, Virgin surrendered, exasperated. The two albums became the stuff of legend.

By the time their new manager, ex-tour manager Paul Bailey, had tied up the new deal with Cooking Vinyl, Andy had decided to combine them into a double album. Colin and Dave didn't agree. They felt that the renaissance of XTC should be punchy and perfect. A concept album almost. Record companies and possible producers for the project all seemed to side with Colin and Dave. But democracy being what it is in XTC, Andy won out. Twenty-one songs would be recorded, possibly split into electric and acoustic/orchestral halves. The producer brave enough to handle the project would be Haydn Bendall, a blast from the past. The man who recorded XTC's *3D EP* in 1977. Drummers lined up to play, including Elvis Costello's tub-thumper Pete Thomas and Prince's Michael Ball, but relistening to *Skylarking* for this book found Prairie Prince reinstated.

With such a large number of songs, a lot of expensive orchestral sessions, and a relatively small budget, it was important to find a cheap but competent studio and thanks to his relationship with Squeeze's Chris Difford, Andy thought he had found the answer in the rural splendor of Chris's Sussex home studio. In late 1997, XTC and Haydn gathered to choose songs. A loose form of democracy prevailed, whittling down Andy's forty-odd tracks to seventeen and Colin's six down to four. But like all good third-world democracies, the dictator cried foul when the voting process between the band, Haydn, and Paul Bailey saw some of his favorites voted down. Eventually, an uneasy consensus was found. What they all agreed was that this was the best collection of songs XTC had ever gathered and that, after a long silence, the album had to be beyond all expectations. After a week or two of preproduction in Haydn's Kent programming suite, they moved into Chris Difford's. It was a disaster. The studio wasn't ready and nothing went to plan. After three weeks with very little recorded they walked out, only to find their tapes impounded until they paid up money they did not believe they owed. Livid, they decided it was easier to start again. They instructed Paul Bailey to hold back Prairie Prince till the new year and book Chipping Norton Studios. This would make a big dent in the budget and Haydn's desired mixing sessions in Abbey Road's extravagantly reconstructed Studio Three seemed more of a pipe dream.

In the end, the record would not be finished by the time this book had to be submitted. So the remainder of the story—the track listing, the credits, the recording anecdotes, and even the album title—will have to be left to the sleeve notes.

"?"

TALKING BETWEEN THE LINES
A CONVERSATION ABOUT THE AS YET UNNAMED NEW ALBUM

ON FALLING OUT WITH VIRGIN

ANDY: *You can strike if you're a coal miner but you're not supposed to if you're a group. But we went on strike from 1992 until 1997 and in the end, Virgin let us go out of sheer embarrassment. They could have given us a decent deal but they wouldn't and they weren't going to let us go, so the only power we had was not to record because any belch or fart we recorded they owned.*

COLIN: *The Virgin stuff was all done with lawyers and I stayed out of it. But I was annoyed because they possessed a lot of Andy's new songs, which he'd sent them on demo. It took a lot to get them back. But it was time to say either we're not going to make another record with you or lump it and we weren't prepared to lump it. It held up our careers for a good six years which was very frustrating.*

ANDY: *I don't resent Virgin giving us a crappy deal but I resent them sitting on us for five years. That was plain vindictive. We were the longest-serving band on the label, we even outlasted Richard Branson. But they never knew what to do with us. In the beginning they tried pushing us as teen fodder. We were young and skinny but our music didn't appeal to many sixteen-year-old girls, at least not normal ones. Then they tried the weird mold but that didn't work because we have our straight pop side. Then we wouldn't play the album-tour-album-tour game so that confused them further. At least we're not going through the square peg in a round hole business in the future, or perhaps in our case, a beautifully baroque, Renaissance, filigree shell into a square slot in a sheet of Formica. We're not an obviously marketable item. We're like HP sauce or Marmite. You either love us or hate us.*

ANDY: *I had the five most difficult years of my life. I went through a period of deafness through an infection in my middle ear. I thought it was something in my brain. The pain was so intense that I was banging my head against a wall and all of a sudden the pain subsided and I felt this wetness on my neck. Blood was pouring from my ear. My eardrum had burst out and I was deaf in my right ear for six weeks. My other ear was blocked from the flu that caused the infection so I was totally deaf for three weeks. Luckily it healed. Then I wore my prostate out. I either drank it or fucked it to death.*

Divorce was very tough, if not a little uninspiring. I think most good music is either made out of extreme depression or extreme joy. The divorce was extreme depression and getting together with Erica at last was extreme joy. The five years put me through the mill but it created these great songs.

COLIN: *The first three years I didn't write a song. I felt stale. I wanted to write something that was different to what I'd done before and reject a lot of stuff. I think it did me a power of good. I think I've got a fresher approach now, less earnest and a lot more light and breezy.*

ANDY: *Because we couldn't work as XTC, Dave and I were busy doing other projects. He played on the Chills and Mark Owen albums and toured and recorded with Martin Newell. I produced Martin's first album in the back garden while our marriages were falling apart.*

I wanted to do the bubblegum album, but when I played the demos to Virgin it was like the scene from The Producers *when they first heard "Springtime for Hitler." Their mouths were dangling open. So I went on to make a sensible album with Harold Budd and cowrote songs with lots of people. Cathy Dennis said she wanted to write with England's best two songwriters and chose me and Ray Davies which was an honor. He told her he was forty and she believed him!*

I tried producing Blur but it didn't work out. They said it came out sounding like XTC. What do they expect? But I like what they do. They had the balls to cite an uncool band like us as a major influence.

COLIN: *Carol was pretty ill for a while but she's much better now. I spent most of the time home building and I did a bit of stained glass, as well.*

ANDY: *He did a few commissions.*

COLIN: *It's quite rewarding but it does take up a lot of time and space. Perhaps I'll take it up again when I'm old and decrepit and have to have everything brought to me on a tray.*

ON COMEBACKS AND LONG ALBUMS AND CHOOSING SONGS

COLIN: *I sometimes wonder whether it was wise to put so many tracks on the record.*

DAVE: *It's just stupid.*

COLIN: *Twelve would have been easier. We've got to come back with something wildly different and the orchestral stuff is more outside our usual field. The electric ones are more old XTC.*

DAVE: *But it's the best collection of songs we've had as a bunch. They're absolutely fantastic.*

COLIN: *One fateful afternoon in Andy's living room, Haydn came down and listened to all the tunes, and we voted on which songs would go on. But it was already deemed by Andy that we should do at least twenty. Then at the end of this Nuremburg trial, Andy said, "Hang on. Some of my favorite songs only got two votes and I want to do them." Dave said, "Why don't you do a solo album then?" but the glare from Andy was enough to answer that.*

ANDY: *We had forty songs which were really the orchestral album we should have made in '93 and the noisy guitar album we should have made in '95. We're trying to do something creative with the two strands now. It's really a two-headed monster.*

ON HAYDN BENDALL

COLIN: *It's great working with Haydn. He's so adept at everything. He's done such a variety of work and he knows his onions and keeps a tight ship.*

NEVILLE: *Such diversity of metaphors.*

ANDY: *His CV reads like a telephone directory: Kate Bush, Elton John, Tina Turner, Be-Bop Deluxe, Mrs. Mills, and films like* The Last Emperor *and* Keep the Aspidistra Flying. *He used to be Mr. Engineer at Abbey Road so he's done it all. And he's funny.*

NEVILLE: *And a masochist!*

COLIN: *He wants to mix in Abbey Road but we'll be there a month, which will cost about £30,000, so I don't know where the money's going to come from.*

NEVILLE: *Sounds familiar.*

ON ALBUM TITLES

ANDY: *I've no idea what it's going to be called. They usually leave it to me and say, "No. Don't like that!" There's a name Gregsy has forbidden me to use. I had a long conversation with him about what it was like to be middle aged and he said, "I'm not middle aged." But I liked the phrase* middle age *and when things were going wrong at Chris Difford's, I took a long walk around Peasemarsh and thought a really honest title would be* The History of the Middle Ages. *I thought it would show the reasons behind many of the songs and the fact that we'd all reached middle age, except Dave, who's just past puberty. He put it under the heading of "not doing us any favors."*

NEVILLE: *So are there any other ideas?*

ANDY: *I thought about* Wonder Annual *but the song got voted out. They didn't like* Bloop! *either.*

NEVILLE: *Can't think why!*

ANDY: *I wanted a three-dimensional sleeve of something being dropped into water but that would have been too expensive.*

NEVILLE: *So you fight for your fair share of royalties for five years and spend them all on artwork, huh?*

ANDY: *Yeah, okay. So it won't be* Bloop! *It'll probably be something dull and witless.*

COLIN: *I've got my ideas, but I'm keeping them close to my chest.*

"?"

ON THE TRACKS

(Provisional Track Listing at Time of Writing—Who Knows What Might Happen During the Recording?)

"River of Orchids"

(Andy Partridge)

Nonsuch piqued Andy's interest in orchestral sounds, as "Rook," "Wrapped In Grey," "Bungalow," and "Omnibus" hinted. It pushed him into the purchase of a collection of orchestral samples for his modest shed studio, which he would blend into loops and riffs. From these came the inspiration for a number of the tracks for the new album, including this epileptic, cyclical nursery rhyme. "I just hit upon this wonderful two-bar phrase and let it repeat around and around. I couldn't stop dancing for hours to it and hundreds of songs came into my head," says Andy. Harkening back to the subject of "Roads Girdle the Globe," he had picked on his pet hate, the automobile, but this time there was no irony in the lyric. "It's much more direct than 'Roads Girdle the Globe,' " he says. "It says push your car off the road and let's spread the highways with grass and flowers. I just thought it would be nice to walk into London on my hands on a river of flowers. This from a man who will never learn to drive." Of course, it is eighty miles from Swindon to London so such a trip might be a little unwise for a man who needs to take care of his hands. Harold Budd already uses the song in lectures in Arizona, as an example of modern cyclical composition.

Colin on Vox bass in Chipping Norton. (CREDIT: NEVILLE FARMER)

"Green Man"

(Andy Partridge)

Dave's playing on Mark Owen's *Green Man* album is bound to stir up conspiracy theories about this track, but it was written long before Mark's release. The fertility symbol of the Green Man, like Mummers and Nonsuch Palace, harvest festivals, and maypoles, is all part of the Partridge passion for British history. The tune was a continuation of his love of nursery rhymes. What appears to be a hint of Middle Eastern influence in the arrangement is apparently nothing of the sort. "It's Vaughan Williams with a hard-on," he explains. "It's a percussive pagan piece with this long glorious 'Blue Remembered Hills' string line to carry the melody," clarifying things still further. "The song has come out as sung by a randy father figure—part fatherly, part horny. I suppose that's the Green Man." Obvious, really!

"FRUIT NUT"

(Colin Moulding)

In America, men have dens, rooms beneath or attached to their houses in which they can live out their childhood obsessions and make a mess in the process. In Britain, where houses are considerably smaller, men have sheds at the bottoms of their gardens. Herein lies escape from the perils of adult manhood. Herein seeds are germinated, models are glued, wood is carved, music is recorded, racing pigeons are nurtured.

Colin's is the only XTC garden large enough to warrant an interest in prize vegetables, but he leaves that to a hired gardener. So "Fruit Nut" is not directly about him. "It's a daft little piece about growing fruit and vegetables," says Dave Gregory. "But it's more than that," says Colin. "It's about eccentricity, about husbands of long-suffering wives who are building sheds all over the country to house train sets or whatever."

Frightfully English, with a hint of the Laurel and Hardy theme tune, "Fruit Nut" is a perfect example of the small town intimacy that Colin loves in his songs, though the acoustic nature of the demo is deceptive. "I don't believe in completing the picture in the demos. That's where Andy and I differ. I like the element of surprise. This reminded me a bit of 'Hi Ho Silver Lining' with its 'trompiness' and I wouldn't mind some chugging cellos and some beefing up with electric guitar." But whether that is what will happen remains to be seen.

"EASTER THEATRE"

(Andy Partridge)

If there is a song that demonstrates how far XTC has come in the twenty years since "Science Friction" it is "Easter Theatre." "I came through Andy's back gate one day and I could hear Andy playing this dirgy riff in his shed, like something by Kurt Cobain, over and over," says Dave. "I opened the door and he seemed really excited but I wasn't impressed by it. The next time I heard it, it was fucking amazing. I couldn't believe what he'd done. 'Easter Theatre' is the cornerstone of the album and a wonderful piece of modern classical music."

The arrangement is almost reminiscent of Michael Nyman or even Benjamin Britten, though still a pop song. Andy knows it's good. "I just hope we can do it justice because it's one of the best things I've ever written. I'm being a real protective mother hen about it at the moment and until it works, I won't believe it exists." Propagated from a seedling chord progression of oboe and bassoon samples, which sounded to Andy as though it burst from the ground, "Easter Theatre" celebrates the life cycle through a theatrical performance. "I have books of old stage sets at home, hence the sleeve for 'No Thugs In Our House,' " he says. "The lyric might seem confusing at first, 'Now the son is dead the father can be born,' but the other way 'round it would be too obvious. It is self-explanatory. It just says one son dies and another is born which will itself become a father."

"I'd Like That"
(Andy Partridge)

Add a few bubbles and this might pass as a McCartney/Dukes of Stratosphear tune. It even features Andy's pantomime thigh slapping to mark out the time, a feature of the demo Haydn wanted kept. "I'd Like That" started as an ode to a sunflower but it evolved into a love song celebrating his relationship with Erica, comparing them to famous couples from history: Hector and Helen of Troy, Victoria and Albert, Nelson and Hamilton, Partridge and Wexler! "I had the sunflower hook line but it was just a tail with no donkey, so I wrote the rest of the song and pinned on the tail. It ended up working backward to my brand-new relationship with Erica."

"Frivolous Tonight"
(Colin Moulding)

Imagine Colin Moulding, Ray Davies, Noël Coward, and Cole Porter meeting at a suburban wine and cheese party and writing a sing-along song, while the wives gossip about their husbands' hairy backs. That about sums up "Frivolous Tonight." "It's very provincial and small and that's what I like," says Colin. "As the evening wears on it just gets worse. It's what people like to do; talk about the stupidest things. But it's not a venomous lyric. It's celebratory." "It's a wry piece of commentary," says Dave. "A bit of Ray Davies and Syd Barrett." "It's probably the best thing I've ever written. It's more lyrically and musically complete," says Colin, characteristically dampening his self-praise by sharing the credit. "It's in the mood of Nöel Coward's 'I've Been to a Marvelous Party.' You can't fault him and Cole Porter lyrically. And it's probably in the Kinks camp, as well. Ray Davies is certainly one of the best pop song writers of this century. His songs transcend the ages." And what about yours, Colin? What about yours?

"The Last Balloon"
(Andy Partridge)

Contrary to discussions on the Internet, "The Last Balloon" makes no reference to "Jew children, Jew women, or Jew menfolk," though Andy's enunciation of "climb aboard you children" could be clearer. "The Last Balloon" is a sad and utterly beautiful plea for the next generation to take this last opportunity to save humanity, to escape the system mankind has created and start afresh. "I want the next generation not to make the same mistakes as us and our parents. There's no need to bring furs, jewels, guns, and knives. As the last few lines say, the children should drop us from the balloon like so much sand if they're going to escape our prejudices and faults. They have to *not* listen to us."

"Knights In Shining Karma"

(Andy Partridge)

The gruesome pun of the title was originally one of the band names for the shelved bubblegum pop project and though punning is the lowest form of wit, Andy couldn't let it lie. From the title, and an afternoon "dicking around" with the chords of Macca's "Blackbird," came a new chord structure and a lullaby telling Andy to cheer up in the face of his divorce. "I think I'm basically a good person," he says. "I'm probably a better person than the members of the Christian Right who wanted to do away with me over 'Dear God.' The song basically says that your good karma will protect you. That rather drippy sentiment keeps me bouyant." Like "Blackbird," simplicity was the key to the demo, so the original guitar from the shed appears on the album.

"Boarded Up"

(Colin Moulding)

Colin's five-year sabbatical from songwriting made him determined to make a new start. His newfound interest in the subtleties of easy listening drove him away from the jagged, jarring prestrike XTC. But "Boarded Up" came along before this change of heart and has a Swindonian lyric more typical of *The Big Express*. "It's not characteristic of what I've been doing lately," he says. "It's a dour but effective piece of world weariness," adds Dave. "It is quite miserable," Colin agrees. "It's a lament for Swindon really. Cut off from civilization. A town bypassed by the arts. It's got some lighter lyrical moments, 'Music venue has had its day/Death Watch Beatle band moves in to play.' I want it cut to the sound of someone walking across floorboards. Like people walking across an empty hall."

"Harvest Festival"
(Andy Partridge)

Why, in his forties, Andy should start writing about schooldays is something of a mystery. Both "Playground" and "Harvest Festival" echo images of childhood, with "Harvest Festival" waxing wistful about what happened to the girls he loved at school and confusing the school ceremony of harvest festival with that of marriage. "There were several girls at school who gave me a look across the hall that would totally inflate me for months after," he says. "There was an incredible radioactivity that came from that look. Then, years later, I'd see them married in the local newspaper and wonder what might have happened if it had been me. I suppose someone seeing my wedding photo in the paper might have thought the same thing about Marianne."

Harvest festival remains an abiding memory for many British kids, coming after the summer holiday at the start of a new school year. Pupils would bring in produce to display at the festival and then give to local old people. Originally this would have been fruits and vegetables, but postwar Britain's fanaticism for processed foods meant cans soon formed the majority of the offerings, as with the tins of peaches mentioned in the lyrics. "Harvest festival was a pagan celebration hijacked by Christianity," says Andy. "I always used to wonder what it was about and I'm sure many of the teachers didn't know. I think they just used to steal the best stuff from the display and give the rubbish to the old folks."

The memory is enhanced on the demo by the fat-fingered school piano chords and recorder solo and the almost hymnal chorus line. Andy wants to add the sound of a school hall full of children standing for prayers, but Colin is nervous about the song becoming a parody. "I don't want it sounding too Clive Dunn," he says in reference to a twee seventies U.K. number one, "Granddad." But Andy wants to capture that special atmosphere. "Part of the confusion of the festival was singing those hymns that you didn't understand yet bathing in the mystical glow that they left on you." The song emanates the same warm glow.

"Your Dictionary"

(Andy Partridge)

There are odd occasions when Andy doesn't get his way. Not often, mind you, but given the choice, he would not have included "Your Dictionary" on the album. Andy's divorce from Marianne was messy and acrimonious, thanks to zealous lawyers and a system devised by but not for human beings. At the time he was eaten up with fury, feeling, perhaps unfairly, that he was the only injured party. "I was extremely bitter and angry about being betrayed in my marriage," he says. "Your Dictionary" captured that mood succinctly and viciously, emphasized by the sinister string quartet and acoustic guitar of the arrangement. "I don't feel that way now and didn't want to use this song as a rusty can opener to prize open old wounds with Marianne. The words are a little petulant, spelling out bad words but given a different connotation. It's a noncommunication song because the nub of our marriage breakdown was noncommunication."

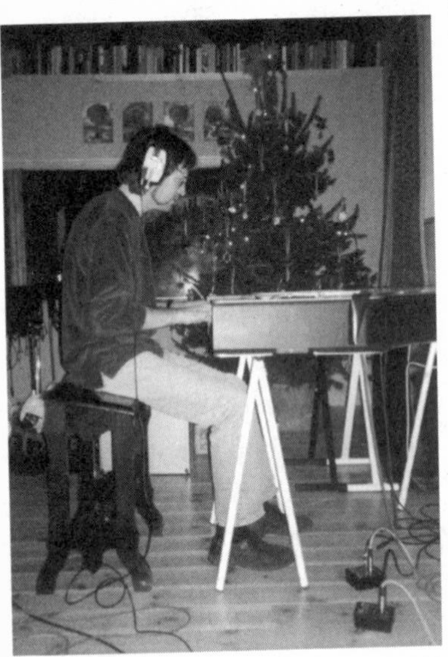

Dave on Baldwin electric harpsichord in Chris Difford's studio. (CREDIT: ANDY PARTRIDGE)

As is so often the case, rage brings out the best in a songwriter and the rest of the band insisted the song remain in.

"PLAYGROUND"
(Andy Partridge)

Andy is convinced that school life is only a dry run for the rest of our lives, that the bullies will always be bullies and the bullied will always be bullied. "You may leave school but it never leaves you," says the lyric. "Kiss chase ends when you're caught." "You're marked by the masters and bruised by the bullies." It's a bit of a sad attitude and, says Andy, true to his life. "It's rather autobiographical. The sweet girl playing my wife did run off with a boy with a nicer bike."

This introspective view had originally inspired a "twinkly," easy-listening arrangement, but the demo ended up as a straightforward electric guitar pop song, which, at time of writing, Andy believes will remain on the album.

"MY BROWN GUITAR"
(Andy Partridge)

John Flansburgh of They Might Be Giants called Andy one day to ask if he would contribute a track for the Hello Record Club, which releases compilations of demos by famous artists and interesting unsigned ones. Teased by the idea, Andy sat down to write something specifically for the project, breaking his normal regime by trying to write without a particular starting point. Two songs resulted, "Prince of Orange" and "My Brown Guitar." The latter was a plodding but striking tune of extraordinary harmonies and grinding guitars which even Flansburgh suggested should be an XTC album track. "It's basically just nonsense," says Andy, who is often unaware of the deeper meaning of his own songs until years after writing them. "I just like the sound of the words. Maybe they mean something. I suppose it's about sex when all is said and done." Well, isn't it all?

"Church of Women"
(Andy Partridge)

Kids never get to play with the toy trains their fathers buy them and Holly Partridge rarely gets her hands on her own guitar. "It's tiny and easy on the fingers so I carry it around with me," says Andy in poor justification. But at least he is productive with it, writing this song in praise of the opposite sex. "I think women are as faultlessly, beautifully, wonderfully perfect as you can get. I buy the romance of that. I was terrified of them when I was younger and I think that has left its magic fallout. I love the smell of them, the shape of them, the things they do and say, and I thought it would be great to have a religion in praise of them because they've been out of praise for too long." Or, to put it more basically, "I love the shit out of them."

The song is a simple plaintive verse that rolls into a glorious, reverent chorus, replete with deep harmonium and a sense of majesty about it. And he claims not to be religious!

"We're All Light"
(Andy Partridge)

"A piece of genius," Dave calls it. So it is somewhat disappointing to know that this uplifting, radio-friendly song comprises Andy's collection of the worst party chat-up lines: "Did you know all your atoms were once part of a star?"

"It came out of desperation really. I found a little rhythm pattern like something by the Wailers and wound up my guitar to maximum distortion and played it like a ukulele," he says. "I put it down on cassette and started jumping around the shed and started scatting this conversational song. It's just party talk. A man trying to impress a woman to get into her underwear. It's a mixture of lame chat-up lines and it came out charming. I don't often get to show the cheesy side of me." Sure you don't!

"I Can't Own Her"

(Andy Partridge)

Like "Your Dictionary," Andy wrote "I Can't Own Her" but didn't want to record it. The rest of the band outvoted him and Haydn was especially determined to include it, though changing it from the "loungy" nature of the demo to include orchestral sounds, guitar feedback, and possibly Celtic harp. "It's a bit too honest," says Andy, cringing. "I think it's about both the women in my life, one coming and one going. Not that I want to own them, but there's a desperation about losing somebody. In some ways I didn't want to lose the one that was leaving and in another way I didn't want ever to lose the one that was coming. It's a desperate and raw little emotional song." But desperate and raw can make for a great song and had Andy really wanted the song to die, he wouldn't have played it in the first place. "Sometimes I write songs that trip me up and maybe expose more of me than I would wish," he says tellingly.

"In Another Life"

(Colin Moulding)

Colin's songs always painted Lowry images rather than Leonardos. His lyrics mirror his own simple life, dismissive of the trappings of stardom and disinterested in jet-setting. "In Another Life's" "let's make the here and now great" storyline is typical Moulding, though the music is an oddball hybrid of the Kinks and Bowie's "Heroes." "I'm marvelously at home writing this sort of stuff. I haven't got a clue about world issues," he says. But although he feels that this is the kind of song he should write at this time of life, he still camouflages the autobiographical lyrics with images of his parents' age. "It's definitely about me and Carol but the Burton and Taylor images are icons of my mum and dad's generation. It's a little disguise really. You can't let the cat out of the bag too much."

Andy was not so sure about the song. It was built from the remains of a song from the *Skylarking* demos, which had been butchered to build the middle of "Cynical Days" for *Oranges and Lemons*. Andy thinks it a bit of an offcut. But Dave and Haydn liked it and so the ayes had it and the song was voted in.

"You and the Clouds Will Still Be Beautiful"

(Andy Partridge)

Late in the *Nonsuch* sessions, when Gus Dudgeon was reaching the end of his tether and trying to lay down the law, Andy brought in another song. Gus had heard enough songs and refused to consider it, though Andy tried to teach Dave Mattacks the Afro-Arabic drum pattern. Six years later, it reappeared for inclusion in the new album. Andy believes it was voted in. Colin thinks differently. "It only got two votes but Andy said it was one of his favorites. So we agreed to do it if, as a trade-off, we got to do 'I Can't Own Her' and 'Your Dictionary,' which he didn't want."

The hip-swinging, almost Latin-American-sounding song was improvised, like "River of Orchids," around an infectious three-chord loop and lives up to the simple sentiment. "It's probably about Marianne," says Andy. "Basically, it's saying that despite all our arguments you're still a good-looking woman. Flying cups and flying saucers and flying plates adequately described my marriage. The stain of the Coco Pops is still on the kitchen ceiling where I threw them in a terrible argument." It's amazing, the significance of Coco Pops in Andy's life!

"The Wheel and the Maypole"
(Andy Partridge)

This is not the first time Andy has built a song from bits of others, but this is certainly the most blatant. "Everything Decays" had already evolved into another examination of the life cycle, "Maypole," but it sounded incomplete. "The Pot Won't Hold Our Love," a metaphorical medieval dance about fashioning a perfect marriage in clay, was even more unfinished. " 'Maypole' is about being tied to this cycle of birth and decay and renewal and 'The Pot' is about becoming tied to somebody to start that cycle. So I thought, Why don't I take a hammer and nail and join the two songs at the hip?" says Andy, proving that he was right to choose songwriting over surgery. "I bent them around so that one is in B and one in E, which are related modally so they harmonize at the end."

During XTC's search for a new record deal, they came close to signing to Richard Branson's new label, V2. This song was a particular favorite of Ronnie Gurr at V2. "He said this must be about the old Scottish tradition of mingling your piss in a pot on your wedding night," says Andy. "But it's not. It's about making a pot. Molding it with clay to get it just right. To get that person you want." And so he did.

"Wounded Horse"
(Andy Partridge)

Simple and direct, Colin saw "Wounded Horse" as a bit of a pastiche of the Rolling Stones' "Dear Doctor" and although Andy thought little of it, the band decided it worked. "They thought it was very charming and autobiographical," says Andy. "It's a very dreary blues kind of song with a clip-clopping drum beat. Basically, it's a betrayal song. Colin calls it an adult lyric."

"Stupidly Happy"

(Andy Partridge)

Diametrically opposed to "Wounded Horse," "Stupidly Happy" was a simplistically ecstatic response to his newfound love with Erica Wexler. "It's talking about that new love blankness, that opiated thing of being in love. I've never seen Dave more doped out than when he got together with Aimee Mann—totally stoned!" The song is driven throughout by a repeated guitar riff that Andy believes is the only one Keith Richard missed. "People hear it and can't believe how moronic the demo sounds, but it has to be that one chord and that one bass note and that placid, opiated style of singing. It's purposefully floating and unchanging and suspended in pink goo."

IN THE SIDINGS . . .

Every XTC album has its casualties. Some songs live to appear on future albums, but never before had Andy had so much writing time to accumulate songs. Because V2 was so convinced that they were signing XTC, they sent demo tapes around the world to prospective producers. Before the Virgin deal ended, they had even sent demos to Australian record shops, hoping to gauge public opinion. The result was a glut of bootlegs, which revealed to XTC fans many of the songs that would be vetoed at a later date, including:

"Ship Trapped In the Ice," *Andy's ode to their five-year strike with Virgin Records.*

"Mates," *a sophisticated little song by Colin that was "so short it got overlooked."*

"Bumper Cars," *combining the long-lost Partridge fairground theme and his hatred of bosses. Complete with a wish that "airguns crack my boss's back" in reference to the Middle Mr. Tunley of* "Earn Enough for Us" *fame.*

"Wonder Annual," *another of Andy's childhood themes that hints at Andy's desire to watch Erica pleasuring herself! It could have also been the album title and was previously mooted as the title of an album of outtakes.*

"Standing In for Joe," *which Colin had written for the bubblegum project and which Haydn liked but, according to Colin, "It sounded rather old-fashioned."*

"The Man Who Murdered Love," *one of Andy's clumsier-sounding songs with a defiant yet defensive chorus line that is undoubtedly autobiographical.*

EPILOGUE

Chipping Norton, where XTC is recording as I write, is a pleasant little town in the heart of the Cotswolds, a hilly area in central southern England. A number of places in the Cotswolds are called Chipping something-or-other. "Chipping" is a Viking word, the pillaging Norsemen having left behind more than a lot of illegitimate redheads, a few burial mounds, and a taste for lager. "Chipping," as with "Copen"(hagen) or various Swedish towns called Koping (pronounced "sheuping"), means "market," and is the origin of the English words *shop* and *cheap*. Being a "Chipping" town gives some hint as to the age of the settlement—at least a thousand years. The nearby Rollright stone circle, a nursery school Stonehenge a few miles outside Chipping Norton, is evidence of local inhabitation a couple of thousand years before that. So Chipping Norton Recording Studios' rock 'n' roll image might seem a little out of place. But many of Britain's recording studios have history going back hundreds of years—The Manor, Abbey Road, Sawmills, and Rockfield are just a few that XTC have worked in. In Britain, it is hard to get away from history.

When you work in this atmosphere, you cannot help but be

influenced by it. Perhaps that is what makes the best of British rock music so different from American. The whole attitude to life is different. The education, the housing, the climate, the government, the cities and the countryside, the sense of tradition as against the sense of newness, cramped against spacious. Any intelligent, sensitive composer/performer is bound to show the influence of his/her personal surroundings—Elgar did, Copeland did, Gershwin did, Bartok did, Woody Guthrie, Dylan Thomas, Robert Johnson, the Beatles, Bob Dylan, Joan Baez, Bruce Springsteen, Aretha Franklin, the Kinks, Joni Mitchell, the Beach Boys, and XTC.

XTC, nurtured in Swindon, a town which epitomizes British history and Britons' contempt for it, from the ancient Celts to the Industrial Revolution. A pretty, historical little hill town massacred for the sake of commerce. One of those places where life can be so miserable that if you didn't learn to laugh you'd kill yourself—like Liverpool or Glasgow, the homes of humor and suicide. Swindon, a place that sold its ancient soul to the money devil and paid the price. A huge pockmark on the complexion of Wiltshire, slashed through by the scars of the Great Western Railway and the M4 motorway. A rich seam for a young songwriter to plunder.

Colin caught unawares not pouting for the camera.

(CREDIT: NEVILLE FARMER.)

It is only visiting somewhere like Swindon that truly helps us to understand XTC's music and why it is the way it is. In return, the songs offer clues to the lives of Andy Partridge, Colin Moulding, and Dave Gregory. The songs themselves are all flavored with Andy's, Colin's, and Dave's continued, if grudging, devotion to their hometown and the things they found there to hold their interests.

Ringo Starr said, allegedly, "Do you remember when they started analyzing Beatle songs? I don't think *I* understood what some of them were supposed to be about." Ringo didn't really need to, he didn't write most of them and didn't sing many of them, though only he could fathom the deep philosophical subtleties submerged in "Octopus's Garden." But the fans needed to know the meanings, especially after the Beatles stopped touring; yet more so after they broke up. Fanaticism is a drug and once you are hooked you want more. You have to know why you are addicted. You have to justify your obsession with something as shallow as pop music by finding something deeper in it.

XTC fans, myself included I suppose, love to know what is behind every nuance of their music. Part of the fun of being a fan is to analyze, dissect, theorize on the hidden meaning in a song. This can naturally lead into reading far more into a piece of music than even the writer intended. And the more remote the heroes might become, the more fans' fascination in the minutiae is amplified.

XTC is an unknown quantity to many of their fans. They retired from live performance before many of their supporters discovered them; they haven't released a record for longer than most pop careers last; and Swindon is not high on the list of holiday destinations. So the fans talk to each other, hold conventions, form tribute bands, communicate via the World Wide Web, debating the music they know and love. Andy, Colin, and Dave know about this and, on the whole, love it. There are few bands as friendly to their fans. They leak demo tapes to the fan club for distribution at XTC conventions. It is not unknown for a fan to receive a late-night phone call from a member of the band in response to an interesting letter. But the in-depth, on-the-couch analysis of XTC's songs bemuses them.

When a song is written, there may be a thread of a lyrical

concept but rarely is there the depth of concealed message that this analysis would imply. Colin, especially, writes straightforward narrative songs about a subject. "Nigel" isn't him. His parents would let him do what he wanted and didn't bully him into any career decisions. The most forceful argument his father ever had with him was about cutting his hair after the summer holidays so that he could continue his schooling (in those days, long hair was an expulsion offense in British schools!). He didn't cut it. He doesn't generally hide anyone in his songs. "Down a Peg" and "My Bird Performs" are messages to himself, not to Andy. "English Roundabout" has nothing to do with the complicated traffic island outside Swindon and is only in 5/4 time because it sounded good that way. Colin doesn't like writing songs about issues and when he does, as in "King for a Day," he is often disappointed with the results.

Dave, "I bought myself a Firebird."

(CREDIT: NEVILLE FARMER)

Andy is more oblique, but he is more likely to write about someone he knows than to target a public figure. "Peter Pumpkinhead" is a generic public hero, but not specifically John Lennon or JFK or Jesus. "Madam Barnum" is not Margaret Thatcher. She is not necessarily even Marianne. She is just an interesting way of creating a song about feeling like a fool when you discover you've been cuckolded. "President Kill" is not Ronald Reagan or even an American. He is an amalgamation of superpower leaders throughout the history of "democracy." He, again, is merely a vehicle for a lyrical idea. In fact, during the writing process, Andy is probably more obsessed with the spark of the idea or a turn of phrase than the message itself. That is probably why he was so unhappy about the delivery of the message in "Dear God." Neither Colin nor Andy handle political or religious matters with subtlety. If they have an idea about something, they say it straightforwardly. They are no more embarrassed about their view on the world than Andy is about his sex life. That makes them easy targets for criticism. "Dear God" expresses Andy's disbelief in the presence of God and, according to his right to free speech, he sees nothing wrong in talking about it. But he does not preach. They do not presume to be evangelists for any creed. The words are just there to provoke thought and to express a mood or an emotion or an idea. The songs don't offer some deep philosophical insight, just the kick start to a bloody good argument.

What XTC's songs do expose are more general aspects of their lives and their attitudes:

ANDY PARTRIDGE—A passion for comics, books, and toys, both American and English; an inquisitive interest in industrial and English history; a love of the mechanics of theater, music hall, circus, and the traditions of English entertainment; a love-hate relationship and quizzical fascination for the effects of power and civilization and establishment; an objective interest in faiths, creeds, and their attendant rituals; a celebratory and unembarrassed attitude toward sex (oft mistaken for sexism by those who have forgotten that sex is, usually, a joyous experience of abandonment equally shared between one, two, or more participants), and an adoration of children, women, and life itself.

COLIN MOULDING—A comfortable acceptance of the joys of growing old in little England that comes from the grounding effect of starting a family so early; an eye for the details of English life akin to filmmakers like Mike Leigh and Ken Loach; a hatred of the insensitivity of town planners and government; a childhood interest in astronomy and local history and a subsequent awareness of his place in the universe; most of all, contentment.

DAVE GREGORY—A scholarly love of music that could only come from a family of teachers; a precision and correctness that carries through from his prerehearsal of guitar solos to the orderly layout of his home, the cataloguing of his video and record collection and his encyclopedic knowledge of guitars and who-played-what-on-which-instrument-with-which-amplifier-in-which-studio-on-which-record-under-the-influence-of-what-star-sign-or-guru-or-drug.

What is less easy to read from their music is their attitude toward each other. There is no significance in one member of the band not playing on a particular record. They long since overcame the "jobsworth" mentality that dictates who plays what. The only tradition is that the writer sings the song. Dave plays keys because he can and the others can't. Colin plays bass because he's the best at it. There are only a couple of Dukes songs in which Andy plays bass and Colin strums guitar. Dave and Andy share guitar duties. Prior to retirement from touring, Dave would get the complicated guitar work on Andy's songs to allow Andy to concentrate on singing. Often, Dave gets the most complicated stuff now because he is a most technical and versatile guitarist. But he is the first to admit Andy's instinctive brilliance on guitar and he bows to Andy's superiority in certain styles of playing as Andy does to Dave's breadth of ability.

Dave still regrets not being a songwriting partner in the team. Though he has written TV music for BBC Television, Manchester, Andy claims that Dave has still never presented a complete idea for a song to the band and Dave admits that it takes courage to offer anything up for Andy's scrutiny.

As personalities, there are all the positives and negatives one expects from a three-way marriage of two decades duration. Andy is the boss—erratic but willful. Dave is the voice of reason. Colin is the voice of calm. Colin is a foil to Andy's radical side. Dave opened up their musical horizons. Andy runs the band on instinct. Dave clears up the mess. Colin lets them get on with it. They do love each other.

In 1997, XTC formed Idea Records as an imprint to license around the world. It was designed as a vehicle for their own output, though they have grander designs to help other artists. For the first time in their history, they could make their own decisions without the influence of a record company or an overbearing manager. This might elicit a repeat of the debacle captured on the legendary Troggs tapes—a band out of control, without a guiding influence. But it has also pulled Andy out of his trench. He is talking about playing live, on the back of flatbed trucks, outside radio stations and record stores. After years of people badgering him to play again, it is now Colin who is reticent, worrying about a bunch of forty-somethings making prats of themselves. That doesn't mean that he won't play, any more than it means Andy will. Andy did get up on stage with Aimee Mann and Dave Gregory but he spent most of the previous week on the toilet. The only time he's played more than a few numbers on stage in the last fifteen years was with his ex-brother-in-law's band, Maltloaf. Robbie Wyborn called minutes before the gig to say his guitarist hadn't turned up and Andy, who had already bedded down for the night, played with his waistcoat pulled over his pajamas. He can play live, and once he finds how different it is from those early, manic tours, he might find he likes it.

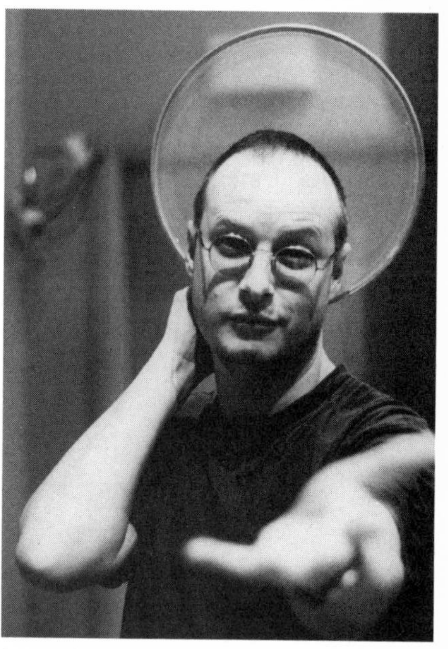

In your dreams, Andy. (CREDIT: NEVILLE FARMER)

Dave, Paul Fox, and John Leckie have all called Andy Partridge a genius, but as Colin says, "Andy knows he's a selfish bastard and so long as you can live with that it's all right." Andy's musical brilliance is countered by a crippling inability to let go, to delegate, to trust. Colin might not be prolific, but his incredible talent for carving a simply perfect melody and evoking a mood are the spurs that kick Andy into action. When Andy wants to stretch himself and doesn't know how, Dave gives him the musical tools. XTC is much more than the sum of its "Parts," and Partsy knows it. When he insisted on recording over twenty songs for the new album, Dave suggested he record half of them as a solo project. Andy refused. He is, quite probably, scared of leading an army of one because he knows how good this musical brains-trust of three is.

When I started out on this book, I was working with Peter Gabriel. I mentioned my connection with XTC and he said this: "I've always looked to XTC for inventive songwriting, innovative production, and a sense of humor. It's their strong blend of personalities that make them one of *the great* British bands." I would only differ on limiting it to "British" bands.

Neville Farmer, 1998

POSTSCRIPT

Dave Gregory's suggestion that Andy should release the acoustic/orchestral songs as solo work concealed deeper feelings. As the album progressed, Dave began to feel left out. Andy had arranged the orchestrations on computer, leaving Dave with little creative work. Guitars and keyboards made way for orchestral instruments on many tracks. At least Andy and Colin got to sing. Unable to have any real say in the direction of Andy's songs, he became increasingly negative about the project.

Early in 1998, Dave, Colin, and Haydn completed most of the work on Colin's songs during Andy's absence in New York. But on his return, tension mounted. In March, annoyed at Dave's negativity, Andy suggested he take a few days off while Andy completed some vocals. Dave started packing his things. After a while, he stuck his head around the door and said, "See ya!" It was only after he had left that they realized he had gone for good. The next day he visited Colin at home and gave him a letter of resignation addressed to him and Andy.

Though Dave had little idea what he was going to do, and though Andy had lost a colleague of nineteen years standing, there was a sense of relief on both sides. Dave wasn't as willing to accept creeping middle age as the others. The only member of XTC able to score orchestrations wanted to be in a guitar band. "I like to hear an orchestra on some tracks, especially if I've had the opportunity to score it, but my principal instrument is guitar," said Dave. Andy and Colin were embracing the second age, delving into Colin's easy listening and Andy's orchestral experimentation.

As this book went to print, neither Andy nor Colin had any idea what would happen next. Mike Batt was brought in to score and conduct the orchestra, but the stretched schedule made it likely that the two discs would be released separately—part one being acoustic/orchestral. It also threw Haydn Bendall's continued availability into doubt. Yet despite all the problems, everyone seemed convinced that this would be the greatest album XTC has ever made.

So the book must just leave the reader dangling. But then, you wouldn't want to know the ending before you'd read the whole story, would you?

SONG AND ALBUM INDEX

1000 Umbrellas, 191
25 O'Clock, 214
3D EP, 22
Across This Antheap, 246
The Affiliated, 224
All Along the Watchtower, 28
All of a Sudden, 122
All You Pretty Girls, 166
Andy Paints Brian (alternative title to Battery Brides), 45
Another 1950, Shoreleave Ornithology, 84
Another Satellite, 194
Are You Receiving Me?, 55
The Arguers (alternative title to Tissue Tigers), 129
Bags of Fun with Buster, 226
Ball and Chain, 117
The Ballad of Peter Pumpkinhead, 262
Ballet for a Rainy Day, 191
Battery Brides (or Andy Paints Brian), 45
Beat the Bible, 58
Beating of Hearts, 147
Beatown, 50
Big Day, 194
The Big Express, 165
Bike Ride to the Moon, 214
Black Sea, 94
Blame the Weather, 128
Blue Overall, 176
Boarded Up, 292
Books Are Burning, 274
Brainiac's Daughter, 224
Bumper Cars, 300
Bungalow, 273
Burning with Optimism's Flames, 101
Bushman President (Homo Safari #2), 81
Buzzcity Talking, 47

Cairo, 84
Chain of Command, 79
Chalkhills and Children, 248
Cherry In Your Tree, 276
Church of Women, 296
Clap Clap Clap, 58
Collideascope, 222
Commerciality, 83
Complicated Game, 78
Countdown to Christmas, 209
Crocodile, 267
Cross Wires, 25
Crowded Room, 47
Cut It Out, 158
Cynical Days, 246
Dance Band, 23
Dance with Me, Germany, 58
Day In Day Out, 71
The Day They Pulled Down the North Pole, 83
Dear God, 199
Dear Madam Barnum, 264
Deliver Us from the Elements, 151
Desert Island, 158
A Dictionary of Modern Marriage, 58
The Disappointed, 266
Do What You Do, 27
Don't Lose Your Temper, 106
Down a Peg, 275
Down In the Cockpit, 126
Drums and Wires, 67
Dying, 197
Earn Enough for Us, 193
Easter Theatre, 289
Egyptian Solution (or Thebes In a Box) (Homo Safari #3), 130
Ella Guru, 250
English Roundabout, 127
English Settlement, 117
The Everyday Story of Smalltown, 170
Extrovert, 201
Find the Fox, 204
Fireball Dub, 57
Fly On the Wall, 126
The Forgotten Language of Light, 83
Frivolous Tonight, 291
Frost Circus (Homo Safari #5), 155
Fruit Nut, 289
Funk Pop a Roll, 154
Garden of Earthly Delights, 239
Generals and Majors, 95
Go +, 57
Gold, 157
The Good Things, 251
Goodnight Sucker, 24
Grass, 188
Great Fire, 150
Green Man, 288
Gribouillage, 275
Hang On to the Night, 34
Happy Families, 251
Harvest Festival, 293
Have You Seen Jackie?, 220
Heatwave, 35
Heaven Is Paved with Broken Glass, 130
Helicopter, 70
Here Comes President Kill Again, 242
History of Rock and Roll, 108
Hold Me My Daddy, 247
Holly Up On Poppy, 267
Homo Safari, 79
Human Alchemy, 151
Humble Daisy, 265
I Am the Audience, 54
I Bought Myself a Liarbird, 170
I Can't Own Her, 297
I Need Protection, 208
I Remember the Sun, 172

I Sit In the Snow, 85
I'd Like That, 290
I'll Set Myself On Fire, 30
I'm Bugged, 31
In Another Life, 297
In Loving Memory of a Name, 153
Instant Tunes, 56
Into the Atom Age, 29
It's Nearly Africa, 124
Jason and the Argonauts, 120
Jump (or Jump, Jump, Love and Swimming Pools), 155
Jumping In Gomorrah, 51
King for a Day, 241
Knights In Shining Karma, 292
Knuckle Down, 125
Ladybird, 152
The Last Balloon, 291
Leisure, 124
Let's Make a Den, 203
Life Begins At the Hop, 67
Life Is Good In the Greenhouse, 50
Limelight, 80
Little Lighthouse, 221
Living In a Haunted Heart, 250
Living Through Another Cuba, 96
Love At First Sight, 97
Love On a Farmboy's Wages, 149
The Loving, 242
Madhattan, 85
Making Plans for Nigel, 68
The Man Who Murdered Love, 301
The Man Who Sailed Around His Soul, 197
Mantis On Parole (Homo Safari #4), 131
Mates, 300
Mayor of Simpleton, 240
Me and the Wind, 153
Meccanic Dancing (Oh We Go!), 44
The Meeting Place, 189
Melt the Guns, 123
Merely a Man, 245
Mermaid Smiled, 195
Millions, 75
Miniature Sun, 248
The Mole from the Ministry, 216
Mummer, 147
My Bird Performs, 263
My Brown Guitar, 295
My Love Explodes, 215
My Paint Heroes, 249
My Weapon, 52
Neon Shuffle, 34
New Broom, 85
New Town Animal In a Furnished Cage, 32
No Language In Our Lungs, 98
No Thugs In Our House, 120
Nonsuch, 262
Officer Blue, 104
Oh Dear, What Can The Matter Be? (alternative title to Toys), 156
Omnibus, 269
One of the Millions, 243
Oranges and Lemons, 239
Outside World, 76
Over Rusty Water, 131
Pale and Precious, 225
Paper and Iron (Notes and Coins), 100
Pink Thing, 247
Playground, 295
Poor Skeleton Steps Out, 243
Procession Towards Learning Land (Homo Safari #6), 157
Psonic Psunspots, 220
Pulsing Pulsing, 80

Punch and Judy, 129
Radios In Motion, 24
Real By Reel, 74
Red Brick Dream, 174
Red, 49
Reign of Blows (Vote No to Violence), 171
Respectable Street, 94
The Rhythm, 48
River of Orchids, 287
Roads Girdle the Globe, 73
Rocket from a Bottle, 98
Rook, 268
The Rotary, 84
Runaways, 117
Sacrificial Bonfire, 198
Scarecrow People, 244
Science Friction, 22
Scissor Man, 77
Seagulls Screaming Kiss Her, Kiss Her, 168
Season Cycle, 192
Senses Working Overtime, 119
Sgt. Rock (Is Going to Help Me), 102
Shake You Donkey Up, 167
She's So Square, 23
Shiny Cage, 223
Ship Trapped In the Ice, 300
Skeletons, 250
Skylarking, 187
The Smartest Monkeys, 265
Smokeless Zone, 106
Snowman, 127
Somesuch, 275
The Somnambulist, 107
Spinning Top, 33
Standing In for Joe, 301
Statue of Liberty, 27
Steam Fist Futurist, 83
Strange Tales, Strange Tails, 105
Stupidly Happy, 300
Summer's Cauldron, 187
Supertuff, 53
Take This Town, 104
Takeaway/The Lure of Salvage, 81
Ten Feet Tall, 72
Terrorism, 202
Thanks for Christmas, 208
That Is the Way, 75
That Wave, 270
That's Really Super, Supergirl, 190
Thebes In a Box (alternative title to Egyptian Solution) (Homo Safari #3), 130
Then She Appeared, 271
This Is Pop, 26
This World Over, 169
Tissue Tigers (or The Arguers), 129
Too Many Cooks In the Kitchen, 207
Towers of London, 99
Toys (or Oh Dear, What Can the Matter Be?), 156
Traffic Light Rock, 36
Train Running Low On Slow Coal, 173
Travels in Nihilon, 102
The Troubles, 202
The Ugly Underneath, 272
Vanishing Girl, 220
Wait Till Your Boat Goes Down, 103
Wake Up, 165
War Dance, 271
Washaway, 175
We Kill the Beast, 58
We're All Light, 296
What In the World??, 215

The Wheel and the Maypole, 299
When You're Near Me I Have Difficulty, 72
White Music, 24
Wonder Annual, 301
Wonderland, 147
Work Away Tokyo Day, 85
The World Is Full of Angry Young Men, 251
Wounded Horse, 299
Wrapped In Grey, 272
XTC's Go 2, 44
Yacht Dance, 121
You and the Clouds Will Still Be Beautiful, 298
You're a Good Man Albert Brown (Curse You Red Barrel), 222
You're My Drug, 223
You're the Wish You Are I Had, 172
Your Dictionary, 294
Your Gold Dress, 216